THE ART OF
ANCIENT MEXICO

Hayward Gallery, London
17 September to 6 December 1992

THE ART OF ANCIENT MEXICO

SOUTH BANK CENTRE

OLIVETTI | ELECTA

Exhibition organisation in Mexico:
Secretaría de Relaciones Exteriores
Secretaría de Educación Pública
Consejo Nacional para la Cultura y las Artes
Instituto Nacional de Antropología e Historia

Exhibition organisation in London:
Hayward Gallery, South Bank Centre

The original project for *The Art of Ancient Mexico*,
including the selection of the items displayed, full
photographic coverage and the design of the
catalogue, was developed by the Olivetti
company for the exhibition shown in Venice,
Paris, Madrid, Berlin, Tokyo and now London

Photography:
Mario Carrieri (except for plate 97)

Translation:
Nicola Coleby

Editor:
Marianne Ryan

Catalogue design:
Egidio Bonfante

Exhibition in London
organised by Andrew Dempsey
with Susan May

Cover illustration:
Anthropomorphic urn (cat. no. 52)

ISBN   1 85 332 091 9

Committee of Honour

Mexico

Secretaría de Relaciones Exteriores

Fernando Solana
Secretario de Relaciones Exteriores

Rosario Green
Subsecretaría de Relaciones Exteriores

Bernardo Sepúlveda
Embajador de México en el Reino Unido

Alfonso de María y Campos
Director General de Asuntos Culturales

Secretaría de Educación Pública

Ernesto Zedillo
Secretario de Educación Pública

Víctor Sologaistoa
Director General de Relaciones Internacionales

Consejo Nacional para Cultura y las Artes

Rafael Tovar y de Teresa
Presidente

Instituto Nacional de Antropología e Historia

María Teresa Franco
Directora General

Mario Vázquez
Coordinador Nacional de Museos y Exposiciones

Maricarmen Serra Puche
Directora del Museo Nacional de Antropología

United Kingdom

The Rt Hon Douglas Hurd CBE, MP
Secretary of State for Foreign and Commonwealth Affairs

The Rt Hon Tristan Garel-Jones MP
Minister of State for Foreign and Commonwealth Affairs

The Hon Mark Lennox-Boyd MP
Parliamentary Under Secretary for Foreign and Commonwealth Affairs

His Excellency Sir Roger Hervey KCVO, CMG
Her Majesty's Ambassador to Mexico

Lord Palumbo
Chairman, Arts Council of Great Britain

Sir Martin Jacomb
Chairman, British Council

Sir Brian Corby
Chairman, South Bank Centre

Dr R G W Anderson
Director, British Museum

Mr Nicholas Elam
Head of Cultural Relations, Foreign and Commonwealth Office

In this comprehensive exhibition of ancient Mexican cultures, we witness the miraculous transformation of limestone, clay and rock into shapes where Mesoamerican man breathed into the objects he created his idea of beauty, his synthesis of the world and his attempts to express his interpretation of the universe. Sometimes the likeness of a ceramic funeral object is so faithful as to suggest that a timely duplicate was made from a live model in order to achieve a perfect and realistic analogy for the afterlife; more frequently, volume and line describe flamboyant convolutions that achieve notable peaks of abstraction and outstanding sophistication. I often wonder how deliberate the aura of anonymous Prehispanic artists was in the creative impulse of the Hans Arps, the Brancusis and even in the sparse marble figures of a Modigliani; at any rate Henry Moore for one avowed in his homeland how great an impact the Pre-Columbian artists made on his own aesthetic conception – particularly once he had discovered the reclining figure of the Chac Mool.

At times art nouveau motifs avant la lettre *enhance the curves of nature and convey us towards animal representations that embody an auspicious Aztec deity or stir in us memories of Loïe Fuller's sensual rhythmic patterns of geometrical precision; exquisite seated figures recall the tender image of everlasting motherhood; delicate shapes lovingly sculpted in Jaina vie for the refinement of the awesome turquoise masks brimming with all the splendour of their colourful regalia. But what surprises incessantly is the variety of language exclusive to Mesoamerica in this art: naturalistic expressions of some physical deformity may flank the most delightful depictions of humour and* joie de vivre *in the same place as a menacing colossus coexists with an overbearing warrior, while the involuntary elegance of the hand and arm of an Olmec child will astonish with the grace and ease of its gestures and the perfection of its proportions.*

Be that as it may, the pieces presented in the ample space of the Hayward Gallery confirm once more man's eternal involvement with beauty, with nature, and with the universe of the gods, as well as his ability to marry the graceful with the useful in artefacts intended for everyday life – all of which stirs in us both amazement and admiration.

For a long-contemplated project which now becomes a reality in London, my warmest thanks to the Hayward Gallery and to the organisers on both sides of the Atlantic, whose generosity made possible this exhibition in which Mexico proudly assembles a revealing collection that conveys an accurate vision of the present and the past of our multifarious country.

Bernardo Sepúlveda
Mexican Ambassador to the
United Kingdom

The art of ancient Mexico has been a subject of curiosity and wonder on the part of other cultures. The exhibition which we are presenting in London is a representative survey of the cultural and artistic achievements of the Prehispanic civilisations which we hope will serve as an introduction to the world full of magic and disquieting symbolism created by those early people.

The majority of the works included in the exhibition are from the collection of the National Museum of Anthropology in Mexico City as well as from important regional museums. They are of such quality that we hope they will convey the wide range of styles, extraordinary creativity and great technical virtuosity with which those ancient people re-created the prodigious naturalism and complex symbolism of their world and expressed their religious beliefs and their attitudes to life with such remarkable aesthetic sensibility.

Behind the variety of styles, subjects and different techniques one can sense a unity and coherence in their universe. This is not just a question of themes and subjects which occur again and again over the centuries and in the widespread regions, nor is it the consequence of a shared system of symbols. It is more a matter of a very special and particular sensibility which is revealed to us in the play of light and shadow, volumes and planes. A fusion between complex artistic forms and the meanings they convey; an entirely original equilibrium between form and meaning, between the permanent and the transitory, between the visible and invisible worlds. This is the eternal preoccupation of art which the people of Mesoamerica were able to resolve with mastery and sensibility. For this reason, and beyond questions of historical and ethnographical relevance, the works in this exhibition, which demonstrate such a high level of aesthetic achievement, belong to another history, that of the great art of the world.

Our exhibition is the result of considerable effort on the part of cultural and diplomatic bodies in Mexico and the United Knigdom as well as the work of the organising teams in both countries. The Art of Ancient Mexico is resuming its international journey in a year of profound significance for the Americas and for Europe. Our most grateful thanks are due to those who have supported the Consejo Nacional para la Cultura y las Artes and the Instituto Nacional de Antropología e Historia in offering successive countries an exhibition of some of the greatest artistic achievements of Mexican art and culture.

Rafael Tovar y de Teresa
President of the Consejo Nacional
para la Cultura y las Artes

ACKNOWLEDGEMENTS

This exhibition began its travels in Europe more than two years ago. At an early stage both the British Museum and the Hayward Gallery were approached as possible London venues. Neither institution could take the exhibition at the time and had to decline the offer, with the greatest regret because of both the splendour of the material and the evident need to present the art of ancient Mexico to a new generation in this country. It has been twenty years since the Maya exhibition at the Museum of Mankind in 1971 and almost forty years since the great Mexican exhibition at the Tate Gallery in 1953.

When a gap opened up in the Hayward Gallery programme for the autumn of 1992, a special year in the history of relations between Europe and the Americas, we approached the Mexican Ambassador in this country, His Excellency Bernardo Sepúlveda Amor, to enquire if the exhibition could be re-assembled and shown at the Hayward Gallery. The Ambassador's response was positive and he has remained crucially supportive in all our preparations.

Further enquiries in Mexico met with an equally positive response, despite the very considerable demands on Mexican cultural and museum organisations during the quincentenary year. We are especially grateful to the following who received us with courtesy and enthusiasm and have been essential to the success of our project: Alfonso de Maria y Campos, Director General of Asuntos Culturales at the Secretaría de Relaciones Exteriores; Víctor Flores Olea who was at that time President of the Consejo Nacional para la Cultura y las Artes and Miriam Kaiser, the Consejo's Coordinadora Nacional de Exposiciones Internacionales; Roberto García Moll, former Director General, and Mario Vázquez Rubalcava, Coordinador Nacional de Museos y Exposiciones, of Mexico's Instituto Nacional de Antropología e Historia; and Maricarmen Serra Puche, Director of the Museo Nacional de Antropología.

It was suggested during discussions in Mexico that the British Museum might be approached to see if some additional material might be lent to the exhibition, making it in a small but important way a collaboration between the national museums in both countries. The Mexicans welcomed this notion and the response on the part of the British Museum has been very positive indeed, not only on the question of loans — which have been numerous and are catalogued separately — but also with advice and help on innumerable other aspects of the presentation of the exhibition at the Hayward. We are grateful to the Director and Trustees of the British Museum and most especially to John Mack, Keeper of the Museum of Mankind, and Miss Elizabeth Carmichael, Assistant Keeper in charge of this area of the Department's collections. They and their staff could hardly have been more helpful or more central to the realisation of our project.

The South Bank Centre was not alone in trying to arrange a showing of this exhibition in the quincentenary year. Mainichi in Japan, together with museum colleagues, were holding similar discussions and the coordination of the showings in both countries has required a considerable degree of collaboration for which we are indebted to the former Mexican Ambassador in Japan, Alfredo Phillips, and Takeo Inada of Mainichi. That it has been possible to satisfy the needs of both countries is a tribute to Mexican diplomatic skills.

This publication represents a full translation of the texts prepared by Mexican scholars for the catalogue of the exhibition when it was shown in Paris and Madrid in 1990 under the auspices of Olivetti (to whom we are grateful for permission to reprint and indeed for their help in gaining access to other material prepared for the original showings). Nicola Coleby has undertaken the major task of translation working with our editor Marianne Ryan. Oriana Baddeley has helped and advised us throughout in ways that are too numerous to mention here — we are greatly in her debt. The display of the exhibition in the Hayward is the work of the designers Stanton Williams.

Many people have been involved on the Mexican side as our arrangements took shape. At crucial stages we have been helped by Sara Bolaño of the Mexican Consulate in Berlin; by both Miguel

Angel Echegaray and Sara Valdés in the Asuntos Culturales department of Relaciones Exteriores; by Elena Uribe and Enrique Alduncin of the Mexican Embassy in London; and by Marcela Ramirez, the British Council's Cultural Officer in Mexico. But our most constant ally during the long period of preparing the exhibition here has been Raúl Ortiz, Minister with responsibility for Cultural Affairs at the London Embassy. To him we would like to express our heartfelt thanks for his patience and tact and good friendship.

Joanna Drew
Director of the Hayward Gallery

FOREWORD

The idea of presenting an exhibition of Pre-Columbian art clearly presupposes a modern concept of art. The pieces in this exhibition were not, however, produced by the Prehispanic inhabitants of Mexico as works of art. They were objects and ornaments used for a variety of ritualistic purposes within the framework of religious beliefs that had their origins in shamanist practices. The latter were transformed into propitiatory rites for the gods of creation, reproduction or destruction, and involved funerary cults which, up to a point, joined death to life through certain rituals. Thus all the pieces exhibited here are animated by an underlying symbolism, the very source of their creation.

The language of form in these pieces, both naturalistic and abstract, expresses a range of feeling concerning nature and the cosmos, and corresponds to the diversity of the cultures that developed in the different regions of present-day Mexico. Similarly, the complexity of the symbols reflects the level of development reached by social groups at different points in their history, and clearly expresses their characteristic way of life; initially, this was primarily agricultural, but militarism was to become increasingly important.

Despite the predominantly religious function of the objects produced by these races, it is evident that value was attributed to well-produced work and to exceptional, precious pieces, and that it was because of this that the objects were used for religious ceremony, the most important activity in the lives of Mesoamerican groups. But it is only in late Aztec testimonies that there is any suggestion of the high regard held for a craftsman able to express himself by means of a beautiful language:

"The good potter puts care into things

Teaches clay to sing,

Talks with his own heart,

Makes things come alive,

Creates them ..."

*(*Matritense Codex of the Real Academia, *fol. 175 v.)*

Here the Aztecs' perception coincides with what Western civilisation since the time of the Greeks has called poiesis.

However, the evolution of three-dimensional form in Western art and the aesthetic concepts that flourished in Europe were radically different from the forms of plastic expression found in Prehispanic Mexico. Although from their earliest contact the Spanish admired these pieces as curiosities, they always saw them as exotic and primitive works. It was only with the emphasis of the Enlightenment on rationalism that the cultural values they embodied began to be viewed with interest, and not until the influence of Romanticism were they seen as important elements for the understanding of folklore and national sentiment. It was well into the current century, when new aesthetic ideas had been generated by modern art, that Prehispanic works came to be seen as art. Not only was it recognised as embodying a language which allowed an understanding of the feeling generated by the specific situations and ways of life of their creators; but it became a source of inspiration and revitalisation for European art itself. It is within this context that the exhibition The Art of Ancient Mexico *is presented; the exhibits are cultural objects that can be interpreted in a variety of ways, and one of these interpretations is that of "art".*

This book is a graphic memorial of the exhibition. The sequence of photographs echoes the sequence of display. It begins with the Central Highlands cultures, starting with the most ancient, in the Pre-Classic period; these are followed by the Teotihuacán culture dating from the Classic period; the city-state cultures of the early Post-Classic period come next, culminating with the Aztec culture of the late Post-Classic period. The cultures of other Mesoamerican regions are then presented: Oaxaca, the Gulf Coast, the Maya, the West and the marginal area of the North, all of which occur at various chronological points during the previously mentioned periods. At the same time the catalogue gathers together several articles giving the reader more detailed information on the concept of Mesoamerica, and presenting a chronological, territorial and cultural framework within which to site the pieces displayed in the exhibition. The following chapter outlines the general characteristics of Mesoamerican art; then comes a chapter that refers specifically to each of the cultures pertaining to the objects on display, followed by detailed information regarding their significance as works of art. Finally there is a catalogue of all the pieces in the exhibition, each one fully illustrated. At the end of the book is a general bibliography for further reading.

Sonia Lombardo de Ruíz

CONTENTS

Catalogue contributors

Carolyn Baus de Czitrom (*c.b.c.*)
Amalia Cardós de Méndes (*a.c.m.*)
Martha Carmona Macías (*m.c.m.*)
Marcia Castro Leal (*m.c.l.*)
Clara Luz Días Oyarzábal (*c.l.d.o.*)
María Dolores Flores Villatoros (*m.d.f.v.*)
Roberto García Moll (*r.g.m.*)
Jesús Nárez (*j.n.*)
Federica Sodi Miranda (*f.s.m.*)
Felipe Solís Olguín (*f.s.o.*)

I. MESOAMERICA

Roberto García Moll

The immense geographical-cultural area known as Mesoamerica evolved over a very long period, within an area comprising present-day Mexico and part of Central America.

Its northern borders were the most stable, extending to the Sinaloa River on the Pacific Coast side and to the Panuco River towards the Gulf of Mexico. There was a clear divide there between the area where hunting and gathering was practised to the north and the traditional agricultural cultures of South America.

Several peoples inhabited this vast territory of Mesoamerica, each with its own distinct ethnic and linguistic traits but, at least by the beginning of the sixteenth century, sharing a certain cultural homogeneity. On the basis of these factors Mesoamerica has been divided into the following regions: the Central Highlands, the Gulf Coast, the Western Region, Oaxaca and the Maya Area.

Towards the north of Mexico are two areas with which Mesoamerica developed cultural links at different periods. The first, known as the North of Mexico, consisted of groups dependent on hunting and gathering and living in a desert or semi-desert environment. The second region, known as the America Oasis, was populated by agricultural groups and occupied land belonging to the present-day United States and a small part of Mexico.

At present the term "Mesoamerica" is not used as a finite concept, but rather as a convenient description for archaeologists. In conjunction with a generalised definition of three chronological periods, each featuring different cultural components, the term enables us to classify an entire world, despite the fact that large gaps persist in our overall knowledge of it.

The three periods generally used – although as research has progressed deficiencies have been discovered in this chronological system – are the Pre-Classic (2000 to 100 B.C.), the Classic (100 B.C. to A.D. 900), and the Post-Classic (A.D. 900 to 1521).

The Pre-Classic period

The Pre-Classic or Formative period was characterised by the existence of sedentary groups living together in settlements, with an agricultural economy based on cultivation of crops such as maize, beans, squash, chillies and cotton. Hunting, fishing and gathering complemented this subsistence.

Ceramic production was to develop during this period, with a notable variety of shapes, colours and decoration. Anthropomorphic and zoomorphic figurines were produced, as well as a range of ornaments, and all forms of stone-working techniques were practised.

Society was clearly structured into different levels or classes during this period, with a pronounced specialisation in crafts.

Mainly towards the end of the period, sophisticated hydraulic systems came into use. The first urban developments appeared, with stepped bases and platforms forming part of large complexes. Time was calculated according to two calendars, one of 260 days and the other, based on the solar system, of 365 days; the use of writing became widespread and the deities of fire and water appeared with their own specific characteristics. A variety of luxury products began to be traded and exchanged over great distances.

The Classic period

For all ranks of society there was a rise in the standard of living during this period, coinciding with a large increase in the population. Agricultural production and the ceramic and stone industries changed very little except in terms of quantity.

Complex links bound the different sectors of society; the State organised and reigned over both civil and religious activities; trade, tribute, war and religion became established institutions, and new deities appeared.

Urban centres of monumental proportion proliferated throughout Mesoamerica during the Classic period and development was clearly perceptible in different regions.

Mural painting and sculpture developed in response both to political necessity, reflecting a clear awareness of history, and to religious demand, expressing the diversification of deities, symbols and rituals.

At the end of this period, violence erupted throughout Mesoamerica. While several accounts or interpretations have attempted to explain this phenomenon, it is generally accepted that this violence was either due to the arrival of hunting and gathering groups from the north or was the result of internal uprisings against the ruling élite.

The Post-Classic period

Few important changes in technology and agriculture occurred during the Post-Classic era. One of the features of the period was the emergence of new regional developments that were shorter-lived than those of the Classic period, as well as being restricted to more limited areas.

The Maya-Toltec culture appeared in the Yucatán peninsula, declining towards A.D. 1200 and afterwards becoming restricted to small urban centres of local influence.

In the Central Highlands, the urban centre of Tula emerged as the heir to Teotihuacán and was succeeded by México-Tenochtitlán, populated by the Mexica or Aztecs. Their extensive domain covered nearly 400 centres over an area occupied today by the present-day States of Puebla, Veracruz, Tabasco, Chiapas, Oaxaca, Guerrero and Michoacán, as well as an important part of the Pacific Coast and Central America; in all these areas the influence of the Mexica is clearly visible. Towards A.D. 1500 the Tarascan peoples enjoyed a unique position; not only did they develop an ornamental type of metalwork but they also possessed tools, which gave them a more advanced technology than that used by the inhabitants of México-Tenochtitlán.

Today, the cultural development of Mesoamerica is interpreted as the evolution of a series of processes that were culturally united but had temporal and regional variations, occurring within multi-ethnic and multi-lingual societies.

Western values must be abandoned when approaching the Pre-Columbian cultures of Mexico, to avoid comparing and contrasting specific characteristics without taking into account the fact that they were part of an original development that occurred completely independently of the European world.

Although the general sequence of development can be seen from the preceding paragraphs, it should be stressed that each area of Mesoamerica had particular characteristics and that in the majority of cases the way one influenced another is a determining factor in their analysis. For example, in the Central Highlands formative developments are represented by early agricultural settlements such as Tlatilco, El Arbolillo, Ticomán and Zacatenco; sites such as Tlapacoya and Cuicuilco exemplify the transition to urbanism and gave rise not only to Teotihuacán but also, after its fall, to important sites such as Tula, Xochicalco and Cholula, which were in turn connected with the formation of the Mexica state.

Similar developments took place in the region of Oaxaca but with several *sui generis* characteristics. These include the formal aspect of sculpture, which either survived from earlier periods or was introduced through the influence of the Olmecs. The sites of Tierras Largas, Monte Albán and Monte Negro belong to this formative period; the development of the last site crystalised in Monte Albán where, as in the Central Highlands, small regional developments flourished, with the Mixtecs dominating the Zapotec group. Examples of Post-Classic sites include Tilantongo, Yanhuitlán, Zaachila and Mitla.

On the Gulf Coast important urban developments took place in sites such as La Venta and San Lorenzo as early as 800 B.C. These were crucial to the evolution of the Classic style in various parts of Central Veracruz. When these particular civilisations disintegrated, El Tajín, Cempoala and Quiahuistlán emerged, as well as the extremely rich Huastec

1. Mesoamerica

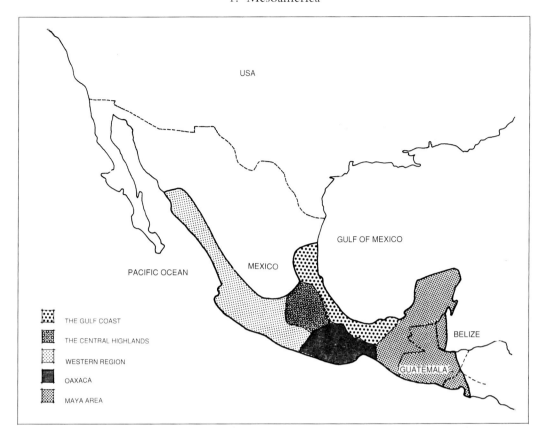

THE GULF COAST

THE CENTRAL HIGHLANDS

WESTERN REGION

OAXACA

MAYA AREA

USA

PACIFIC OCEAN

MEXICO

GULF OF MEXICO

BELIZE

GUATEMALA

civilisation in the north of Veracruz, San Luis Potosí and Tamaulipas.

Certain specialists argue that Maya culture underwent a unique development, but arguments indicate that the Olmec culture was the principal component of that of the Maya. Maya development was at its height during the Classic period; it incorporated a range of cultural variants linked to developments in other cultures throughout Mesoamerica, particularly those of the Central Highlands and the Gulf Coast. Regional developments continued towards the end of the Classic period until A.D. 1400, as in the case of Chichén Itzá where the Toltec component gave rise to a formal style and the use of symbols.

The western part of Mexico is probably one of the least studied regions, but in general the elements that distinguish other Mesoamerican cultures are recognisable here too. It is associated with evidence of the influence of Ecuador and Peru, as well as with the development of the copper industry. By the Post-Classic period, sophisticated instruments with a range of uses had appeared in the region, such as knives and arrow heads; this gave the Tarascans (or *purépechas*) an advantage over the Mexica, who for a great many years put pressure on the cultural frontier of the West.

Lastly, the North of Mexico was inhabited largely by hunters and gatherers until the arrival of the Spanish.

Outstanding among these were agricultural groups that had connections with the southeast of the South American continent, achieving important developments, such as those of the Mogollán, Anazazi and Hohokán cultures. As a result the Casas Grandes culture emerged in what is now Chihuahuan territory. Its principal exponent is Paquimé where the influence of the Central Highlands clearly played a part until A.D. 1000.

II. THE ARTS OF ANCIENT MEXICO

Beatriz de la Fuente

The art of Pre-Columbian Mexico has today assumed its rightful place in the history of world art. Its re-evaluation only began at the end of the nineteenth century but it is now appreciated as an art of extreme subtlety and originality.

In fact, what is generally termed Pre-Columbian or Prehispanic art comprises a diversity of styles which are subject to geographical and chronological variation, as well as cultural circumstances that were endemic to each of the peoples inhabiting Mesoamerica. Each style displays unmistakable hallmarks – for example, Teotihuacán is distinct from the Classic Maya – but nevertheless, all share common foundations.

Thus, each style's identity is established through formal systems of representation and is anchored chronologically; certain deep-rooted codes consisting of symbols lasted for hundreds of years and were manifest throughout different parts of Mesoamerica. In other words, the style can be recognised from the forms, while the signs that make up the system of communicating concepts are based on the beliefs, rituals and visions of the cosmos that united Mesoamerican civilisation. The forms were variable and it could take centuries for the appearance and meaning of changing symbols to alter.

In a different category, the use of stone for monumental works, such as stepped pyramids and colossal sculptures, changed only gradually; by contrast, the changes that took place over a period of time in mural painting and ceramics were more marked.

A brief account of Prehispanic art styles in Mexico with their fundamental characteristics, both changeable and permanent, will give a better understanding of the great creations of Mexico's ancestors, as well as of their significance today. A fundamental influence on style was geography, or landscape, which conditioned it to a certain degree. Thus, the arts and architecture of highland groups are generally more severe in style than those of lowland groups, where there is greater liberty in form and design. In highland areas space and volume are regulated by strict order; in the lowland areas greater movement and fluidity exists.

THE PRE-CLASSIC PERIOD AND THE OLMECS

The earliest artistic manifestations occurred during the long Pre-Classic period, when a large quantity and variety of clay shapes were produced: these include human figurines, mostly female, and different types of pots, vessels and jars with surfaces covered by lively designs or geometric drawings. They have been found in agricultural settlements scattered throughout the whole of Pre-Classic Mesoamerica; hence their enormous variety.

Numerous small terracotta figurines were produced from early Pre-Classic times. The predominance of nude female images suggests the existence of a fertility cult linked to the concept of "mother earth". The features of these delicate figurines began to diversify during the Middle Pre-Classic period, revealing the particular character of the site in which they were manufactured. The relative simplicity of earlier times evolved to allow elaborate headdresses and hair styles; the female shape became more precise, particularly in the so-called "pretty ladies" with their slim figures, narrow waists and thickset legs (known as "onion" legs). Arms end in stumps and feet are shortened, sometimes with incised markings for the toes. The artist modelled each piece individually and used appliqué to add such extras as hair, necklaces and bracelets. There was an unmistakable desire to represent the female attributes, hence the nudity and the inclusion of breasts and the sexual organ. Although most of the female images represent beautiful young women of child-bearing age, there are also older women with heavier bodies and softer flesh, suckling babies or holding children in their arms.

With the emergence of the vigorous Olmec culture the clay figurines acquired a new and different character. As well as the "pretty ladies", gentle clay figurines of acrobats, ball-game players and dwarves were modelled, and beautiful black vessels with shapes and designs depicting natural and imaginary animals, were produced together with outstanding large hollow figures with child-like faces and plump bodies, usually with no indication of their sex. Such transformations in the methods of representation and formal language were indicative of deep changes in the community, as the simplicity of rural life evolved into the complexity of urban society. The Olmecs established the basis of civilisation in Mesoamerica: the planning of cities, monumental basalt sculptures and small jade pieces, and an elaborate code of communication based on symbols. Their powerful religion was expressed via complex imagery and signs and their enormous influence spread along trade routes connecting the metropolitan area located in the south of Veracruz and the east of Tabasco to all the contemporary settlements; as a result their culture was widely diffused.

Our present understanding of Olmec culture has changed radically by comparison with our knowledge of two decades ago; important discoveries in Teopantecuanitlán in Guerrero and at other sites along the Pacific coast of Mexico and Guatemala indicate that the culture of this civilisation was far more widespread than previously thought. At that point it was known that Olmec culture had made an impact on the highlands of central Mexico, principally in Chalcatzingo, and in the states of Puebla and Morelos, as well as at isolated points in Maya territory and El Salvador. Today, however, it is perceived as a culture and style of representation that was of crucial importance in the development of Mesoamerica as a whole; only thus can its geographical range and the unmistakable presence of its style be explained.

Here I will concentrate on the art and architecture of the best-known sites of the metropolitan area along the Gulf Coast of Mexico: San Lorenzo, possibly the eldest site, La Venta and Tres Zapotes. At La Venta the urban layout is determined by a central north-south axis with a slight eastward deviation; the principal constructions maintain a bilateral symmetry in relation to the axis and were made largely out of clay; occasionally they were faced with stone slabs. It was here that the fundamental pattern of Mesoamerican architecture was established: the "negative" spaces formed by the plazas are limited and defined by the volume of the mounds, temple structures and pyramids.

The consistent formal and thematic representation in the approximately 300 colossal stone sculptures in this area – which in themselves indicate a desire for permanency – is immediately recognisable. A noticeable preference for volume predominates, with heavy masses, geometric structures, rounded surfaces and, above all, balanced and harmonious proportions. There are three outstanding groups of sculptures: human figures, comprising the largest group; composite figures with human bodies and animal or fantastic faces and extremities; and a small number of animal figures.

The first group is composed of impersonal seated figures which may represent priests, deity impersonators or supernatural concepts, and the sixteen colossal heads – nine from San Lorenzo, four from La Venta and three from Tres Zapotes – which are undoubtedly portraits of deified rulers. The second group of representations consists of large sculptures of mythological significance and ritualistic aspect: the "thrones" or "altars" (blocks in the form of rectangular prisms), on the front face of which was carved a creation myth: man emerging from the cave or earthly womb. Ritualistic aspects are portrayed by figures bearing heavy-bodied children in their arms; some emerge from the caves in the "altars", while others are freestanding sculptures, such as the celebrated statue of Las Limas, an imposing effigy carved out of smooth, well-polished dark greenstone. The children have large heads with fantastic facial features. These heads are also found in other colossal sculptures and in numerous small figurines, and were once thought to represent the principal Olmec deity: the jaguar-monster, combining human and feline features. Today they are recognised as images incorporating the traits of other animals – serpents, eagles, monkeys – and their true identity remains unclear.

The Olmecs were the first to carve the attractive greenstones and jades, both the translucent blue-green and other jadeites of varying shades of green. Out of these were created small but perfect human figurines, masks, dwarves and other esoteric pieces, such as axes, celts, canoe-shaped objects and perforators used for sacrifice.

The West

In relatively recent times, probably between the second and first centuries B.C. and the first five centuries A.D., a region in the West of Mexico was inhabited by groups with very similar artistic and cultural traits. I refer essentially to the region comprised of the present-day States of Colima, Jalisco, Nayarit and, towards the south, part of Guerrero. Shaft tombs are the unifying feature found throughout this area. Offerings and accompaniments for the dead were left in the chambers of these tombs: clay figures that share the same expressive traits and have similar features, produced for identical purposes and in response to the same cultural stimulus.

The shaft tombs illustrate the funerary architecture of that period; to date no other type of contemporary permanent construction is known. The basic structure of the tombs consists of a circular well or shaft, dug into the earth to a certain depth; on reaching a harder substance, at least one chamber was opened out to the sides with passageways leading to the shaft. The top of the shaft was sealed with a stone slab, whose surface was covered with earth so that no trace of its existence remained.

The surviving sculpture indicates that there were two main stylistic regions in the West: that of Guerrero, in which carvings of hard stone predominate, and the Colima-Jalisco-Nayarit region with its terracottas. For many years the theory that the early sculptures of Guerrero bore similarities to the Olmec style of the Gulf Coast was mere conjecture; today these similarities have been proved by recent discoveries at various sites in Guerrero. The Balsas River in the north-east forms the border between two regional styles within the state : the Mezcala and the Chontal styles. Mezcala sculptures, carved out of fine-grained stone with green and grey tones, demonstrate an unmistakable purity of line and precision and, above all, above all, a remarkable abstract form. Almost all represent human figures, which basically feature flat surfaces and depressions. There are also models of temples and masks; hundreds of masks, used as offerings, were discovered during excavations at the Templo Mayor of Tenochtitlán, and although they display greater formal and expressive freedom than those of the Olmecs, their style denotes a common affiliation. The Chontal style, by comparison, is less powerful, using greater detail for the facial features, hands and clothing, and with a certain ambiguity in the projection of masses which contrasts with the definite striving towards plane surfaces in the Mezcala style.

The general Colima-Jalisco-Nayarit style is easily recognisable in that the sculptures, which are always of clay, represent either whole figures or vessels in the form of human beings, animals, plants or, occasionally, fantastic hybrid combinations. The imagery ranges from naturalism to simple stylised deformity. Charming aspects of life are illustrated anecdotally: pregnant women, maternity, young figures performing daily tasks, rituals and also warriors. Not even in the numerous images of deformed or sick characters are there any signs of drama or tragedy. It is a naturalistic and secular art, but with strong symbolic overtones that are inherent in its role as accompaniment for the dead. Its character is predominantly based on living forms, and the various regional styles highlight the docility or ferocity of fat dogs, the softness of ducks and birds, and the rounded silhouettes of gourds made out of the reddish, burnished clay of Colima. The Nayarit stylistic depiction of men and women amounts almost to caricature, their bodies covered in brilliant colours, while in Jalisco a number of varying styles are united by their common animation of everyday life, and the fact that they are destined to be burial offerings in the chamber of the dead.

Little is known about the art of the West prior to the late Post Classic period, when the Tarascans settled in the present-day state of Michoacán. The imposing *yácatas* (tiered pyramidal structures) testify to their presence; a unique feature of these is that several circular pyramids share a rectangular platform; the best preserved are found in Tzintzuntzán and Ihuatzio. The Tarascans were also notable for their manufacture of metal, copper and silver objects, as proved by the surviving masks, pectorals, discs and axes. A brief mention should be made here of the agricultural groups that settled in the vast region marking the northern border of Mesoamerica. Their simple culture is reflected in basket work and, particularly, rich and multicoloured ceramics. Many of these come from Casas Grandes – a large city built out of adobe – and consist predominantly of variously-shaped pots and bowls. Some are zoomorphic in form, others have animal handles and all are decorated with lines, spirals, rhomboids, squares and parallel lines on flat, brilliantly coloured surfaces.

After the decline of the Olmec culture, a number of centres of art emerged. Over a period of two or three hundred years, these evolved into the splendid and varied conurbations of the Classic period, with their own idiosyncratic art: Teotihuacán in the Central Highlands, Monte Albán in Oaxaca, El Tajín in the centre of Veracruz, and Tikal, Copán, Palenque, Yaxchilán and Piedras Negras, among the most outstanding, in the centre of the Maya area. The artistic language of the Olmecs changed dramatically and the evident desire for sculptural three-dimensionality was gradually subsumed by the use of relief carving. Formal solutions acquired particular expression at each site: relief carving, frequently incorporated into architecture, was the most common, but occasionally there were great achievements in sculpture. High-quality mural paintings from this period also survive, and characteristic styles of architecture developed at each site.

Izapa

During the transition from the Pre-Classic to the Classic period the distinct Izapa style emerged in stone altars and stelae. It spread throughout a region that extended beyond the site in Chiapas after which it is named, and has been found at sites along the Gulf Coast and in Oaxaca and the centre of Mexico. Characterised by elaborate mythological scenes carved in low relief, its forms range from naturalistic imitation to abstract renderings of nature. Most of the monuments are commemorative and combine history and mythology; scenes of supernatural images and primordial myths related to the human life cycle predominate. The Izapa sculptors used a perspectival system with large figures in the foreground and smaller ones in the background; they were also adept at depicting the movement of figures, producing highly animated scenes. The Izapa style forms a bridge between late Olmec and early Maya imagery.

THE CLASSIC PERIOD

Teotihuacán

The enormous metropolis of Teotihuacán imposed a severe geometric style which can be seen in its urban layout, its constructions, its sculpture and, to a lesser degree, in its ceramics and paintings, both on walls and on vessels. The vast area was divided into square and rectangular plazas bounded by pyramids and platforms that echoed the geometric forms of the plazas. The two main causeways – the Avenue of the Dead and the avenue running along one side of the Ciudadela – form a cross, the basis of a rigid urban grid within which the city's buildings were organised. Pyramids, temples, civic buildings, palaces and large residential complexes were built there. The language of the architecture is defined on the basis of two simple forms: the *talud*, a talus or sloping wall, and the vertical wall; a particular feature of Teotihuacán can be seen in the latter, consisting of a *tablero* or entablature with mouldings framing an inset frieze. In early periods the friezes were painted in brilliant, flat colours, and during the period of greatest splendour they were decorated with polychromatic sculptural reliefs.

Monumental stone sculpture repeated these weighty, geometric architectural forms. Similarly, the granite, serpentine and onyx masks of Teotihuacán portray rigid faces devoid of individual features, echoing the classic Teotihuacán canon. The conventionality of the official art is revealed by the urban planning, architecture and sculpture, while the cosmopolitan aspects of the city are manifest in several ceramics and certain mural paintings. There are thousands of baked clay figurines, the most ancient of which have flat bodies with simple outlines. The figures from the Classic period are notable both for their careful modelling and for their lifelike qualities, for which reason they have been named "portrait-type". Large clay incense burners or braziers also date from this period, made in imitation of scenographic temple façades.

During its centuries of splendour, the city must have appeared spectacular: the exterior walls of buildings were painted in brilliant colours and the interior walls bore rich symbolic scenes. Among these, large impersonal images of gods or their representatives can still be admired, with colourful attire and masked faces, participating in ceremonies focused on water, war and the earth's fertility. Various animals are also present: the mythical plumed serpent, stalking jaguars, birds with colourful plumage and flowering trees with glyphs at their base. In the mural scenes at Teotihuacán, a range of colours were used: reds, blues, greens, ochres and shades of black were combined with line to produce illusory images with a gentle projection. The faithful, rhythmical repetition of images indicates that stencils may have been used. This repetition is one of the distinguishing features of Teotihuacán art and architecture. Concrete forms of sublime abstraction and rhythm suggestive of cosmic order invariably characterise the Teotihuacán style.

Oaxaca

The fully developed Classic Zapotec style can be seen at Monte Albán, a funerary and religious city built on a mountain-top in the Valley of Oaxaca. The architectural language of the Zapotecs can be seen with pristine clarity: spaces enclosed in plazas and the flattened volumes of pyramidal bases. Each tiered platform of the pyramids consists of a wall formed by the *talud* and a *tablero* which has an open space at the bottom in the shape of an inverted U, formed by two mouldings with different levels of projection, which produce a pleasing effect of chiaroscuro. The north-south orientation of the main part of the city is reminiscent of Teotihuacán, as is, to some extent, the distribution of the buildings, but there is no direct imitation. Thus the east and west sides of the Main Plaza are formed by constructions of different elevations, avoiding the rigorous symmetry found at Teotihuacán and reproducing the visual effect of the distant mountains. The north and south sides of the Main Plaza are enclosed by large architectural complexes consisting of plazas and buildings of limited access. This intentional degree of privacy indicates that access was restricted to the ruling class, and is echoed by other structures in the city.

Oaxaca boasts a strong tradition of sculptural relief, evident in the Danzantes (Dancers) at Monte Albán and in the Ball-game Players at Dainzú. Very flat relief is combined with carving to produce images of highly animated human figures in ritualistic postures. Following a tradition that reached the Zapotecs from the south, a similar kind of relief carving is found on the stelae, recording the principal actions of governors or warriors. However, the Zapotecs revealed their greatest skill as sculptors in their singular clay urns. These generally represent gods and goddesses of human appearance; the three-dimensional image affixed to the front of a hollow cylinder is their most notable characteristic. The expressive realism of some of the urns from the earliest periods is surprising, and each piece is highly individual; at the peak of Zapotec splendour a number of forms proliferated, while the size of the headdresses became exaggerated and faces were covered by masks with fantastic features. However, despite the wealth of ornamentation, the human figure is rigid and inexpressive; it is almost invariably shown in a seated posture and represents the official art imposed by a ruling élite.

The few remaining mural paintings in Monte Albán are restricted to funerary chambers. On either side of the recess anthropomorphic images of gods covering the walls seem to lead in opposite directions, while a form of directional perspective orientates the viewer towards the principal image. The figures are schematic, painted in flat colours with sharply outlined silhouettes. A splendid tomb, excellently preserved and recently discovered at Huijazoo, an archaeological site near Oaxaca, provides an unsurpassed example of Classic Zapotec painting.

Towards the end of the Classic period Monte Albán ceased to be the principal Zapotec city and other cities in the surrounding valleys came to the fore, such as Mitla and Yagul. Here, elegant buildings that extend horizontally feature typical Zapotec façades that appear to have been faced with the stepped frets characteristic of the Mixtecs. In both cities groups of buildings are composed of square or rectangular patios enclosed by precincts; the decoration of stone mosaic frets and a variety of designs lends singular expression to the Mixtec architectural style. Its very precise form of expression is also found in goldwork (above all in the rich gold jewellery that was manufactured using the delicate lost-wax technique) and in the paintings in codices and a very fine and individualistic type of polychromed ceramic.

THE CLASSIC AND POST-CLASSIC PERIODS IN THE GULF COAST AND MAYA REGIONS

The central and northern coast of the Gulf of Mexico
Like their contemporaries, the inhabitants of the central part of the Gulf Coast during the Classic period also left their particular mark. The city of El Tajín is the principal example of their architecture, while stone and clay sculpture abounded at smaller sites. The buildings reveal a freer spirit than those of Teotihuacán or Monte Albán. They adapt naturally to the surrounding topography by means of structures grouped around plazas. Both civic and religious buildings vary in height and ornamentation, producing an elegant and dynamic visual effect which is enhanced by the cornices projecting from the individual tiers of the pyramids. The Pyramid of the Niches is an outstanding example, so-named because of the regularly spaced niches on each of the six tiers. They total 365, which indicates that, like the Pyramid of Tláloc and Quetzalcóatl in Teotihuacán, they had a ritualistic and calendrical function. Eleven ball courts are situated in the central part of the city alone, indicating the importance of the ceremonial ball game. Stone reliefs on the vertical walls of the South Ball Court display scenes of the game depicted in the characteristic double-outline linear style, which includes interwoven scrolls and bands.

Three types of stone sculpture appear to have originated in this region, although they are also found in distant areas. All three, *yugos, hachas* and *palmas,* are associated with the ball game, and all were carved with astounding mastery and sensitivity. The *yugos* (yokes) are symbolic representations of the players' belts, hence their horseshoe shape. The image most commonly found on them is a toad surrounded by characteristic interlacing. The *palmas* resemble oars and have notches at the front which fit the *yugo*, as portrayed in the ball-court reliefs. The *hachas*, which may have been used as scorers in the game, are composed of two faces in profile joined together at the forehead and becoming broader at the back of the head, splitting the image into two planes.

In contrast to these esoteric stone carvings, the three-dimensional terracotta sculptures lend a notably human dimension to the art of Central Veracruz. They have gentle curved forms, and their faces in particular display a high degree of naturalism. The famous "smiling faces" have genial expressions, while other splendid examples are fully-fledged portraits.

Several of the sculptures are large and hollow; the upper torso is naked and the figures wear narrow-waisted skirts with belts formed by fork-tongued snakes. The half-closed eyes, like crescent moons, suggest that the figures represented are either dead or in a trance-like state; they have been described as Cihuateteo (Snake Woman). Many smaller clay pieces also represent women, standing upright with their arms extended and their hands held up in a ritualistic posture. Several of the clay sculptures incorporate *chapopote* (the black gold or natural petroleum found in abundance along the coast), as an ornamental element on the facial features, the headdress and the body. The art of Central Veracruz encompasses a rich and little-known world combining two complementary elements: the enigmatic ritual of the ball game and the pleasing softness of the human figure.

The northern region of the Gulf Coast was inhabited by the Huastecs. Little remains of their simple architecture, and there have been few archaeological excavations. The repeated use of circular layouts in the buildings is an original feature, and the buildings are thought to have been dedicated to the god of wind. No ornamentation remains on the façades, but one building in Tamuín had mural paintings with scenes demonstrating the regional Mixtec-Puebla pictorial style. Twelve figures, possibly gods, were portrayed in a procession, framed by frets and painted in Indian red. The figures stood closely together and wore large, colourful ornaments. Sharp angular lines echoed the composition of diagonals which gave a sense of direction to the figures.

Sculpture was the Huastecs' most outstanding form of artistic expression. Of approximately 400 known pieces, all except one are sculpted in soft, easily carved sandstone and date from between the ninth and eleventh centuries A.D. Their basic form is a thin rectangular prism or slab. In the sculptures of ordinary human figures the broadest surface of the slab depicts frontal and rear views; by contrast, in the figures of hunchbacks and men holding rods, this surface depicts the figure in profile. The principal theme is the human figure: women, men and a small number of hunchbacks and elderly figures. In the group of female figures, the system of representation is repetetive, consisting of upright figures with arms held at the sides of the body and hands resting on stomachs; breasts are modelled on naked upper torsos and limited by a lower border. The headdresses are the distinctive Huastec feature. A consistent fan-shaped part and other variable elements are combined with a rectangular block and a conical cap. Some of the fans are composed of serpent heads or radial spokes imitating folded paper crests and the figures bearing these are thought to represent the mother-earth goddess Ixcuina-Tlazoltéotl.

A greater variety of forms is found among the ordinary male figures. Some of these are schematic, naked and without a headdress or bearing only a close-fitting cap which allows the accentuated cranial deformation to be seen. Others are notable for their fine, careful carving: delicate relief designs cover the body or loincloth. In others the ribs are portrayed, with a hollow containing the heart beneath them. Many wear a conical cap which always rises up above a band, and circular hooked earflares, thought to be the attributes of Ehécatl-Quetzalcóatl, god of wind. Some male sculptures are composed of two figures; some bear the figure of a child on their back, others a skeleton.

A third group of figures consists of hunchbacks, while a fourth comprises a unique group within Mesoamerican sculpture, consisting of just over 40 male figures holding a rod or a serpent in their hands. These may be related to the ancient god of fire, with the rod representing the *mamal-huaztli*, an instrument that was used to set the god alight.

The slabs of sandstone appear to have determined the characteristics of Huastec sculpture to a large degree. Thus the use of flat forms was established, and the body, limbs and headdresses were synthesised in hieratic predominantly abstract and geometric figures.

The Maya region

The Maya are the people that have aroused the greatest interest among those concerned with the history of mankind, due, I believe, to two fundamental reasons: their art – reliefs, mural paintings, painted vessels and small ceramics – which is always expressed in human dimensions to which we can easily relate; and their hieroglyphic writing, which has still not been completely deciphered. Maya art is like an enormous mosaic displaying a multitude of regional styles. I will refer only to a few of the sites located in the Mexican Republic (although the region extends to Central America): Palenque, Yaxchilán and Bonampak, as great examples of the Classic period, and Chichén Itzá as the great city of the Post-Classic period.

Palenque is built in a style that extends through the Usumacinta River basin and includes the cities of Yaxchilán and Bonampak in Mexico and neighbouring Piedras Negras in Guatemala. The unifying style of these sites centres on the human figure, represented in sculpted relief. Buildings were constructed for the edification of man, and reliefs and paintings were executed for his glorification. The buildings are generally of different sizes and elevation and the plazas are never closed at the corners, so space can flow in harmonious movement, creating an equilibrium with the volume of the pyramids. The buildings are grouped in complexes adapted to local topography and are linked together by wide flights of steps, ramps or avenues. The structure of the pyramids is made lighter as a result of walls broken by pillars alternating with open spaces. Graceful pierced roofcombs reinforce the sensation of movement and lightness. No two constructions are the same at these sites, and although the characteristic patterns of the region's architecture

– porticoes of pillars, sanctuaries with the typical Maya vaulting, the volute cornice and pierced roofcomb – are repeated, the individuality of each building prevails. Some, like the building with paintings in Bonampak, incorporate features displaying affinities with the Puuc style of the northern Maya region, while others, like the Palace Tower and the Temple of Inscriptions at Palenque, are unique in Maya architecture.

Relief stelae were not erected at Palenque. All sculptural creativity was concentrated in the stuccoed façades: the walls, friezes and roofcombs. Interior spaces were decorated with splendid stone panels and tablets carved with animated human shapes. The form and content of the Palenque reliefs reveal a definite human orientation, in which the concept of the universe and historical awareness are brilliantly integrated.

In the stelae and lintels at Yaxchilán, the carving of several individuals is apparent: so much so that today the work of at least eleven sculptors or masters of workshops is recognised in the large number of carved monuments in this city. Yaxchilán has more carved lintels than any other Maya city. They are carved out of soft limestone or sapodilla wood, perpetuating scenes of victory and subjection, of religious rituals and political alliances. Two main types of relief appear: the first, which may be the most ancient, is characterised by deeply carved figures that project and stand out from the background plane beneath, creating a chiaroscuro effect which contributes to the strongly lit images. The second type is a flatter form of relief with less well defined outlines; the profiles of the principal figures merge with the secondary elements formed by ornaments and clothing. It should be pointed out that in Yaxchilán, as in Palenque and Bonampak, the vast majority of representations are portraits, although not in the same vein as the academic concept of the Western portrait. Nevertheless, the Maya artists at these and other sites shared a definite desire to capture likeness according to their own systems of representation.

Bonampak is a minor site, and although imposing stone stelae and excellent sculpted lintels have been found there, it owes its fame to the masterly murals painted on the walls of one of its buildings. They have recently been cleaned and carefully restored almost to their original splendour. Apart from the beauty of the images, their importance is due to the fact that they reveal how significant this form of art was when Maya culture was at its height. They show a command of naturalism, line and colour, as well as having enormous documentary value. The fresco paintings cover the interiors of three chambers and extend over about 100 square metres. Hundreds of Mayas are depicted in a unified work portraying the celebrations and rituals of the last dynastic accession at Bonampak. On the walls of the first room the main focus of the scene is the presentation of the infant heir to the nobility; he is accompanied by his family, noblemen dressed in white mantles and processions of musicians and dancers. The action takes place in horizontal bands which indicate the way the scene should be read at the same time as structuring the composition, and which culminate at the highest point of the vault with representations of celestial images. Three walls in the second room describe a fierce contest in the jungle, a historical battle played out against a mythological background. The figures are free from conventionality, and different pictorial planes and shades of colour create an effect of perspective and volume. Physical strength and a variety of expressive gestures are clearly illustrated in the scenes. A dead body, rendered with the use of foreshortening, lies across two steps of the pyramid, at the feet of the victorious warrior-ruler. The scenes in the third room represent the celebration of the victory, when musicians, dancers and courtesans reappear. The ruler, his family and retinue are engaged in the ritual of autosacrifice; a dance is portrayed on three walls of the chamber, taking place in front and on the steps of a pyramid. Masks of gods cover the upper part of the vault and a sort of procession of deformed characters bearing an enormous figure seem to descend from the vault. The Bonampak murals form part of the world's history of mural painting and have their own originality and dignity.

At a time when cultural and artistic life was in decline in the cities of the Usumacinta River basin, a large number of structures were being built in the Puuc style of Uxmal at Chichén Itzá, the great Maya-Toltec city in the Yucatán peninsula. However, in contrast to the precision of the masonry carving and stone mosaic designs which decorate the friezes at Uxmal, the constructions at "old" Chichén show crude stonework and a certain carelessness in the proportions of the decorations of frets and masks.

The astronomical and calendrical purpose of many of the constructions at Chichén Itzá was already evident in the building known as the Caracol (spiral shell) built in ancient times. Thus, the openings in the walls of the Caracol were used for observing the movements of Venus, and the imposing radial pyramid called the Castillo is positioned in accordance with the movements of the stars and planets. The steps of its four stairways total 365, indicating its adaptation to the solar year, and on the days of the equinox the nine stepped tiers of the pyramid form a shadow like nine segments of a serpent.

The Toltec presence is concentrated in the buildings at the northern end of the city. Serpent columns are placed at temple entrances, the head resting on the ground, the upright body forming the shaft of the column and the tail with its rattles supporting the lintel. Pillars and columns fill wide spaces, as in the Temple of the Warriors, the Court of a Thousand Columns and the Market. The use of the column signals a radical change in the concept of space: the narrowness of the Maya vault was transformed into the simplicity of the colonnaded gallery. True interior space was created for the first time in Mesoamerica at both Tula and Chichén Itzá.

Further themes of Toltec architectural relief are apparent in the warriors sculpted on the pillars, in the friezes with stalking jaguars, in the plumed serpents that alternate with eagles, in the rows of skulls and in the image of a human face in the jaws of a fantastic plumed serpent creature.

The standard-bearers, atlantean figures and the famous Chac Mools are also Toltec sculptures, and are considered by contemporary sculptors to be masterpieces of world art. These images are indicative of substantive changes in the language of sculpture, with a return to the three-dimensional figure sculpture that had been relegated to the background during the Classic period of Maya art. Because of Toltec presence the art of Chichén Itzá is imbued with a singular character: the harmonious fusion of two styles, Maya and Toltec. Legacies from different times and places in Mesoamerica were united and recreated in this city, hence its originality.

THE CLASSIC PERIOD IN THE CENTRAL HIGHLANDS OF MEXICO

Tula

The power of the Toltecs from Tula was acknowledged by the Mexica when they accorded them a prominent place in the Mexica history they created, within which they are the Toltecs' successors. Here it is worth mentioning that the perfection of Toltec crafts and the mastery of their constructions, according to the information given by the Mexica to Fray Bernardo de Sahagún, does not coincide with what is revealed by the surviving art and architecture. Buildings, sculptures and reliefs are all badly made and bear no trace of the "interest and skill of the works they made", as described by Sahagún. In fact, the originality of Toltec art lies basically in the introduction of new architectural solutions such as the vast colonnaded gallery covering an enormous interior space, and to images that are innovatory and reveal, above all, their military strength. As the sun warrior nation, the Toltecs are the ancestors of the Mexica. Architectural space and pyramidal volumes are conceived on a monumental scale; new elements, apart from the colonnaded gallery, include the construction of a wall of serpents, the *coatepantli*, built as protection for the most strictly religious part of the city: large warrior figures dedicated to the cult of the sun were carved, known as atlanteans, although it is thought that they may have served as caryatids bearing a flat roof on the summit of Pyramid B; upright plumed serpents were erected with the same roof-bearing function, the head resting on the ground and the tail serving as a support for the upper part; benches with relief scenes of figures were also placed against walls. The characteristic Toltec pillars, found in both Tula and Chichén Itzá, have antecedents in Teotihuacán in their function as architectural supports; however, the custom of covering the four sides of a pillar with reliefs of warrior figures is typically Toltec. Another Toltec custom was the facing of pyramids with flagstones that were carved with stalking feline figures or eagles and vultures bearing heart symbols in their beaks, as well as with the image of the man-bird-serpent previously mentioned.

The free-standing sculpture at Tula is remarkable for its innovatory images within Mesoamerican iconography: the Chac Mool, the atlantean figures with their arms held high and the standard-bearers. In three-dimensional sculpture the forms are hard and the volumes tend towards geometricality without reaching the purity of Teotihuacán. The basic shapes are synthesised in masses and planes, but particular details, such as clothing and ornament, are profusely detailed by means of square or rectangular plaques, and are abruptly divided into sections. The innovation of the forms and images lies in the vigour expressed by means of the cube, the cylinder and the rectangular prism.

The Mexica

The art of the Mexica, the ancient inhabitants of the most magnificent city of Mesoamerica, is awe-inspiring in its richness, and in the variety of its forms of expression. Their architecture, their plastic arts and their literature reveal a young and vigorous people, profoundly religious, who were heirs to a thousand-year-old culture that they were to transform into their own complex cosmic vision. In approximately 200 years, from the beginning of the fourteenth century to 1519, when Hernán Cortés reached the metropolis, the Mexica converted the small island at the west end of the great lake of Texcoco into the capital of the empire, the *axis mundi* of Mesoamerica.

During the period of Mexica power, Tenochtitlán, built on land reclaimed from the lake, was constructed on a square grid formed by canals and streets. Three large causeways – Tlacopan, Tepeyácac and the one that branched towards Coyohuacan and Iztapalapa – led from the centre and linked the island with dry land. Four quadrants framed the ceremonial centre enclosed within a wall, and next to this but outside the precinct lay the palaces of the rulers. In the first volume of his memoirs, Fray Sahagún describes the twin pyramids of Tláloc and Huitzilopochtli in the centre of the city – the group now known as the Templo Mayor – the circular temple dedicated to Quetzalcóatl, the *tzompantli* or altar of skulls, the enclosed Ball Court and the wall that closed off the precinct. The location of the religious buildings was based on the movement of the sun, which, depending on the time of year, rose from behind the temple of Tláloc, the god of rain and agriculture, or from behind the temple of Huitzilopochtli, the god of war and fire. On mornings of the equinox the sun faced the temple of Quetzalcóatl.

Many of the monumental stone sculptures are exceptional, incorporating forms and subject-matter from earlier cultures but developing new solutions. Mexica sculptors borrowed the colossal scale of the remote Olmec tradition, but overlaid the pieces with elaborate designs and symbols in low relief. The Classic Veracruz style made a dramatic return in the extraordinary clay sculptures found in the Templo Mayor: effigies of young eagle warriors, possibly anthropomorphic images of the god of the sun as he began his flight through the skies. An eclecticism existed in Mexica sculpture that hovered between naturalism and abstraction, depending on the artists who were brought from distant parts of the empire to work in the capital.

The characteristics that distinguish Mexica sculpture from other Mesoamerican works are the impeccable structure and deep, concentrated energy that underlie the diverse regional styles it incorporated into its strong aesthetic expression: integrated forms, preferably in rounded volumes, always within a balanced composition. This strength of vision is found both in apparently simple works (the elusive simplicity of great art) – such as the red cornelian grasshopper, the obsidian monkey, the carved serpentine serpents or the eagles of the Templo Mayor – and in works combining a plurality of images and complex symbolism – the goddess Coatlicue, the two Coyolxauhquis, the Tláloc Chac Mool, and the Sun Stone. Many Mexica sculptures of human figures lack the attributes that would identify them as gods; among them are some of the masterpieces of sculpture. Other sculptures portray deities in their anthropomorphic guises, combined with symbols from a different order. These never disappeared completely from the artistic and religious iconography, even when anthropomorphism reached perfection. This phenomenon can be seen in the Mexica sculpture that represents gods and supernatural images; the signs of their supernatural and religious appearance have to be represented in a visible form; sacred art has to represent the invisible using material means; and the response to the search for the representation of divinity was often to use fantastic images endowed with hybrid attributes that have no likeness in nature. In effect, the vast majority of stone gods carved by Mexica sculptors display complex combinations of forms that range from naturalism to abstraction.

The cosmopolitanism of Tenochtitlán is also evident in its minor arts, which include polychromatic vessels, feather objects (headdresses, mantles, fans) and goldwork. But while the variety of this Mexica art is indicative of the empire's dominion, the powerful hidden energy that appears nowhere else in Mesoamerica is found only in the Mexica's great sculpture.

During two brief centuries Mexica artists mastered many different types of expression. They organised forms into structures that express the wisdom of reason and which now, from a distance of five centuries, comprise the basis of pride and world fame.

1. VILLAGE CULTURES IN THE CENTRAL HIGHLANDS

Martha Carmona Macías

The Central Highlands of Mexico comprise the present-day states of Morelos, Puebla, Tlaxcala, Hidalgo, Mexico and the Federal District; this mountainous region sits on a northern latitude of about 20°, with a temperate climate which rarely encounters frost.

The region is bordered on the south by a transversal volcanic range; the interior plateau, known as the Anahuac tableland, is in fact a high valley, lying at an altitude of over 2000 metres. Where there used to be a large rain-water lake, there are now only a few small stretches of water.

The southern part of the central plateau consists of mountainous foothills of volcanic origin, over which the legendary volcanoes of Popocatépetl (5.452 metres high) and Iztaccíhuatl (5.286 metres high) preside. The Valley of Mexico, an area of approximately 9,600 square kilometres, is situated within the central Mexican plateau, lying between raised ground on one side and high mountains on the other, and formed in the transversal neo-volcanic axis. The mountainous landscape that surrounds the central lacustrine valley is the result of the last volcanic eruptions. In addition to the above-mentioned volcanoes are the sierras of Tepozotlán, Las Cruces, the Ajusco Hill and the Xitle Volcano, responsible for the dramatic destruction of Cuicuilco, the capital of the region during the Late Pre-Classic period. Finally, there are the sierras of Frío River and the Sierra Nevada, notable for their beauty.

It was these geographical conditions that formed the background to the first human settlements developing in the Central Highlands, with their material and technological progress and their political and social organisations, ritualistic practices and the increasingly complex cosmic bel;iefs that were to serve as the basis for future developments.

The Pre-Classic cultures of the Central Highlands
The beginning of the Pre-Classic period, which has been subdivided into Early (2000-1200 B.C.), Middle (1200-800 B.C.) and Late (800 B.C.-A.D. 250), is marked by a knowledge of agriculture and ceramics, and several traits such as maize-based subsistence, which are evident in certain settlements or villages.

Two main cultural currents can be distinguished in Mesoamerica during this period: the first is a village-type culture found in valleys and highlands; the other is the semi-urban culture characteristic of semi-tropical or coastal regions, generally known as the Olmec culture. This group came into contact with the Central Highlands settlements around 900 B.C., and made an important cultural impact.

During the Pre-Classic period, materials such as bone, wood and vegetal fibres continued in use, as did techniques that had been employed since prehistoric times. Clay began to be used intensively for the production of many forms of pottery, whose decoration, which was simple to start with, became more varied and artistic, using polychromy, by the end of the period. Baskets, nets and snares were used for hunting and fishing, together with spearheads made out of different materials and in different shapes. Grinding stones and mortars were used, as well as large pots for the storage of water and food.

The fine clay figurines that were produced at the time enable us today to appreciate the physical appearance of these peoples, their activities, their use of ornament and what may have been a cult of fertility.

The Pre-Classic period witnessed a combination of hunting, fishing, gathering and agriculture, the last of two kinds, grazing and arable; irrigation was developed during the Middle Pre-Classic. A system of bartering probably existed among the villages.

It was during this period that a construction system for residential units (as they are termed

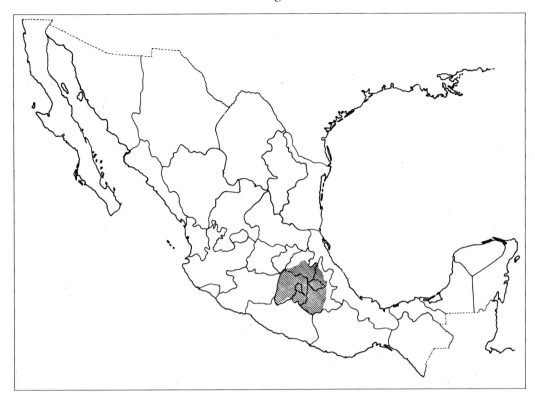

in archaeology) was introduced. The units were initially simple huts (houses made from branches), which gradually evolved to include platforms and several rooms, culminating in the construction of the first temples. The foundations generally consisted of adobe and stone, while the walls were either of mud or simple adobe bricks; the floors were made out of tamped-down earth or stone blocks, except at Tlapacoya (Late Pre-Classic), where they were made of stucco; the roofs were of straw, and access to the rooms was usually by means of stairs or ramps. Patios, stoves and ovens appeared in association with these constructions, and simple maize fields (cultivated fields) have been found near the residences.

At first the Pre-Classic groups generally walked around naked, but adorned themselves liberally with necklaces, bracelets, earflares, nose-plugs, bangles and so on, and made intensive use of facial and body paint; their appearance was enhanced with elaborate hairstyles and headdresses, including partial or total shaving of the head.

The development of magical thought was much affected by natural phenomena and other factors beyond human control, such as life, death, sleep, fire and other related forces. Reality was mixed with superstition, and animals and inanimate things were endowed with human attributes: sun, moon, rain, earth, death, mountains, and animals such as the jaguar and the serpent, all became mythologised.

It was at this time that the cult of death began to appeare: the cemetary of Tlatilco in the state of Mexico provides an example of the habit of burying the dead with offerings. While there is little evidence of human sacrifice, discoveries at Tlatilco also prove the existence of this practice.

The impressive cultural manifestations that characterised Mesoamerican cities during later periods were built on the pillars of Pre-Classic achievement, including not only ceremonialism and the establishment of centres of power, as well as architectural advances such as platforms and temples, but also technological progress and calendrical knowledge.

The earliest inhabitants of the Highlands subsisted on animals and plants. The discovery of maize and its cultivation enabled these hunting and gathering groups to share a more sedentary life, and they began to settle near lakes and rivers.

During the Early Pre-Classic period (2000-1200 B.C.), peasant groups in the Valley of Mexico settled in higher altitudes to avoid the flooding of their settlements and crops. The north-east region includes the sites of Tlatilco, Coapexco, Tehuacán and Zohapilco among others; Tlatilco was first established around 1200 B.C., and because of its proximity to the banks of the Hondo River, benefited not only from crops and fish but also from a considerable degree of freedom for movement and hunting. One group settled at the site of Zacatenco in about 1100 B.C., occupying the foothills of the Guadalupe Sierra and the area next to the extensive plain at its foot. In the area of Zohapilco, at the south of the Valley of Mexico, research has investigated the lengthy development that occurred between the sixth and first centuries B.C. This site is located on the banks of the former Chalco Lake, now dry, near the settlement of Tlapacoya; Zohapilco is an archaeological site characteristic of the ancient human settlements found on the banks of a lake with a large quantity of fauna and fertile soils. During this period the groups already possessed a degree of simple but effective technology. They used native materials, such as all types of stone, as well as bone, wood, vegetal fibres and clay; various kinds of tools were in use, such as hammers, perforators, knives and scrapers, as well as accurate snares, and there is evidence of simple forms of basketry and ropemaking; doubtless they wove nets and *petates* (mats woven from vegetal fibres).

The settlers had large and small projectile arrows, with or without shafts, which they used to wound and kill animals; also in use were rods for sowing, blades or wooden hoes for digging earth, bodkins and awls of deer antler or tibia, bone needles, serpentine and bone gimlets used to bore holes in stones and softer materials, flint or serpentine chisels for

3. Valley of Mexico

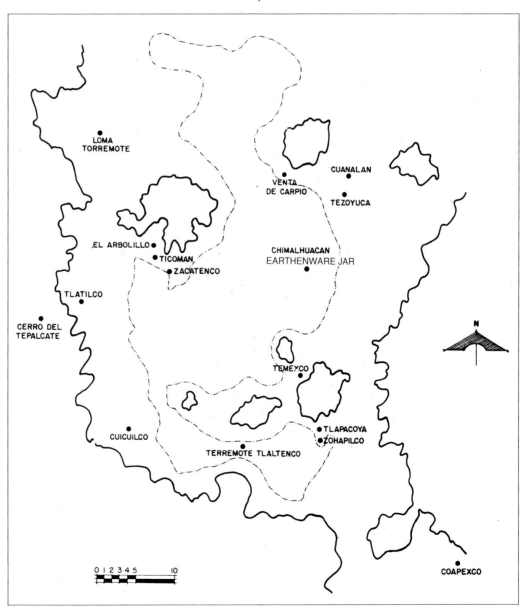

stone engraving, and possibly bone or wooden borers for starting fires. Rounded volcanic stone mortars were employed for grinding; flat, slightly oval, rectangular or square grinding stones with or without supports were also in use, as were stones used as anvils.

Basketwork and woven objects have not survived, mainly due to the passage of time; however, at Zacatenco a piece of ancient cloth has been found, combining cotton threads with a fibre similar to yucca; at Arbolillo and Copilco the impressions of large baskets were discovered, and in Ticomán the remains of what seems to have been a skin cape were found. Recently excavated residences on the Terremote Ridge show clear signs of ropemaking and basketry. The Pre-Classic peasant groups also made rather crude clay figurines with applied features. These seem to have been linked to a fertility cult, but at the same time may represent the physical appearance of the ancient inhabitants.

Bracelets and necklaces adorn these figurines, which also have holes in their earlobes and nostrils, from which earflares and nose-plugs were hung; they wear bangles and sandals; their hair is worn up, in some cases showing simple or elaborate turbans; the female images are nude and display facial and body painting.

With regard to pottery, large pots were manufactured for storing water and food; other, smaller pots were used for cooking, and simple bowls were made for eating out of. Vessels were also manufactured as burial offerings or for religious ceremonies and rituals. The decoration of the vessels is usually incised, with geometric motifs picked out by bone engravers. Characteristic are vessels with composite silhouettes and incised triangular designs filled with parallel lines; in Arbolillo, Tlatilco and Zacatenco in particular, plates with engraved centres and short-necked pots have been found.

The Zohapilco phase (2500-2000 B.C.) evolved in the area of the same name, where a simple figurine was found which had a cylindrical body and superficially traced features, dated by Carbon 14 to 2200 B.C. (plus or minus 100 years). The Nevada phase which followed (1400-1250 B.C.) is characterised by gourds, jars with composite silhouettes and vessels with flat bases. Later periods at the site are datable to the Middle and Late Pre-Classic.

Between 1200 and 800 B.C., a certain style developed in the Central Highlands that reflected the specific beliefs of the Gulf of Mexico region. Pottery had close affinities to that of the Gulf area, consisting predominantly of flat-bottomed plates, and highly polished black, white or dark-red bottles. Extremely fine clays were used, made with white kaolin or grey volcanic ash bases. This pottery is generally decorated with abstract motifs, either incised or in relief, in the form of lines or stylised motifs; masks, figurines and stonework are delicately modelled or sculpted.

The central theme of decoration during this period (1200-800 B.C.) was the jaguar. Jaguar teeth, jaws, paws, markings and eyes were represented, combined with anthropomorphic features creating man-jaguar superimpositions, in what was evidently a complex combination of mythological beliefs. For some researchers, the jaguar represents force, wisdom, occult powers, the subterranean world, night, caves and fertility; it can also be seen as the earliest incarnation of nascent Mesoamerican deities, and as such has been interpreted as the "jaguar-bird-serpent" antecedent of a water deity.

Notable settlements in the Valley of Mexico at this time included Tlapacoya, Arbolillo, Ticomán, Tehuacán, Zacatenco and Tlatilco, as well as Chalcatzingo in Morelos, and Moyotzingo and Las Bocas in Puebla; other villages, which include Atoto, Xico, Xalostoc, Coatepec and Lomas de Becerra, also began to take shape in the Valley of Mexico. At Tlatilco fine representations were made of the animals and plants found in the surrounding area, such as ducks, rabbits, turtles, pumpkins and *guajes* (a fleshy tree with an edible fruit similar to pumpkins). Two pottery styles emerged, one that developed in the Central Highlands, characterised by geometric and linear motifs, and a second style, using symbols, introduced by Olmec groups and applied to vessels and figurines that continued to be produced using local techniques. In addition, however, figurines began to be manufactured in a polished white or marble colour, with slit eyes, down-turned mouths, and a head that is generally deformed and shaven; they were represented in a seated posture, giving rise to new types of figurine, such as the so-called "baby-face" and "pretty lady" types, as well as hollow figures in a polished red colour, and other variants. These features, combined with the Olmec influence that was characteristic of the Middle Pre-Classic, are found in villages in Puebla, Morelos and in the Valley of Mexico. Various activities of daily life in the villages are represented by the figurines, and it is possible to distinguish shamans, dancers, ball-game players, deformed beings, elderly figures, acrobats and musicians, for example. The figurines also reveal the physical appearance of the villagers, as well as their attire and ornament: it seems that society was governed by a shaman who, as well as being the ruler of the group, was the guardian of magical and herbalist secrets and the intermediary of the supernatural forces that were the subject of worship. Singing and dancing ceremonies undoubtedly took place, as there are representations not only of musicians and dancers, but also of musical instruments, such as clay bells, whistles, flutes, rattles and notched bones used as resonators. Different pigments continued to be used for painting the body, and bead necklaces, circular earflares, nose-plugs, pectorals, bracelets, wristlets and bangles were worn. As part of the aesthetic pattern and body decoration, scarification, intentional cranial deformation, dental mutilation and the shaving of heads, either total or partial, sometimes combined with beautifully combed locks of hair, were all fashionable, together with colourful and elaborate headdresses.

The cult of the dead acquired new forms, like the multiple burials which, in some cases, suggest that human sacrifice might have taken place. Funerary offerings were placed according to the status of the deceased, and occasionally the body was covered with cinnabar; Tlatilco in the state of Mexico is outstanding in this respect. The site was inhabited from prehistoric times, and has provided archaeologists with detailed cultural information on Pre-Classic human groups.

Researchers at Tlapacoya have divided the Middle Pre-Classic into the Ayotla and Manantial phases. The first evolved between 1250 and 1000 B.C. (representing the site's Olmec phase) while the Manantial evolved between 1000 and 800 B.C. These phases were studied in the region of Zohapilco on the banks of the former Chalco Lake, near the settlement of Tlapacoya in the state of Mexico. Numerous burials with finely wrought offerings from the Ayotla phase (1250-1000 B.C.) have been found there, as well as ancient dwellings belonging to the inhabitants of this area. Population density increased during the Manantial phase which followed, when objects carved out of jade were introduced to the area. During this period, Tlapacoya and Tlatilco became the ruling villages, controlling the economy and giving political cohesion to the Central Highlands sites. The same Gulf of Mexico influence is apparent in sites such as Gualupita, Atlihuayán, Chalcatzingo, Iglesia Vieja, Ajalpan, Las Bocas and El Caballo Pintado in Morelos and Puebla.

Middle Pre-Classic village communities were the first to introduce hydraulic technology for the irrigation of their fields, a great cultural advance which improved food production and led to excess produce. As a result certain settlements became wealthier, grew larger, and exerted control over smaller villages, thus achieving economic and political power which transformed them into the so-called "ruling villages".

This phenomenon is apparent at the archaeological site of Moyotzingo in Puebla (1200-800 B.C.), where settlements were established in terraced dwellings, and certain villages became ruling sites in the Puebla-Tlaxcala valley; similar developments are apparent throughout the Central Highlands.

Although such rural villages as Zacatenco, Atoto, Tetelpan, Xico, Chalco and Ticomán were to continue their existence in the Valley of Mexico, from the year 700 B.C. the first ceremonial centres also began to appear, including, for instance, Cerro del Tepalcate, Tlapacoya, Cuicuilco and even the initial phases of Teotihuacán. This signalled the beginning of a new cultural development, the Late Pre-Classic, characterised by the emergence of centres acting as integrating focal points.

From 800-700 B.C. until the begining of the first century A.D., increasingly rapid cultural developments in the Valley of Mexico lead to the birth of urbanism and the growth of civilisation. These were the years in which the great Teotihuacán state was formed, and in which villages and towns were replaced by large cities. Although the methods by which this change was brought about are as yet unexplained, archaeological evidence points to an increasingly complex society.

Towards the year 800 B.C., the inhabitants of the Valley lived in small sites which varied in size from 10 to 60 hectares. There was a greater number of settlements in the south of the area; in the valley of Teotihuacán there were relatively few. Cuicuilco must have existed by this time, but had not acquired the dominant role it would later assume. There was as yet no monumental architecturet, but towards 450 B.C. the first known religious building in the Valley of Mexico was erected at Cerro del Tepalcate: this was a platform for a temple. Its proportions were modest, with two tiers leading to the upper part where there was a temple consisting of a mud hut. Various extensions were added to it, used to accommodate offerings and burials with offerings.

As time passed the population of the valley continued to grow, especially in the south where some sites now reached 100 hectares in size. By around 400 B.C., construction of the main pyramid at Cuicuilco had begun, heralding the beginning of monumental religious architecture in the Central Highlands. The pyramid consisted of an oval base made out of adobe, with three tiers and a total height of 17 metres. A circular temple was built at the summit of the pyramid, with a mud altar inside it. About 100 years later, towards 300 B.C., the size of the base was increased, reaching a height of 27 metres and now in a circular form, with a diameter of 80 metres, and faced in stone. Cuicuilco was to become the main centre of the southern part of the valley, although as the site is now covered by a layer of lava, it is difficult to obtain much detail about it.

The complexity of the site and its society during that period is indicated by a number of findings at the site: ceramic representations of a deity associated with fire; radial burials in front of the circular pyramid; a circular-roomed structure made out of flagstones painted with red motifs. The discovery in 1968 of other stone altars situated close to the circular base further implied the relative importance of Cuicuilco, which is calculated to have had up to 20,000 inhabitants, and to have occupied an area of 400 hectares towards the year 50 B.C., when the eruption of Xitle caused its destruction.

The pyramid at Tlapacoya is contemporary with Cuicuilco, and presages the architectural style of Teotihuacán. The base, which has sloping walls, reaches a height of five metres, and was built in three stages. Tombs were found in the interior, constructed with stone walls and roofs made from basalt slabs. The offerings found there can be considered luxury items, as among other objects they include jade beads, obsidian knives, and vessels decorated in fresco with "negative painting". The earliest bottles to bear a representation on the bottle neck, showing a deity associated with rain, come from Tlapacoya.

The archaeological remains at Cuicuilco aand Tlapacoya imply great technological advances in both architecture and pottery, a high degree of division of labour, the existence of social classes with different functions, and ritual activities centred on two deities whose basic traits suggest that they were later to become known as the Old God, or Huehuetéotl, and the god of rain, or Tláloc. The priestly caste continued to perform both religious and political functions.

During the last hundred years of Cuicuilco's existence, the valley of Teotihuacán began to show signs of great vitality. Between 150 B.C. and the early first century A.D., the settlement of Teotihuacán alone reached a population of ten thousand and covered 6 square kilometres, from which beginning it was to develop into the great urban centre of Mesoamerica. The exploitation of obsidian deposits in the valley and the exportation of obsidian artefacts are thought to have been among the principal factors favouring the development and peak of Teotihuacán's growth during this period, and it is probable that some of the main temples, such as the Pyramid of the Sun, already existed, but that they were later covered by other structures. Thus, Cuicuilco in the south and Teotihuacán in the north-east were two large centres which polarised and integrated smaller settlements, simultaneously competing for resources in the Valley of Mexico. The eventual destruction of Cuicuilco (due to the eruption of Xitle), however, was to contribute to Teotihuacán's superiority, as was Teotihuacán's economic potential; Teotihuacán absorbed part of the population of Cuicuilco, thus winning the battle for supremacy in the Valley of Mexico, and acting as a starting point for the Classic period that was to follow.

2. VILLAGE NATURALISM

Sonia Lombardo de Ruíz

Most of the surviving sculpture from the cultures of the Central Highlands of Mexico in the Pre-Classic period is made of clay. The objects are masterpieces of modelling; the ones presented in this exhibition were given a well-polished finish that results in a smooth, glossy texture.

A particular genre is represented by the small female figurines – between 7 and 15 cms high, which are generally represented naked, or with small skirts or belts; sometimes they are decorated with colourful body paint, and they always have fine hairstyles, or headdresses in the form of crowns, bows and turbans. During the Middle Pre-Classic, the figurine type known as "pretty ladies" had vertically elongated heads that were large in proportion to the body (plate 5). The torsos are long and slender, while the arms, which are very short, are held out from the body, without any differentiation for the hands. This forms a strong contrast to the bulky hips and legs, which make the figures appear very solid. The open forms and rounded outline produce a graceful overall effect. In some cases, the same type of "pretty lady" is found in large-scale sculptures – up to 54 cms in height – which comprised tomb offerings (plate 1). The principal features are incised, including eyes, mouth, navel and sex. The emphasis on feminine physical characteristics in the context of agricultural village peoples links the figurines to a cult of fertility.

There are many forms of ceramics; some were for everyday use, others were of a ceremonial nature, generally associated with death rituals.

Depending on the firing process used, the vessels acquired different tones: yellow, light brown, a reddish brown or grey and black.

Vessels of the Late Pre-Classic are remarkable for their elegant silhouettes. Some are extremely simple, their only decoration consisting of a slight curvature that swells out at the base and rim of the tubular body (plate 9). In others, the horizontally fluted sides of the vessels project a series of graceful crest-like forms, creating shadows and reflections of light (plate 10).

Bottles in the form of acrobats (plate 2) are particularly significant. The acrobats are represented in elaborate positions, with their bodies bent double and their feet held up above their heads and curving down to touch them. They are masterful compositions of balanced volume and great expression, which at the same time fulfill their functions as jars. The fact that some of them have been found in tombs suggests that these acrobats were destined to be linked to some religious function.

Elements associated with the Olmec culture appeared in the Central Highlands during the Middle Pre-Classic in the form of black or grey ceramics with incised or printed decoration. Among them are numerous bottles with high cylindrical necks and spherical bodies (plate 4), as well as zoomorphic and even anthropomorphic vessels whose forms adopt ingenious positions in accordance with the function of the vessel (plate 8). All of these are characterised by their bulky volume, which gives a sense of generosity and opulence to the elements of nature they reproduce. Small fauna from the edges of lakes, as well as aquatic life (an important element in these village peoples' subsistence), inspired the ceramic motifs: armadillos (plate 3), *tlacuaches* (a type of marsupial native to Mexico), ducks (plate 6) and fish, among others. Their presence in burials may be related to the *nahual* (animal spirit) of the buried individual, that is, to the daily influence of the person's tutelar animal.

The appearance of decorative designs with feline elements, such as schematically stylised jaguar paws, indicates the conceptualisation of one particular deity, possibly totemic and connected with fertility and rain, who was given form as a symbolic element in ceramics.

Pre-Classic sculptural conception, expressed in ceramics, also includes small-scale sculpture – between 10 and 54 cms in height. Softly rounded volumes dominate the formal language of this sculpture, which was based on symmetrical composition, although considerable freedom was exercised in using one single element to break this symmetry, seeking to adapt it to the functional shape of the vessels.

Representation was naturalistic, but at the same time deformities were employed to express or accentuate elements that were important or of interest. The use of colour in the Middle Pre-Classic was fairly restricted, with only one, two or, exceptionally, three colours appearing; by contrast, in the Late Pre-Classic period ceramics were polychromatic. The subject-matter reflected natural elements found in the local environment, but it also had a social function connected with magical-religious practices – related to fertility, subsistence and death – which gave it symbolic significance. The use of ideographic elements, such as the jaguar paw to symbolise the rain deity, indicates an important element of esotericism in religious belief, exercised by an emerging priestly caste.

1. FIGURINE

Pre-Classic Central Highlands culture. Tlatilco, State of Mexico. Middle Pre-Classic (1200-800 B.C.). Clay. Height 54.5 cm, width 17.2 cm. In store. MNA, Cat. no. 1-2545, Inv. no. 10-202223.

Pre-Classic figures portray daily village life through a variety of activities, which in some cases involve beautifully constructed scenes; infants and pregnant women are common, as well as representations of infants' cots. These hand-modelled figurines show us life in all its different stages, as well as giving precise details of physical appearance and human activity. They also allow us to deduce the level of cultural development of the groups who produced them.

The Middle Pre-Classic (1200-800 B.C.) was the period of Olmec domination (1000 B.C.), a situation reflected in the character of the figurines. Some display intentional cranial deformity, dental mutilation, slit, slightly slanting eyes and downturned lips of a white or marble colour; they are represented in the classic seated posture of Olmec figurines.

This Olmec style influenced the indigenous style of the Central Highlands, as is evident from such types as the "baby face" larger-scale figures, like the one illustrated here, which is hollow and modelled in the Olmec tradition. However, the characteristic red colour of the Central Highlands has been kept, and the figure stands upright, naked and delicately polished, and displaying facial and body painting. The intentional cranial deformity is beautifully framed by a headdress, which is well complemented by earflares.   *m.c.m.*

2. ANTHROPOMORPHIC BOTTLE

Pre-Classic Central Highlands culture. Provenance Tlatilco, State of Mexico. Middle Pre-Classic (1200-800 B.C.). Clay. Height 35.5 cm, width 17 cm. Pre-Classic Hall. MNA. Cat. no. 1-2520. Inv. no. 10-77582.

Pre-Classic village communities practised the cult of death and human sacrifice, especially of children, associated with funerary rites. Research on individual and multiple burials has revealed the predominance of inhumations with the body in a curled-up position, shrouded in cotton cloth or matting. There are also burials in which corpses are stretched out in a variety of positions; occasionally dogs were sacrificed to accompany the dead; offerings that were directly related to the social status of the deceased were made; the remains were often sprinkled with red pigment and cinnabar, possibly representing blood, the symbol of strength and life. The burials were generally in holes or pits dug in cultivated fields or close to huts.

Radial burials dating from the Late Pre-Classic have been found at Cuicuilco, where the custom of cremation was initiated; in Tlapacoya, tombs were constructed with stone walls and flagstone roofs in the centre of the pyramidal base, and contained rich offerings of ceramics, basketry and other objects.

The Middle Pre-Classic site of Tlatilco is a particularly significant case, where numerous burials have been excavated, all with offerings containing outstandingly beautiful and delicate vessels of different shapes and decoration.

This vessel represents an acrobat and may be of a ceremonial type; it is modelled in light brown clay with a polished finish, and its ornament and features are applied with clay fillips. The acrobat's body is beautifully arched, with one foot resting on the head; the right leg has been cut off to act as a spout.

A similar example has been excavated from burial No. 154 at Tlatilco.   *m.c.m.*

3. BOTTLE IN SHAPE OF ARMADILLO

Pre-Classic Central Highlands culture. Tlatilco, State of Mexico. Middle Pre-Classic (1200-800 B.C.). Clay. Height 25cm, width 28.7 cm. Pre-Classic Hall. MNA. Cat. no. 1-2519. Inv. no. 10-77581.

During the Pre-Classic, materials such as stone, bone, wood and vegetal fibres continued in use, but clay became more popular, with the development of a fine, delicate pottery; large pots were manufactured for water and food storage, while smaller pots were made for cooking. This type of pottery is known as domestic ware, of common usage, as opposed to the ceramics used in ceremonies and funerals, which comprised incense burners, jars and a variety of beautifully shaped and decorated vessels.

Fine representations of animals like the armadillo can be seen in these ceramics. This modelled zoomorphic version has a polished finish. Notable decorative techniques include the use of incised line on the animal's body, as well as arching bands of geometric decoration on the carapace, filled with a zig-zag motif and produced by rocker stamping using a shell.

The armadillo was hunted for its meat, while its shell was used to manufacture the percussion instruments that were played in rituals and religious ceremonies. It is likely that at this early period its tail was used to strengthen the blowpipes used in hunting.   *m.c.m.*

4. CEREMONIAL BOTTLE

Pre-Classic Central Highlands. Tlatilco, State of Mexico. Middle Pre-Classic (1200-800 B.C.). Clay. Height 22.5 cm, diameter 14.5 cm. In store. MNA. Cat. no. 1-2142. Inv. no. 10-221977.

Between 1200 and 900 B.C., in the early years of Mesoamerica's development, specific beliefs and ways of life were to be reflected in a particular type of stylistic expression; the pottery of this time comprises a rich range of forms, notable among which are bottles that are frequently highly polished and black or fawn-coloured. Some of the black vessels have a light-coloured border as a result of a particular firing process. In general they are decorated with abstract symbols, either incised or engraved: motifs in the shape of crosses and spirals, as well as the eyes, paws, fangs, eyebrows and markings of the jaguar, appear. The jaguar represents a most powerful iconographic theme: one body of opinion sees it as symbolising strength, power and wisdom, associated with the nocturnal world, caves, water sources and fertility; it is also seen as evolving into certain deities from later periods. Other research has identified in the jaguar the earliest sculptural interpretations of four future deities: spring, fire, death and the plumed serpent.

Thus at Tlatilco there is one representation of an aquatic serpent with iconographic elements representing the jaguar. The fusion of the two components enables us to identify an ophidiano-jaguar animal, which may be related to water, land and fertility. The jaguar theme is not merely decorative; it has a graphic and abstract function, reflecting indigenous philosophies and religious beliefs. A clear example of this pottery is the vessel illustrated here, with its decoration symbolising a jaguar's paw; this hand-modelled vessel comes from Tlatilco, and has a polished black finish, while the designs on its body have been both incised and scratched on.   *m.c.m.*

5. ANTHROPOMORPHIC FIGURINE

Pre-Classic Central Highlands culture. Tlatilco, State of Mexico. Middle Pre-Classic (1200-800 B.C.). Clay. Height 11 cm, width 4 cm. In store. MNA. Cat. no. 1-2159. Inv. no. 10-47362.

During the Pre-Classic period, the groups who had settled in the Valley of Mexico modelled delicate clay figurines, mostly female, symbolising the earth's fertility.

Early in this period, these were executed using the technique of appliquéd clay fillips for the features and body ornaments; they were shown naked, but with facial and body decorations. Pigments of vegetal and mineral origin were used to draw a variety of geometric designs or bands on the body and face, red and yellow being the preferred colours. Notable features are the headdresses and elaborate hairstyles, together with adornments such as necklaces, earflares and bracelets.

During the Middle Pre-Classic, the first figurines to wear items of clothing and a type of footwear appeared. The practices of cranial deformation and dental mutilation began in the Central Highlands around 1000 B.C. (Middle Pre-Classic) under the influence of the Gulf of Mexico region, and these traits appear in a large number of figurines.

In this delicate example modelled in clay, the appliqué technique has been used for the features, the necklace and tresses of hair; the figure represents a naked adult woman. Traces of red and white paint decorating the body and face can still be seen; there is also a fine headdress, and the hair is elegantly styled in locks and tresses.   *m.c.m.*

6. DUCK VESSEL

Pre-Classic Central Highlands culture. Tlatilco, State of Mexico. Middle Pre-Classic (1200-800 B.C.). Clay. Height 22 cm, width 21 cm. Pre-Classic Hall. MNA. Cat. no. 1-2518. Inv. no. 10-77580.

The principal craft practised by Pre-Classic groups was pottery and the modelling of figurines. Notable among the former are organic and zoomorphic representations, with vessels that faithfully reproduce different types of pumpkins, as well as anthropomorphic and zoomorphic likenesses.

This duck is a fine example of a zoomorphic vessel. Modelled in black earthenware, it comes from Tlatilco. The staining is the result of a paricular firing process, and there is a hole at the top of the head for pouring water.

Tlatilco was located close to a lake, and aquatic animal representations are frequent and realistic; turtles and fish modelled in clay illustrate the animals that were found locally.

Ducks were initially used for food; however, by the Post-Classic period they were thought of as messengers of the clouds and bearers of seeds in agricultural fertility rites. Whistles imitating birdsong and in the shape of birds were modelled from Pre-Classic times, as well as flutes and rattles that were used in magic-religious rituals and ceremonies.   *m.c.m.*

7. ANTHROPOMORPHIC FIGURINE

Pre-Classic Central Highlands culture. Valleys of State of Puebla. Middle Pre-Classic (1200-800 B.C.). Clay. Height 27 cm, width 12.5 cm. In store. MNA. Cta. no. 1-2558. Inv. no. 10-135812.

Pre-Classic figurines come in the form of masked shamans, acrobats, musicians, dancers and even loving mothers suckling their young. Seen as a whole, they reflect customs, dress and ornament.

From these we can deduce that village communities were governed by shamans; their role as intermediaries between man and supernatural forces meant that shamans were both feared and respected.

Within society there were craftsmen, stone workers, weavers, painters and basketmakers. In the figurines, the various crafts are represented by small skirts, trusses, coifs, turbans, headscarves, short trousers, sandals, loose-fitting jackets, blouses and ribbons, all of which testify to the development of weaving using vegetal fibres such as *ixtle* and cotton, as well as *tule* (American reed) and palms for the manufacture of mats. The figurines wear bead necklaces, circular earflares, nose-plugs, bracelets, bangles and, as a form of breast decoration, pyrite mirrors. Many of the personal ornaments that inspired this decoration have been discovered in the excavation of burials. Villages undoubtedly traded with each other, as some of these items have clearly been exchanged.

A widespread custom at this time was the decoration of the face and body, using a number of techniques: through the use of paint applied with stamps or brushes; scarification; cranial deformation – tabular, vertical and oblique; dental mutilation, in which the natural form of the incisors was altered without damage to the root; and total or partial shaving of the head, sometimes combined with tresses and headdresses that emphasised this practice. Although during the Middle and Late Pre-Classic period, male figurines were modelled, there was always a higher percentage of females, possibly associated with Mother-Earth, as she was responsible for giving birth to life.

The nudity associated with fertility is apparent in this figure, modelled in clay; she is delicately polished and wears earflares; her roundedness suggests that she represents a woman in the first months of pregnancy.   *m.c.m.*

8. ANTHROPOMORPHIC JAR

Pre-Classic Central Highlands culture. Tlatilco, State of Mexico. Middle Pre-Classic (1200-800 B.C.). Clay. Height 19.6 cm, width 9.8 cm. In store. MNA. Cat. no. 1-5301. Inv. no. 10-226449.

In Nahuatl, Tlatilco means "Where there are hidden things"; the town is currently called San Luis Tlatilco and forms part of the Municipality of Naucalpán in the state of Mexico. From a cultural point of view, Tlatilco was one of the largest and most complex sites in the Valley of Mexico, equal in importance to sites located in the states of Puebla, Morelos and Guerrero. The diversity and beauty of the ceramics suggests groups of craftsmen who produced polished vessels using a variety of decorative techniques, such as incising, scraping, engraving, rocker stamping and finger-nail prints, as well as painting on dry stucco and negative painting.

The motifs tend to be geometric, either covering the whole surface or in bands, together with symbolic and abstract designs that are related to the jaguar, introduced into the Central Highlands – via Oaxaca-Guerrero, Puebla and Morelos – by Olmec groups from the coast of Veracruz and Tabasco. Vessels such as bottles and jars started being produced when the Olmec tradition amalgamated with the local one, in a beautiful combination of the two. The piece represented here is a fine example of Tlatilco's ancient inhabitants' skill in ceramic production. Two different colours have been used so that elements of the vessel stand out, such as the light brown band around the red face of the figure, which has curly hair; there are holes in the head, possibly so that the figure could be suspended; it displays cranial deformity and wears earflares. Its clothing consists of a large loincloth and a belt around the waist, and its open mouth serves as a spout. *m.c.m.*

9. FUNERARY VASE

Pre-Classic Central Highlands culture. Tlatilco, State of Mexico. Late Pre-Classic (800 B.C. – A.D. 250). Clay. Height 27.5 cm, diameter 12 cm. Pre-Classic Hall. MNA. Cat. no. 1-1139. Inv. no. 10-42028.

During the Late Pre-Classic period, the Central Highlands were to witness some of the earliest religious constructions, such as the platform of Cerro de Tepalcate and the pyramidal base at Tlapacoya. Population increased, and towards the end of the period certain villages and towns had evolved into densely-populated settlements that can be considered to be pre-urban, and in which true ceremonial centres were to emerge.

Tlapacoya is an archaeological site located on the east side of the Valley of Mexico, and provides important information on cultural development, which ranges from the earliest period of hunter-gatherers, through the first farmers, to the first villages; the density of its population and the presence of finely-wrought objects, such as haematite and jade mirrors, suggest that during the Middle Pre-Classic period it rivalled Tlatilco for supremacy in the Valley of Mexico, and was an important ruling site that rapidly developed into a ceremonial centre (from 300 to 100 B.C.). The elegant piece shown here comes from this important archaeological site, and was excavated from one of the tombs located in the centre of the pyramidal base.

The slender and fragile form of the vase is modelled in clay; the technique used to give the polished, dark-brown finish results in a uniform texture that emphasises the concave curve of the body, framed between a wide circular mouth at the top and an annular base. The result, a piece of great delicacy, displays all the mastery of the Pre-Classic peoples. *m.c.m.*

10. TRIPOD FUNERARY VESSEL

Pre-Classic Central Highlands culture. Tlapacoya, State of Mexico. Late Pre-Classic (800 B.C. – A.D. 250). Clay. Height 22 cm, diameter 15 cm. Pre-Classic Hall. MNA. Cat. no. 1-1128. Inv. no. 10-42017.

Tlapacoya was initially sited on an island in what later became known as the Chalco Lake. Over a period of time, the water level changed, and a number of shores were formed. The hill on which the human settlement was established during Pre-Classic times was the result of volcanic activity. During the Middle and Late Pre-Classic period, an agricultural group settled at Tlapacoya and built terraces on the hill — a great technological advance preventing the erosion of soil and seeds.

Funerary rites which involved ceramic offerings were performed by these inhabitants of Tlapacoya; this funerary pottery was initially decorated in light colours, but later dark and even black finishes were substituted, as in this vessel with a horizontally fluted body, excavated from Tomb I at Tlapacoya. Modelled in clay and covered with a highly polished black finish, it has a convex base, a hollow interior and a circular mouth, and stands on three solid supports. It is dated to between 300 and 100 B.C. *m.c.m.*

1. FIGURINE

2. ANTHROPOMORPHIC BOTTLE

2. ANTHROPOMORPHIC BOTTLE

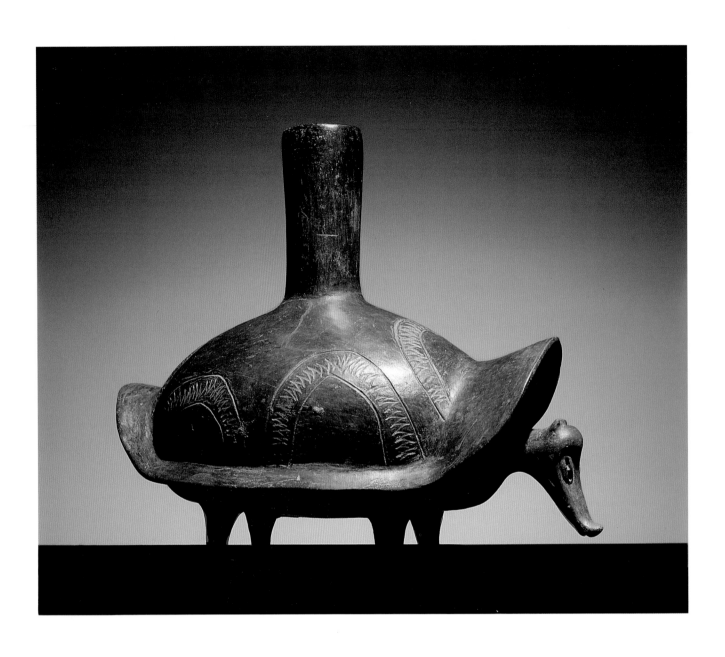

3. BOTTLE IN SHAPE OF ARMADILLO

4. CEREMONIAL BOTTLE

5. ANTHROPOMORPHIC FIGURINE

6. DUCK VESSEL

7. ANTHROPOMORPHIC FIGURINE

8. ANTHROPOMORPHIC JAR

9. FUNERARY VASE

10. TRIPOD FUNERARY VESSEL

3. TEOTIHUACAN, METROPOLIS OF PRIESTS AND MERCHANTS

Clara Luz Diaz Oyarzábal

In the 1950s it was usual to speak of the Classic period (around 100 B.C.-A.D. 900) – which included the Teotihuacán culture – as a theocratic period *par excellence* in which war was unknown, and of Teotihuacán as a ceremonial site of great importance, where Tláloc, the god of rain, was the pre-eminent deity. However, intensive research from the 1970s onwards has led to a rapid change of outlook, and today views on Teotihuacán have become so complex that it is no longer feasible to sum up its significance in only a few words.

The Teotihuacán culture developed in the Central Highlands of Mexico between 100 B.C. and A.D. 750. During this period, Teotihuacán was to influence nearly all the regions of Mesoamerica, originally dominating the communities closest to it in the Valley of Mexico, and later, through commercial links, affecting far more distant sites, such as Chalchihuites in the north of Mexico, the areas of Veracruz, Oaxaca, the Guatemalan Highlands and even the Yucatán peninsula. Its metropolitan nature, its trading system and the religious prestige that must have been generated by its enormous pyramids and ceremonial centre, were all to attract a transient population that would have enriched and given colour to the life of the great city and its inhabitants.

Teotihuacán is situated in the valley of the same name, 40 kilometres north-east of the Federal District, in the state of Mexico. At the north, the valley is bordered by the Cerro Gordo, and at the south by the Sierra Patlachique; it is irrigated by the San Juan River and other smaller sources, and its fertile land is well suited to cultivation, providing its inhabitants both with animals for hunting and with basic materials for the construction of their city and for the production of items that might be used for trade purposes.

Certain specialists are of the opinion that the original founders of Teotihuacán spoke a language of Yuto-Nahua affiliation, although this cannot be definitely proved. As regards the inhabitants' origins and ethnic characteristics, we can say hypothetically that physically they resembled the earliest inhabitants of the Central Highlands.

One method of finding out about the population has been the study of skeletal remains. On the available evidence, the people who lived in some of the "palaces" at Teotihuacán appear to have had rounded skulls, the average height of men being 1.61 metres, and of women 1.46 metres. While skeletons of both infants and adults have been found, there are very few of elderly people, suggesting that the average lifespan of the inhabitants would have been between 35 and 40 years, and that the death of children younger than one year was a frequent occurrence.

Both human bones and figurines reveal methods of personal embellishment that conform to an established aesthetic pattern: tabular, vertical and oblique cranial deformation, scarification and several forms of dental mutilatition.

The skeletal remains also indicate to some extent the type of diet followed by this group; the basic food appears to have been agricultural produce such as maize and beans, which are represented in certain mural paintings. Vegetal remains discovered in the process of excavation testify to a diet of products such as pumpkin, tomato, avocado, *alegría* (a type of grain), plums, chilli and *nopal,* and further archaeological exploration provides evidence of the consumption of animals, including venison, dog, rabbit and turkey. The proximity of Lake Texcoco, as part of the lagoon area of the Valley of Mexico, enabled this diet to be complemented with turtle, fresh-water fowl and fish.

One of the principal characteristics of Teotihuacán, revealed during relatively recent excavations, was the high level of urban development reached by the Prehispanic settlement. The latest discoveries indicate that it was a true "city" in the present sense of

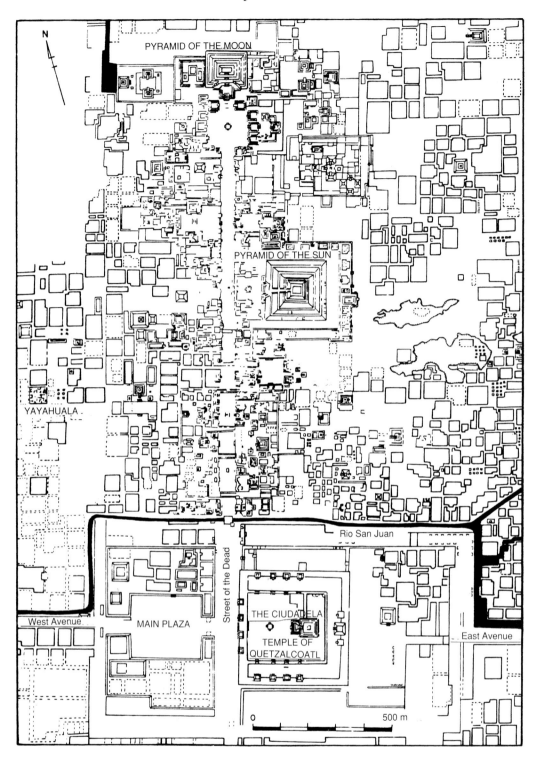

the word. Architecturally it was conceived compactly, with wide avenues and adjoining residential structures, each housing a number of families and separated by narrow streets. Residential and ceremonial structures were built in accordance with an urban grid; subterranean drainage systems were installed in residential units, which, in many cases, flowed into a large canal running the length of the Street of the Dead and flowing eventually into the San Juan River. As well as hundreds of specialist workshops for the production of artefacts made from ceramic, shell and, in particular, obsidian, there was a central market and a merchants' quarter.

At the height of its powers, Teotihuacán extended over an area of 22.5 square kilometres, with a population of approximately 150,000 – 200,000.

The city layout seems to have been the result of a master plan, conceived in Teotihuacán's infancy when its main buildings were constructed: the Pyramid of the Moon, the Pyramid of the Sun and the Ciudadela. The layout of the Street of the Dead, the principal avenue, was probably planned at this point; it was named by the Mexica, when they arrived at Teotihuacán and found the buildings in ruins and covered in undergrowth. This avenue forms the north-south axis, and the city's most important buildings are located along its length. At right-angles to this axis, starting at the Ciudadela and the Great Compound (two of the main architectural groups), lie the East and West Avenues. The two axes divide the settlement into quadrants, giving a grid-like aspect to the layout.

Together with the Pyramids of the Sun and the Moon which dominate the city, the Ciudadela is one of the most important sites. It consists of a virtually square precinct, each side measuring approximately 40 metres, with a large sunken patio in the centre and four platforms along its borders. Occupying one end, inside the Ciudadela, is the Pyramid of Quetzalcóatl. Units consisting of a number of rooms line its sides, and are thought to have been the residences of the ruling class of Teotihuacán. To the west of the Street of the Dead, and facing the Ciudadela, is the Great Compound, an esplanade of similar size to the Ciudadela, which has been sounded by archaeologists but not yet completely explored. It appears to consist of both a central plaza (which must have functioned as the city's main market) and a precinct with two gigantic wings, on top of which were built the residences of state officials.

Typical residential buildings in the metropolis are commonly known as "palaces", which can be defined as "residential units" each housing several families. The second term is the one currently used with the greatest accuracy. These residential units, square or rectangular, vary in size, but usually measure between 25 x 25 metres and 50 x 50 metres. Windowless walls form an outer boundary enclosing the space; inside are numerous rooms, with walls decorated with paintings, passageways and sunken patios. It has been calculated that between thirty and sixty people lived in them, depending on the size of the structure. There was almost always a main sunken patio, which functioned as a local ceremonial area specifically for the use of the unit's inhabitants, and which in some cases had a temple in the centre. Religious rituals were undoubtedly celebrated here by the most important person in the unit, involving everyone who lived there. This type of structure provided the city with considerable architectural unity, while simultaneously facilitating the state's supervision and control of the inhabitants. These residential units existed only in the city and in a few sites that came under its administration, and disappeared in Mesoamerica after the fall of the city in which they had been conceived. They should not be confused with the so-called "palaces" of Maya architecture.

The most sumptuous residential building known so far is the Palace of Quetzalpapalotl (or Quetzal-Butterfly), situated in the Street of the Dead to the south-west of the Pyramid of the Moon. Its privileged position, richly decorated carved pillars and mural painting suggest that it housed the highest social class. Other totally or partially excavated residential units that are famous for their architecture and their mural painting include those of Tetitla, Tepantitla, Zacuala, and Yayahuala. Archaeological investigations indicate that approximately 2200 units of this type existed throughout the city.

One feature typifying Teotihuacán architecture is the *talud-tablero* or talus-entablature, in which a rectangular element (*tablero*) rises from a sloping base wall (*talud*). The height of a monument could be increased merely by repeating this combination in a vertical direction. The *talud-tablero* recurs endlessly within the city; wherever it is found in the rest of Mesoamerica it is considered an indication of the influence of Teotihuacán. The remains of pottery workshops have been found in the ancient city, and the potters distinguished themselves in the production of both utilitarian and luxury ceramics. As well as supplying the city, they also, via commercial networks, reached sites as far away from the Central Highlands as Kaminaljuyú and Tikal in the Maya region of Guatemala, and Matacapan in the state of Veracruz.

Approximately thirty workshops were dedicated to the production of *San Martín Orange*, a type of ceramic vessel in very common domestic usage in Teotihuacán, which seems to have been exclusively made for the city as it is rarely found at other archaeological sites. The location of these workshops at a fair distance from the Street of the Dead indicates

5. Typical Teotihuacán temple and cross-section showing the *talud-tablero* (sloping panel)

that the Teotihuacán state did not have any particular interest in controlling their production. By direct contrast is a workshop producing ceremonial braziers that has recently been discovered near the Ciudadela. Its location in such an important part of the city, situated next door to the Ciudadela, a building considered to have been the religious and political centre of the city, indicates that the production and distribution of these very special religious artefacts was directly controlled by Teotihuacán's rulers.

The famous *Anaranjado Delgado* ceramic, or thin orange ware, is an excellent chronological indication of the Classic period, as it ceased to be produced after the fall of Teotihuacán. It is characterised by extremely thin-walled vessels and by an orange finish in which white dots are clearly visible. It has not been determined whether it was produced in the state of Puebla or in Teotihuacán itself; but in either case, Teotihuacán was undoubtedly its centre of distribution and controlled its commercialisation throughout Mesoamerica.

While its architecture and sculpture are of high quality and have an unmistakable and characteristic hallmark, Teotihuacán was completely unrivalled in the field of mural painting. Paintings decorated buildings both in the centre of the city and on the outskirts, in ceremonial centres and in residences. The large number of polychromatic murals has earned Teotihuacán the title "city of colours".

Although the principal subject-matter appears to be religious and is conveyed through a language of symbols that are extremely difficult to interpret, these murals also illustrate many of the more practical and concrete aspects of life in Teotihuacán: customs, dress, ornament, games, plants, fruits, trees, animals and other domestic features are represented.

The techniques employed and the origin of the colours used in Teotihuacán paintings have long been subjects of interest. From what is known about the disposition, dimensions and composition of the murals, we can conclude that these paintings were carefully thought through. The painters were specialists who conceived their work as an entity from start to finish.

Walls built from stone and mud were then covered with a layer of mud and small fragments of *tezontle* (a porous stone found in the area) approximately ten centimetres deep. A smooth finish with a lime base, between two and four millimetres deep, was applied to this layer. Next, the area to be painted was marked off using horizontal and vertical threads, and the outline of the principal figures was sketched in in red or black. A colour, nearly always red, was then applied to the background of the composition, and finally the figures were painted with different colours. The operation was generally carried out using the *al fresco* technique, while the lime finish was still damp, except where colours such as blue and green were applied, which were not resistant to the action of the lime because of their chemical composition. In these cases a process known as *al temple*

44

was used, in which pigment was applied to a dry wall, but mixed with some sort of paste or adhesive, which may have been nopal sap.

Once the composition was finished, the outlines were often emphasised with a dark-red line to heighten them or to give greater contrast. This line was executed with such thin brushes that some lines were only two millimetres wide. The brushes were probably made of dog's hair or another organic material, which has naturally disappeared over the years.

The glazed appearance or hard finish of some of the murals seems to have been obtained by burnishing the painting when it was still fresh, using a fine-grained stone instrument. The pigments were derived from iron compounds for the reds, ochres and yellows, and copper compounds for the blues and greens. Black was obtained from charcoal.

The Teotihuacán economy was based primarily on agriculture, hunting and lakeland resources. However, the economic impulse which initiated the urban development referred to above seems to have developed from the exploitation of obsidian, the extraction, carving and commercialisation of which was as important during Prehispanic times as the steel industry is today.

Hundreds of workshops specialising in obsidian are calculated to have existed in the city, and there were at least as many others who concentrated on shell, basalt, slate, stonework, ceramics and figurines, without taking into account other types of work that have left no archaeological trace. A large quantity of this production was destined, among other objects, for trade as part of Teotihuacán's intense commercial activity, for which specific routes were established radiating north, south, east and west from the metropolis, but especially towards the Gulf region in the east, and towards the Maya region in the south. Teotihuacán exported the surplus of its specialised production via these routes, receiving in exchange mica, cacao, cotton, jade, alabaster, rubber, shells, precious feathers, jaguar pelts and other exotic produce.

Trade was so important in the Central Highlands that, while armed conquest may have played a part in certain cases, in general it was Teotihuacán's commercial system that spread the city's influence through Mesoamerica. In archaeological terms this influence is expressed with different degrees of intensity: from the discovery of isolated vessels considered to be the product of sporadic commercial contacts, to the probable establishment of colonies as far away as the Maya region.

On the other hand, if instead we examine the effects of outside contacts on Teotihuacán, it is easy to see the mark left by other cultures, especially those of the Gulf Coast and of Oaxaca.

Archaeological excavations carried out in the so-called Oaxaca Quarter, located in the south-west of the city, reveal architectural characteristics native to Teotihuacán alongside Oaxacan domestic ceramic ware and mortuary customs. While this points to a strict Teotihuacán state power, it also indicates the presence of foreign ethnic groups resident in the metropolis.

The influence of the Gulf region in Teotihuacán, on the other hand, is evident both in the ceramics found in the Merchants' Quarter, and, in archaeological terms, in the persistent presence of marine and caracol shells from the Gulf, as well as in the Tajín style of artefacts and ceramics found in Teotihuacán.

The Maya area had a less marked effect, visible in ceramics and in some of the details of the city's murals.

Teotihuacán, with its social strata and clearly differentiated social classes, was imbued with a strong sense of religion. The numerous pyramids and temples found in different parts of the city testify to this fact, as does the unequivocally religious subject-matter of most of its frescoes. Among the many gods venerated, the most important was Tláloc, the god related to water and agriculture, but other gods, identified as Quetzalcóatl, Huehuetéotl or the Old God of Fire, and Xipe Totec or the god of spring, were also represented.

However, the concept of Teotihuacán as a theocratic and peaceful ceremonial centre, held in high religious esteem throughout Mesoamerica, is undergoing rapid change as a result of data which suggests that the final years of the metropolis were not as peaceful as previously thought.

For example, the figurines with helmets and shields which appeared during this period, and the protective walls erected in key parts of the city, are unmistakable symptoms of political and social unrest. Although no battle scenes appear as such, an incipient militarism is evident in the murals of the residential unit of Atetelco, where warriors are represented disguised as animals, as in the case of the paintings of coyotes★ bearing spears and spear throwers; there are also symbols that refer to sacrifice involving human hearts.

Although it is still a little early to make an adequate assessment, the most recent findings – which are still being studied – imply that in the Pyramid of Quetzalcóatl in the Ciudadela mass sacrifices took place, dated around 150 A.D., at the time of the pyramid's construction. These discoveries will provoke a radical change in certain theories about Teotihuacán, especially those concerned with the period of the emergence of militarism in this culture.

Many of the city's buildings reveal traces of fire, a fact which certain research has interpreted as accounting for the violent collapse of the Central Highlands' main city. Several theories have been postulated: that there were invasions by nomadic groups from the north; that a great famine destroyed the population; that perhaps there was an internal uprising by oppressed social classes; or even that sites such as Xochicalco and Cholula held Teotihuacán's commercial network in a stranglehold. Possibly it was a combination of all these factors that led to the sudden collapse of a city that had achieved great splendour, political as well as religious and economic, whose legacy of impressive remains has suffered such ravages of time.

The glory of Teotihuacán did not pass unnoticed by the peoples who succeeded it; on the contrary, many Teotihuacán cultural traits were to be absorbed by following generations. Five hundred years after the fall of the city, when it was in ruins, the Mexica elevated Teotihuacán to mythical status, attributing to the city the creation of their Fifth Sun, the sun which gave birth to their world.

The Fifth Sun was born after the world had passed through four previous stages or suns, ending in catastrophe. According to Mexica cosmography, in order to create the Fifth Sun the gods had assembled in Teotihuacán:

"It is said that when it was still the era of the night, when there was still no light, when it had not yet dawned, the gods gathered together; it is said that they called out to each other, there in Teotihuacán" (*Matritense Codex* of the Real Palacio).

Among other things, the legend narrates how, through their sacrifice on a pyre, two gods transformed themselves into the Sun and the Moon, and began their movement in the firmament. Thus, in poetic terms, began a new era.

At the beginning of the twentieth century, the indigenous population of the Valley of Teotihuacán were still practising religious rituals at the pyramids. However, scientifically controlled excavations began at Teotihuacán at this time, and the cult, with its Prehispanic roots, was more-or-less forced to come to an end, although the city "where the gods were born" is still held in high regard.

★Coyote: *Canis latrans*, an American mammal similar to the wolf.

4. CONCEPTUALISATION AND ABSTRACTION:
THE ART OF TEOTIHUACAN

Sonia Lombardo de Ruíz

The production of artefacts for inter-regional trade was one of the pillars supporting the economic development of the great centre of Teotihuacán. It was also one of the means by which the culture's religion was disseminated, since figurines representing the Teotihuacán gods were traded, as were objects used in the cult of the gods, such as pectorals, earflares, braziers, masks and vessels.

Cylindrical tripod vessels, with or without lids, are among the most typical of Teotihuacán trade goods and, at the same time, some of the most interesting because of the variety of motifs used. Several different decorative techniques were employed: polychromy based on fresco or natural clay colours; and smooth or fluted surfaces, with low relief and scraped or incised decoration. These vessels tend to be of horizontal proportion, so that their diameter is frequently greater than or equal to their height. Raised borders along the rim and the base are common, further accentuating the horizontality of the vessel, and the area between the two is used as a field for the representation of various motifs. These are almost always deities or their symbols, and also depict scenes in which priests appear, as in the vessels from Tikal or Kaminaljuyú in Guatemala, sites showing evidence of Teotihuacán influence.

As already mentioned, Teotihuacán was in its turn influenced by the regions which its own culture had infiltrated; as a result, a Teotihuacán vessel is sometimes decorated with motifs that are, for example, affiliated to those found in the Gulf region; the diagonal bands that appear on the vessel in plate 11 are an example, showing a series of volutes typical of the Gulf region style.

The ancient tradition of clay figurine production persisted throughout this period, articulating the process of evolution towards a more structured religion. Initially, female figurines were modelled; later, shaman figures were made in large numbers and, little by little, deities or their representatives began to appear, featuring symbolic elements such as the circles around the eyes – "spectacles" – that characterise Tláloc, the god of rain, who was all-powerful in Teotihuacán religion.

Physical appearance conformed to a particular aesthetic, a fact that emerges clearly in the figurines. Horizontal lines, also emphasised in the ceramics, are accentuated through the eyes and mouth, and are further reinforced by tabular, vertical and oblique cranial deformation. The faces consistently adopt the shape of an inverted trapezium: the widest part is uppermost, and enormous earflares are hung as a counterbalance, giving the form of a horizontal rectangle to the overall composition.

While the figurines of priests and gods wore increasingly complex attire, one series represents naked men of highly naturalistic proportions. Of greatest interest — although their meaning is unknown — are the ones represented in seated postures, with crossed legs and a completely symmetrical composition, and with a hollow in their chests in the form of an inverted trapezium, harmonising with the shape of the head. The hollow is lidded, and contains other figurines inside.

Despite the naturalism of these figurines, their general composition is governed by strict geometric form; thus, for example, in the figurine in plate 12, the arms and legs form a perfect hexagon, resulting in a stability that gives the figure great dignity, in spite of its small size. Naturalistic representations found in Teotihuacán also include several almost life-sized stone sculptures, whose function is equally unknown. The aesthetic impact of some of these is quite extraordinary, as in the figure in plate 13. The mastery of the stone-carving, the proportion and composition all conform to the classical concept of beauty.

Masks were an important element of the religious ritual of the inhabitants of Teotihuacán.

They were worn by deities and priests as part of their insignia, and were symbolic in themselves, incorporating the features of the deities or priests and thus representing them. One example of this is the ceremonial brazier in plate 18.

This ceramic piece was designed as a vessel in which fire could be built. Its function, however, is concealed behind a geometric composition in which a series of plaques – rectangular, trapezoidal and circular and held within a structure of superimposed horizontal bands – combine to form a temple bearing the face of a great priest of the god of fire, the representative of the god himself. Bearing an enormous headdress of feathers and symbols, as well as luxurious attire, and occupying the most important central point of the composition, is a mask with the large earflares of a dignitary and a butterfly nose-plug, the symbol *par excellence* of fire and thus, through association, of the god.

The composition of another very similar mask (plate 14), possibly a fragment of another brazier, once again plays two trapeziums against each other. An inverted trapezium corresponds to the mask's face, while a second one, with its widest edge at the bottom of the mask, is formed by the earflares and the border along the upper edge of the mask. The formal language of Teotihuacán, conceived on a basis of pure geometry, is clearly displayed in this piece, in which plane surfaces and an emphasis on horizontality predominate.

Funerary masks also existed (see plate 15). These were tied around the head of the deceased as a form of protection, and had magical-religious significace. The use of greenstone – jade, jadite, serpentine – derived from an ancient tradition of the Pre-Classic period, alluding to water, and to the fertility of the earth. Thus, among these agricultural peoples, the covering of the deceased's face with a green mask symbolised transmission of the power of fertility; it assured his sustenance and thus survival in the next world.

Death was a constant theme in Teotihuacán culture: so much so that on some occasions skulls were decorated with sculpted ornaments and a tongue as if they were a "living death". Such is the case of the monumental sculpture in plate 16, which also picks up on an ancient tradition that persists in Mesoamerican sculpure of various regions and all periods: the representation within a single object of its appearance in both life and death, two opposed forces united in one form. This concept alludes to human sacrifice as a source of life for the gods.

The cult of the god of fire, the most ancient of all the gods and of whom there are representations dating from Pre-Classic cultures, was never discontinued, and the god became part of the Teotihuacán pantheon; the traditional image of a bent old man, seated cross-legged, continued in use, and the only change was his adaptation to the sculptural language of Teotihuacán (plate 17).

His general form became strictly geometric, inscribed within a rectangle that is itself constructed from three rectangular elements, with an overtly horizontal accent: legs, torso, headdress. At the centre of the composition, further accentuated by its exaggerated size in relation to the body, is the face, which differs from the masks previously described only by the noticeably deep wrinkles that give the god his identity.

The god of fire, whose iconography was defined by the earliest Pre-Classic manifestations, is presented in the naturalistic image of an old man, but the rest of the Teotihuacán gods relied on conceptualisations that took form through symbols. They were the product of speculative thought on the part of a priestly group which conceived a religious system not only to explain its own existence but, at the same time, to control the world.

Tláloc, god of rain and storms, is an example of this process. He is represented as a large mask, vaguely anthropomorphic (plate 19), in which the distinctive elements are his spectacles, fangs and curved lips. Occasionally the lips alone are sufficient to evoke the god; when they are combined with pointed teeth (plate 20), they refer to his destructive aspect.

Tláloc himself, his representatives or his symbols are essential motifs in the mural paintings of Teotihuacán. They are found in a variety of forms – as central figures, in borders, and also in processions. In the fragment that comes from Zacuala, for example (plate 21), the god is painted with his fangs and spectacles, and displays the earflares normally worn by a dignitary, as well as a large headdress; surrounded by symbols representing water – blue bands in the form of waves, and also starfish – the god is singing and scattering seed.

Mural paintings are one of the most interesting archaeological discoveries of Teotihuacán. They covered large areas within the temples and residential buildings, and consisted of simple blocks of colour, or used geometric, botanical, zoomorphic and anthropomorphic motifs. Arranged in bands, borders and panels, they always emphasised architectural elements such as plinths, doors, columns, cornices or merlos (plates 22 and 23), as well as bearing symbolic meaning. Panels in walls were nearly always surrounded by frame-like borders, generally deriving from serpents' bodies decorated with quetzal feathers, sometimes interwoven, and often featuring aquatic elements or symbols of Tláloc, such as marine shells, snail shells, star fish, and "water eyes". The streams of water that gush from the jaws of these serpents allude to agricultural fertility, the prime source of survival for the inhabitants of Teotihuacán.

Another type of border, like the one in plate 25, consists of symbols of the deity known as *la grandiosa* (the magnificent one): zig-zag bands and a series of dots and lines. Feathers, thought of as a precious element, are also important, as are braided serpents. As the giver of life, this god is associated not only with fertility but also with death, and embodies both benevolent and terrible aspects.

Numerous motifs fill the central panels in the walls. There are flowering trees with different elements (plate 22) that have been interpreted as hieroglyphic; mythical beasts, like the green birds with outspread wings and crest-like plumes, letting forth a song in the form of a volute (plate 26); or the great coyote who also sings and wears a feather headdress (plate 27). The coyote bears an enormous obsidian knife of the kind used to extract hearts in human sacrifice, and the image clearly represents a scene from a ritual, in which the protagonist, a warrior-coyote, sings a hymn while going to sacrifice his victim.

The relationship of warrior orders with certain animals – the coyote in this case – and of war with the sacrifice of prisoners as an offering to the gods, is widely known because of its persistence until Aztec times. Scenes are expressed symbolically and economically, but all of them are charged with meaning.

Seen as a whole, the plastic arts of Teotihuacán take two forms. One involves naturalistic representation, and its affiliation with the social group that practised it has not been established. The other, geometric in its general manifestation and with the objects theselves being symbolic, corresponds to the needs of priestly groups, and uses an esoteric language on different levels, to be understood only by individuals or groups with a distinct level of initiation. This included the art of writing, making possible the communication of knowledge which was used as a source of power, for the appropriation of economic excess and, at the same time, as a way of exercising social control.

11. TRIPOD VESSEL

Teotihuacán culture. Teotihuacán. Classic (A.D. 0-750). Clay. Height 20 cm, diameter 23 cm. In store. MNA. Cat. no. 9-2024. Inv. no. 10-78074.

Ceramic tripod vessels are symptomatic of Teotihuacán culture. They consist almost entirely of a series of sumptuary and trading objects, which appear fairly frequently in funerary offerings and in sites with which Teotihuacán had contact, particularly in the Maya area. Different techniques were used for decoration, such as fine polishing, or applying and then painting a layer of stucco, or by means of incising or scraping. Their supports were solid or hollow, cylindrical or rectangular; the latter sometimes also boasted incised or fretwork decoration.

Nearly all of these vessels, particularly the ones found at Teotihuacán itself, are profusely decorated with an iconography comparable to that of the murals.

The example shown here came from a residential building in Teotihuacán; its base has individual decorative border ornaments applied to it, while the vessel itself is incised with curvilinear motifs, clearly implying connection with the style of El Tajín, in the Gulf of Mexico region. The complexity of the fretwork design on the supports and the elegance of the motifs on the main body of the vessel make this a unique piece.

c.l.d.o.

12. ANTHROPOMORPHIC FIGURE

Teotihuacán culture. Central Highlands. Classic (A.D. 0-750). Clay. Height 13.9 cm, width 10.4 cm. In store. MNA. Cat. no. 9-3585. Inv. no. 10-223779.

Ceramic figurines were to play an important part in the ceremonial equipment used by the Mesoamerican peoples from very early times until they came into contact with Europeans. It has been suggested that these figurines served as fetishes and that they were undoubtedly used in agricultural and general fertility rites. Particularly useful in archaeological terms, they contribute to our knowledge of the physical appearance of the ancient inhabitants and of their customs, as well as their ornamentation and clothing. Careful study of these figurines reveals the existence of social classes, and of the commercial relationships that the Mesoamerican peoples had with one another.

The ample range of figurines discovered at Teotihuacán are so typical that some are considered to be diagnostic of this culture. Produced in massive quantities in specialised workshops, they have been found in their thousands during excavations of the city's residential buildings, leading to the hypothesis that they formed part of a popular and domestic cult.

Among the most typical examples are the so-called "puppet" or "articulated" figurines, "portrait" figurines and those with hollow chests, of which, in contrast to those previously mentioned, very few examples are known.

Although several different theories have attempted to explain these figures with hollow chests, which contain a second figure, the true reason behind this type of representation is not known. Perhaps the most appropriate suggestion is that they are linked to the indigenous concept of the *nahual*; that is, to a double that each of us possesses and into which we can transform ourselves.

c.l.d.o

13. ANTHROPOMORPHIC SCULPTURE

Teotihuacán culture. Teotihuacán. Classic (A.D. 0-750). Stone. Height 71 cm, width 23 cm. Teotihuacán Hall. MNA. Cat. no. 9-3158. Inv. no. 10-81806.

Representations of the human body were not typical of Teotihuacán culture, which was more preoccupied with gods than with men. Not even in the case of this anthropomorphic sculpture, with its excellent linear quality, can we assume that it truly represents a human body. On the contrary, the piece almost certainly played a role in Teotihuacán ritual as a god or as a figure to be decked out with the attributes of a deity, such as a mask, necklaces and headdress. It has been attributed to the early years of the Teotihuacán culture because of its style.

The piece is an excellent example of Teotihuacán stonework, and comes from a building close to the Pyramid of the Sun, called the The Priests' House, which was excavated by Leopoldo Batres at the beginning of the twentieth century.

c.l.d.o.

14. CEREMONIAL MASK

Teotihuacán culture. Teotihuacán. Classic (A.D. 0-750). Clay. Height 10 cm, width 18 cm. Teotihuacán Hall. MNA. Cat. no. 9-2065. Inv. no. 10-373.

This anthropomorphic clay mask formed part of the decoration of a ritualistic brazier of the kind that represented a temple. Research has revealed that this is the mask of a priest.

Earflares and nose-plugs were ornaments used by the upper social classes. This mask uses both, indicating the high class of the important individual or the priest to whom it alludes.

c.l.d.o.

15. FUNERARY MASK

Teotihuacán culture. Central Highlands. Classic (A.D. 0-750). Stone. Height 21 cm, width 25.5 cm. Teotihuacán Hall. MNA. Cat. no. 9-1703. Inv. no. 10-228047.

In Teotihuacán, masks were used not only in ritualistic braziers and to cover the face of a sculpture that represented a particular deity, but also as part of the attire of the deceased on his journey to the next world. They are found both on clay figurines and in mural paintings.

Death masks, which were placed on the faces of important corpses, were probably an attempt to perpetuate the live image of the deceased. However, in many cases the face is represented with open eyes, frequently made from shell and obsidian inlays. Teotihuacán funerary masks are notable for their sober and realistic style. The mask presented here is an excellent example of this type.

c.l.d.o.

16. CEREMONIAL SCULPTURE IN THE FORM OF A SKULL

Teotihuacán culture. Teotihuacán. Classic (A.D. 0-750). Stone. Height 71 cm, width 96 cm, depth 37.5 cm. Teotihuacán Hall. MNA. Cat. no. 9-2567. Inv. no. 10-958.

Teotihuacán representations of mortuary symbols are so rare they are almost non-existent. The two monumental sculptures of skulls that have been known, since 1917, to come from the area in front of the Pyramid of the Sun, are exceptional. One of these is the piece shown here.

Originally this skull was painted red, the symbol of death; the sculpture features two further elements: a vertical cord and a group of flames. A surprising feature is the tongue lolling out of the skull's mouth.

The image is highly symbolic: the knotted band signifies the idea of being "tied up for death", that is, sacrifice; the tongue refers to autosacrifice, alluding to a Mesoamerican custom of making the tongue bleed with maguey spines; the flames refer both to the act of burning incense to the gods, and to the cyclical celebration of the New Fire.

Thus, this monument is not a representation of the god of death, but a reference to the blood sacrifice that was performed in connection with the ceremonial celebration of the New Fire; that is, with the end of a calendrical cycle.

As the piece has no peg for fixing it to a wall, and has a flat base, it is thought that together with the other known piece it formed a pair which was used to define the space in which sacrifice took place, and that possibly both sculptures were originally placed on a platform in front of the Pyramid of the Sun. *c.l.d.o.*

17. HUEHUETEOTL OR THE GOD OF FIRE

Teotihuacán culture, Teotihuacán. Classic (A.D. 0-750). Stone. Height 44 cm, width 34 cm. In store. MNA. Cat. no. 9-4187. Inv. no. 10-222234.

The Old God of Fire, Huehueteotl, one of the most ancient of Mesoamerican gods, was represented in statues as an old man with a wrinkled face, hunchbacked, sitting cross-legged and bearing a brazier on his head. The iconography of this stone sculpture persisted from the period of the first villages in the Central Highlands (approximately 800 B.C.), until the end of the Mexica culture.

The cult of this god is said to have emerged in Cuicuilco, an archaeological site in the Valley of Mexico, where the eruption of the Xitle volcano would have been observed by the inhabitants.

The braziers borne on the heads of these sculptures indicate without doubt that they were used in rituals dedicated to a sacred fire, which was conceived of as different to a common domestic fire.

The outer border of this brazier shows a design consisting of rhomboids with a central disc, which have been interpreted as "eyes", and which, because of this, also signify light or fire. *c.l.d.o.*

18. DOUBLE-CONED CEREMONIAL BRAZIER

Teotihuacán culture. Azcapotzalco, Mexico City. Classic (A.D. 0-750). Clay. Height 76 cm, width 41.4 cm. In store. MNA. Cat. no. 9-2407. Inv. no. 10-81803.

Braziers are among the objects typical of Teotihuacán ritual. Generally polychromatic and decorated with exotic materials such as mica and cinnabar, they are considered to be ceremonial objects that were characteristic of this culture.

This type of brazier represents a priest inside an altar; the priest's face or mask appears within, framed by the temple jambs and lintel, architectural elements that are generally decorated with discs and designs related to the butterfly, the symbol of fire.

This brazier is a work of art combining ceramics with architecture. The chimney or flue for the smoke can be seen at the rear.

The piece comes from Azcapotzalco, a Teotihuacán centre of great importance in the Valley of Mexico, which must both have controlled and served as an intermediary for the lesser sites surrounding it and Teotihuacán. Azcapotzalco copied both the daily lifestyle and the rituals of the metropolis on which it depended; hence the existence of such an object among its archaeological remains. *c.l.d.o.*

19. VESSEL REPRESENTING TLALOC, THE GOD OF RAIN

Teotihuacán culture. Teotihuacán. Classic (A.D. 0-750). Clay. Height 45 cm, width 30 cm. In store. MNA. Cat. no. 9-3102. Inv. no. 10-224372.

The most frequently represented god in Teotihuacan was Tláloc. On this ceramic vessel he is shown with his typical attributes, spectacles, fangs and a water-lily emerging from his mouth. *c.l.d.o.*

20. ARCHITECTURAL ELEMENT REPRESENTING TLALOC

Teotihuacán culture. Teotihuacán. Classic (A.D. 0-750). Stone. Height 129 cm, width 104 cm, depth 12 cm. In store. MNA. Cat. no. 9-4565. Inv. no. 10-136721.

There are six known pieces of this type, found during excavations carried out at the end of the nineteenth and beginning of the twentieth centuries, and all from the building called Los Subterráneos (The Subterraneans) in Teotihuacán. Traditionally known as La Cruz de Tláloc (The Cross of Tláloc), the piece represents the god Tláloc schematically: the lips are represented by bands, and show large fangs and a forked tongue. The piece was originally covered with a layer of stucco painted red.

Its function has been the subject of speculation; while certain researchers believe these pieces to be sepulchral, others suggest that they formed part of the roof of a corridor. However, the weight and size of the sculptures suggest that they were more likely to have been placed vertically on the floor, although it is not known whether they were aligned or used to define a space. *c.l.d.o.*

21. MURAL FRAGMENT WITH REPRESENTATION OF TLALOC

Teotihuacán culture. Teotihuacán. Classic (A.D. 0-750). Stucco and paint. Height 75 cm, width 145 cm. In store. MNA. Cat. no. 9-4716. Inv. no. 10-136067.

This mural fragment, from the residential unit of Zacuala, represents the god Tláloc or one of the deity's priests, scattering seeds on the earth which are to sprout and multiply. The piece can be considered a typical mural in terms of its subject-matter, its red background and the fact that it forms part of a series of repetitive images. *c.l.d.o.*

22. MURAL FRAGMENT WITH BOTANICAL IMAGE

Teotihuacán culture. Teotihuacán. Classic (A.D. 0-750). Stucco and paint. Height 30 cm, width 51.5 cm, depth 4 cm. In store. MNA. Inv. no. 10-229226.

The fragment shown here originally formed part of a much larger painting representing a sequence of nine trees with a distinct glyph painted on each trunk; the sequence was repeated after the first nine trees. A plumed serpent approximately 3.5 metres long extended above the trees. The mural is dated just before the final years of Teotihuacán, being attributed to the period A.D. 600-750.

The nine trees represented are very similar to each other, although they have different types of flowers and glyphs. All their roots are visible.

The fragment exhibited here displays the glyph known as "yellow platform". Other glyphs represented are "feathered eye" and "maguey leaf".

Our limited knowledge of the system of writing used in Teotihuacán makes this mural particularly important, as the glyphs on these trees may represent a writing system. *c.l.d.o.*

23. ARCHITECTURAL CREST

Teotihuacán culture. Teotihuacán. Classic (A.D. 0-750). Stucco, paint and stone. Height 27.5 cm, width 17.5 cm, depth 5.5 cm. In store. MNA. Inv. no. 10-229215.

Teotihuacán's architecture was governed by horizontal lines; nevertheless, the roofs of many buildings were crowned by architectural crests or merlons, which gave them greater height and emphasis. These merlons were of different sizes , occasionally reaching over one metre in height.

As we have noted, the residential units usually had a sunken main patio, in the middle of which a very small temple was constructed, almost a replica of the larger temples in the city's ceremonial centre. Within the temples in these patios, ceremonies were conducted under the direction of the residents' leader. Like the temples in the city centre, the domestic ones also had merlons, but naturally they were in proportion to the size of the temple. This merlon probably comes from one of these temples, and has the distinguishing feature of well-preserved stucco and paint. *c.l.d.o.*

24. ARCHITECTURAL CREST

Teotihuacán culture. Teotihuacán. Classic (A.D. 0-750). Stucco, painting and stone. Height 33 cm, width 27 cm, depth 9 cm. In store. MNA. Inv. no. 10-229216.

The stepped-fret form adopted by this architectural merlon, is symbolic, referring to the serpent with its mythological character. *c.l.d.o.*

25. MURAL FRAGMENT WITH SYMBOLIC REPRESENTATION

Teotihuacán culture. Teotihuacán. Classic (A.D. 0-750). Stucco and paint. Height 53.5 cm, width 92.5 cm. depth 3.3 cm. In store. MNA. Inv. no. 10-229201.

This fragment formed part of a painting of the "Great Goddess" of Teotihuacán, a deity that seems to have had associations with both life and death. This duality is not unusual, and was represented from very early periods in Mesoamerica. The piece is notable for its polychromy: green, light and dark red, yellow and blue. *c.l.d.o.*

26. MURAL FRAGMENT WITH ZOOMORPHIC REPRESENTATION

Teotihuacán culture. Teotihuacán. Classic (A.D. 0-750). Stucco and paint. Height 84.5 cm, width 114 cm, depth 4 cm. In store. MNA. Inv. no. 10-229198.

Birds are widely represented in Teotihuacán iconography. However, only in a few cases can the actual species be identified; in this mural fragment, it is not possible to determine whether the bird is a quetzal or an owl, which are the two most likely candidates.

Here, the bird is shown surrounded by a green line which could be interpreted as a platform, and on which various human marks are painted. The bird is shown in profile with a thin line coming out of its beak, indicating speech. Thus, this is a bird that speaks and dances. Its meaning still cannot be deciphered, but it may be that the bird symbolises a priest or, perhaps, a social or political group. *c.l.d.o.*

27. MURAL FRAGMENT WITH REPRESENTATION OF COYOTE

Teotihuacán culture. Teotihuacán. Classic (A.D. 0-750). Stucco and paint. Height 77 cm, width 190 cm, depth 5 cm. In store. MNA. Inv. no. 10-229196.

Mural painting in Teotihuacán, especially that of the city's final years, reveals a symbolism that is still unclear, but definitely linked with human sacrifice. The relationship of the coyote with human sacrifice and with military orders is documented in various murals located *in situ* in the archaeological city, where coyotes appear with anthropomorphic traits.

The coyote represented here wears a feather headdress and a bead necklace; from his mouth emerges the curvilinear motif, widely used in Mesoamerica, that is known as the "speech line", indicating that the coyote is speaking or perhaps singing. Tied to the left leg is a terrifying weapon, an enormous obsidian knife of the kind used for human sacrifice – the extraction of the heart. The fragment probably comes from Techinantitla, a residential building in Teotihuacán that has been only partially explored. *c.l.d.ó.*

11. TRIPOD VESSEL

12. ANTHROPOMORPHIC FIGURE

13. ANTHROPOMORPHIC SCULPTURE

14. CEREMONIAL MASK

15. FUNERARY MASK

16. CEREMONIAL SCULPTURE IN THE FORM OF A SKULL

17. HUEHUETEOTL OR THE GOD OF FIRE

18. DOUBLE-CONED CEREMONIAL BRAZIER

18. DOUBLE-CONED CEREMONIAL BRAZIER

19. VESSEL REPRESENTING TLALOC, THE GOD OF RAIN

20. ARCHITECTURAL ELEMENT REPRESENTING TLALOC

21. MURAL FRAGMENT WITH REPRESENTATION OF TLALOC

22. MURAL FRAGMENT WITH BOTANICAL IMAGE

23. ARCHITECTURAL CREST

24. ARCHITECTURAL CREST

25. MURAL FRAGMENT WITH SYMBOLIC REPRESENTATION

26. MURAL FRAGMENT WITH ZOOMORPHIC REPRESENTATION

27. MURAL FRAGMENT WITH REPRESENTATION OF COYOTE

5. XOCHICALCO, TEOTENANGO AND TULA, CITIES OF ATLANTES AND PLUMED SERPENTS

Federica Sodi Miranda

Our knowledge of the prevailing sociological environment of the Central Highlands at the beginning of the tenth century is dependent on archaeology and historical sources. Many years had elapsed since the disintegration of the great state or empire of Teotihuacán. After the fall of the City of the Gods, other centres were to come to the fore, some inhabited by peoples from distant regions, whose social and religious policies bore their own particular hallmark. A case in point is El Tajín in the Totonac area; another is the city of Monte Albán, ruled by the Oaxacan Zapotecs. Both had been under the influence of Teotihuacán during the Classic period.

The decline of the metropolis of Teotihuacán made it possible for both El Tajín and Monte Albán to achieve greater expansion in separate parts of Mesoamerica. A similar situation arose in the Central Highlands, although to a lesser degree, in the city of Xochicalco in the present-day state of Morelos. For several centuries Xochicalco was an active city, vigorously influencing the cultural development of various different peoples, especially the Chichimecas, invaders from the north who were soon to settle in the central region.

However, the disintegration of Teotihuacán did not mean the loss of its cultural heritage, nor the annihilation of its people, either through death or through amalgamation with other groups. People of Teotihuacán origin survived in different parts of the Valley of Mexico. Among other things, the ceramic ware known as *Coyotlatelco* testifies to this fact. With red on light brown colouring, it seems to have naturally evolved from the pieces produced during the last stage of Teotihuacán's development. This type of ceramic ware and other cultural elements derived from the City of the Gods have been discovered in such centres as Azcapotzalco, Oztotípac, Coyoacán, Cerro de la Estrella and Culhuacán, among others, so it is feasible to describe some of these sites, including Azcapotzalco, as Teotihuacán strongholds.

The city of Cholula, a great religious centre, evidently also remained under Teotihuacán domination until the beginning of the ninth century. Around this time, groups from the north of Oaxaca and the lower-lying lands of the present-day state of Puebla violently seized control of the Cholula site. The peoples who displaced the Teotihuacán rulers in so rudely were known both as the Olmec-Xicalancas and as the "historical Olmecs", thus clearly distinguishing them from the more ancient or "archaeological" Olmecs, creators of the mother-culture in Mesoamerica. The Olmec-Xicalanca victory began a new process of migration and scattering of the Teotihuacán peoples. It is a fact that many of them reached the land of the Totonacs via the area of El Tajín, and continued towards the south of Veracruz, to the area known today as Los Tuxtlas. Of these Teotihuacán emigrants, the few that remained in these sites became known as *pipiles*, a title probably deriving from the word *pipiltin*, meaning nobleman, since they were recognised as such by the peoples with whom they came into contact; some of these *pipiles* persevered to reach more distant sites, such as Chiapas, El Salvador, Honduras and Nicaragua.

In a nutshell, the central area of Mesoamerica towards the beginning of the tenth century saw former cities such as El Tajín, Xochicalco and Cholula, far from having disappeared, flourishing and expanding in different ways, having absorbed new groups from the south. As a result, these centres constituted a sort of cultural bridge between the development that had occurred during the Classic period and what then took place during the Post-Classic period. These nuclei of civilisation, and likewise less important communities that had become places of refuge for Teotihuacán groups, played an important role in the subsequent chain of events: they were occasionally able to exert influence on the

Chichimeca hordes that had already begun to penetrate from the northern borders of Mesoamerica. These groups from the north, called the Toltecs in historical sources, established their capital at Tula, in the state of Hidalgo, and developed their own culture.

Thus, certain sites already in existence as important centres, such as Xochicalco and Cholula, became even more significant after the fall of the great Teotihuacán, while other less prestigious places were to become more powerful, such as Cacaxtla, Teotenango and the previously mentioned Tula. All of these, alongside other social groupings that were more inclined towards militarism, typify the Early Post-Classic period which extended from A.D. 850 to 1250.

Xochicalco

Xochicalco, whose name means "Place of the House of Flowers", is located in the state of Morelos, approximately 25 kilometres south-west of Cuernavaca, the capital of the state.

Vegetation around the city is relatively scarce, despite the Tembembe River, which flows to the west and is a tributary of the Amacuzac river. Ruins of buildings are found not only on the Xochicalco hill, but also on the Coatzin or Bodega hill, which is separated by a ravine; here, a wide stone causeway leads to the summit, where there are remains of constructions. Ruins of ancient monuments survive on much of the high ground in the hilly area.

Xochicalco had been a residential site since Pre-Classic times, but was to achieve its greatest importance in the intervening period between the fall of Teotihuacán and the peak of Tula's prosperity.

The hill on which Xochicalco stands was artificially altered by means of stepped terraces, which took advantage of the topography of the area and involved the further levelling of areas that were already flat. The sides of these terraces were faced with stone; in some cases there were up to five in number. The finely proportioned Pyramid of the Plumed

6. The Ball Court at Xochicalco

The Ball Court at Xochicalco is a very long rectangular patio closed off at right-angles by channels at either end, forming the shape of a capital I. On either side of the court is an elevated bench which rises up at an angle from the level of the court until it meets the wall, in which two ring-shaped stones pertaining to the game are embedded. The Court is 52 metres in length and 9 metres wide. The benches are 1 metre wide and the walls are 8 metres in depth. Because of the unevenness of the land, the different sides of the building are arranged in different ways: in the north-west corner the *talus* or sloping walls which border the ·central platform rise directly from ground level, whereas, along the west side and particularly along the south side, a series of *talus*, porticos and stairways compensate for the changing levels.

A sculpture was found in the middle of the court in the form of an offering in a special crafted box which was tightly sealed and placed in the ground just beneath the surface. It represents the head of a *guacamaya*, similar in size and shape to those found in Copán which were used as markers in the ball game.

Serpent is situated on the highest part, completely faced with low reliefs carved in an extraordinary style, combining elements from the Mexican Highlands with others of Maya, Oaxacan and El Tajín origin. The structure consists of two tiers with *talud, tablero* and volute cornice; it is orientated towards the west, and has a flight of steps at the front. The principal motif, repeated eight times around the four sides of the first tier and interrupted only by the stairway, is the plumed serpent, symbol of Quetzalcóatl, which has magnificent heads with plumed crests and forked tongues. In beween these motifs are seated human figures, as well as a series of hieroglyphs, the meaning of which is still controversial, but which seem to indicate a calendrical change.

Another building of great importance is the palace, which must have been the residence of the great leaders or ruling lineages; following the Mesoamerican system, it consists of several patios surrounded by rooms. There is also a Ball Court here, whose features make it identical to the one at Tula. This proves once again that Xochicalco, which was contemporary with Teotihuacán, survived its fall and continued to thrive throughout the Toltec period.

Teotenango

During Teotihuacán's final years, a substratum of Otomí groups existed, widely spread out throughout the Valley and state of Mexico. They used *Coyotlatelco* ceramics and developed an indigenous style which in some cases made considerable progress, as in the case of the Matlatzincas of Teotenango.

This site, built on the Tetepetl hill, lies in the Toluca valley, in the municipality of Tenango del Valle, a name derived from Teotenango, which means "In the True Place of the Rampart".

A series of architectural and urban elements that give cohesion to the city are apparent in the architectural complex known as the Northern System, and in the part that has been explored to date. They indicate not only a sense of planning that made the most of the local geography, but also a stylistic tradition, a concept of space and a knowledge of construction techniques; the most important of these will be mentioned below.

Platforms and plazas are two elements that are fundamental to the organisation of space, and were conceived with a degree of generosity that is reminiscent of large centres or theocratic cities such as Teotihuacán. The builders of Teotenango took into account the topography of the hill, which rises in a north-south and east-west direction, building up the surface to form platforms on different levels, contained by high stone walls that often covered the hill's rocky flanks and outcrops.

Most of these platforms were rectangular in layout, and were divided into two sections, one high and one low, creating an L-shaped form with a corridor or passageway in between the two levels; the placing of ceremonial structures on the lower section formed the plazas, which were either totally closed or open along one of their sides.

The distribution of the platforms and plazas on different levels and the superposition of these planes at different heights gives the city an air of majesty in relation to its surroundings. A play of light and dark is created, in which an ascending horizontal line dominates the panorama, while the buildings constructed on these planes accentuate the balance of volume without needing to be of different heights, as the sense of elevation is given by the platforms themselves.

The most characteristic structures of Teotenango are the bases for temples, of which a fair number survive in the ceremonial area – four have been discovered to date – and the Serpent structure, all of which are formed by three or four tiered layers at the front and a high sloping wall at the rear, giving the layout the shape of a T. The tiers generally consist of a *talud* and a cornice, projecting in some cases and inset or vertical to the *talud* in others.

These bases have stairways with borders at the front of the plazas, giving access to the temples that would have been located on the upper part of the base, but of which no traces remain, partly because they were constructed from perishable materials and partly because of the destruction that took place during the Spanish colonisation.

The Ball Court dates from the climax of the ceremonial centre's prosperity; the character of its architecture, together with that of the temple-bases, give an indication of the comparative relationships with Tula and Xochicalco. Also to be taken into account are the complex ceramics that have been found buried in layers in the area and which come from Tula and Xochicalco.

Teotenango happens to be one of the Mesoamerican sites where fortification reached a certain degree of perfection, and where it is possible to see the development of the city's defence system. From the start, it was constructed on the summit of a hill with steep, rocky sides, themselves forming a natural defence which was emphasised by the construction of stepped platforms faced with high perimeter walls that were difficult to scale. These rising platforms and their sloping stone walls made the north side of the hill impregnable, and when it was ultimately conquered by a group of Chichimecas-Matlatzincas, who brought warrior customs with them, the defensive aspect of the city was reinforced, with a rampart built on the west side, next to an area of lava which could have been a place of potential entry for the enemy. The rampart was continued, at right angles, to defend the north side of the city up to the Street of the Frog, where the high walls of the platforms rose. Additional stone or dry-stone walls were constructed all along this trajectory, as well as along the Street of the Frog, in the form of trenches, as a strategy to make the enemy retreat to a place that could be attacked.

The same structures were built around the southern part of the hill, so that in the map attached to the *Relación de Teotenango* of 1582 the site is shown surrounded by a crenelated rampart.

Tula

The archaeological city of Tula lies in the southern part of the state of Hidalgo, approximately 60 kilometres directly north of Mexico City, and the same distance north-west of the archaeological city of Teotihuacán.

Tula was built on a plain irrigated by a river which surrounds the Coatepetl or Serpent's Hill. The present-day town occupies only part of the former capital, and minor ruins were found in its main square. According to linguistically-based maps of Mendizábal and Jiménez Moreno, Tula lies very close to the limits of the areas where Otomí and Yuto-Aztec languages are spoken. The name *Tula* means "metropolis", and its Otomí name, *Mamenhi*, signifying "The place of many neighbours", echoes this meaning.

The city extended to the nearby hills of Nonoalcatepetl, today La Malinche, El Cielito and El Jicuco, and is known as Tula-Xicocotitlán. Further to the north are the desert plains of Teotlalpán, the point reached by the incursions of the barbarians known as Teochichimecas.

Historical sources and chronicles mention Tula as the most important centre in the Central Highlands during this period. Records exist documenting both the rulers of this site and its daily life, enabling us to refer to it in greater detail below.

Origin and foundation of Tula

The last Maya date known within the Long Count system [see page 225] is the year A.D. 909. By curious coincidence, it was only one year earlier that the tribes headed by Mixcóatl, coming from the north, broke into the Valley of Mexico. For the first time in the history of the centre of Mexico, we find not an anonymous group but one of clear-cut identity and, what is more, a leader whose name is known. Mixcóatl must have been an extraordinary individual, whose qualities and influence reverberate throughout the chronicles of Mexico's Prehispanic history. It was he, with the Toltec, who initiated the historical period about which some form of written information exists; the documents referring to earlier periods tend to be based on mythology. The legend of the suns recounts how, after the death of four previous suns, the gods themselves gathered in Teotihuacán and out of their sacrifice the Fifth Sun was born:

"The Fifth Sun was born and remained motionless for days. The gods managed to put him in motion, conceding defined periods of predominance and recession to each of the fundamental principles. The years were allocated time and space, and because of this he is called Ollin Tonatiuh, the Sun of Movement. Quetzalcóatl, through his sacrifice, was destined to create humanity for the Fifth Sun, those of us living on earth today ".

Archaeology has verified the basic concept of this myth: by the time these new, future rulers arrived, the grandeur of Teotihuacán was long gone and it was time to begin a new epoch. The Toltecs found other groups in the valley who had preceded them and who had assimilated the remains of the Teotihuacán world. Little by little, the Toltec culture emerged from the ensuing amalgamation of races. Mixcóatl and his people imposed themselves and in time established a political structure.

It seems that Mixcóatl did not take long to conquer the valley, and established his capital in Culhuacán. At that point this was a peninsula in the Cerro de la Estrella, surrounded by water, a description which not only calls to mind what would later be Tenochtitlán, but also implies the necessity of a defensive position. Mixcóatl's empire grew rapidly. Extending beyond the margins of the valley, it took over the regions of Toluca and Teotlapán; in Morelos, Mixcóatl met a women called Chimalma with whom he had a son known as Topiltzin.

Myths and legends tell us that "...the woman Chimalma came out to meet him, and placed her shield on the ground, and threw down her arrows and spearthrowers, and stood upright, naked, without underskirt or shirt. When Mixcóatl saw her, he aimed his arrows at her; the first one he fired passed above her and she merely bowed her head; the second one he fired passed by her side and simply swerved away; the third one he fired, she caught with her hand, and the fourth one he fired passed between her legs. After having fired at her four times, Mixcóatl turned round and left. The woman immediately fled and hid herself in a cave in a large ravine. Mixcóatl re-equipped himself with supplies of arrows, and again came to find her, but this time found no-one. He then abused the women of Cuernavaca. And the women of Cuernavaca said: "Let us find her." They went to fetch her, and said to her, "Mixcóatl is looking for you, and because of you he is abusing your younger sisters." Mixcóatl returned once again, and again she came out to meet him; in the same way, she stood up and laid bare her sex; in the same way she placed her shield and arrows on the ground. Again Mixcóatl fired at her repeatedly, to no effect... After this, he seized her; he lay with the woman whose name was Chimalma, and she later became pregnant".

While Chimalma was pregnant, Mixcóatl was assassinated by one of his captains, who usurped the throne of Culhuacán. The widow fled to her parents and died giving birth to the son who never knew Mixcóatl: Ce Acatl Topiltzin Quetzalcóatl. The child was raised by his grandparents in Tepoztlán, a town where the long-standing tradition venerating Quetzalcóatl was still strong and which had cultural affinities with Xochicalco, as both sites sustained a cult to Quetzalcóatl. Although Mixcóatl was not a devotee of this cult, Topiltzin was educated in its doctrine and taught to venerate Quetzalcóatl.

A group of noblemen who defended the lineage of Mixcóatl called on him to succeed his father to the throne of Culhuacán. Quetzalcóatl accepted, sought the remains of his father, buried them in what is now known as the Cerro de la Estrella and built a temple on the tomb, elevating his father to the status of a god. He overcame the usurper and determined to establish himself in Tula.

Once the Chichimeca groups had settled down, their original social structure, which was tribal, evolved into a more complex society ruled principally by militarism. This was the point at which the city started to be governed by ruling lineages.

Tula, a city on a par with Cholula, Cacaxtla, Xochicalco and Teotenango, did not have the same ecological conditions at a geographical level; nevertheless, as a city-state, it had a military organisation that allowed it to use contributary labour from other regions for the construction of its monuments. It could also obtain tributes in the form of produce which enabled it to complement its economy and to import specialised craftsmen from different regions of Mesoamerica.

Toltec civilisation established the structure of imperial tribute, which was later adopted by the Aztecs. Their influence was to reach from one extreme of Mesoamerica to the other, but was particularly powerful in the Yucatán. After their brief empire had come to an end and its religious centre had been destroyed, the Toltecs, according to tradition and archaeology, founded dynasties in other regions; they continued to occupy Culhuacán, where less civilised Chichimeca groups, who later invaded the Valley of Mexico, married their women, adopting a large proportion of their culture and learning to speak their language.

Tula at that time was an area which had been tamed by several centuries of experience in plant cultivation and animal domestication. By intercepting slow-flowing rivers, the semi-desert area had been transformed into a productive region, capable of sustaining a metropolis like Tula which relied on irrigation of the land.

Cultivation by hand and the use of the *coa*, or pointed dibble stick for sowing, led to the cultivation of maize, pumpkin, chilli, beans, *chía* or sage seed (used for drinks and oil and as a gloss for paintings), maguey (used for mead), syrup, *pulque* (an intoxicating drink made from fermented maguey juice) and paper; cacao was also produced, as were potatoes, cotton, sweet cassava, pineapple, avocado, papaya, zapote and several varieties of plums. There were other signs of civilisation: maize mash with ash or lime (tortilla); irrigation; the use of rabbit fur to decorate woven textiles; cotton garments, turbans, heeled sandals, one-piece warrior suits; and finally, earflares, necklaces, bracelets, bangles and pectorals, often manufactured from precious metals.

As already mentioned, the Toltecs, relying on military strength, were able to use extra labour brought in from other regions to help with the construction of hydraulic works (crucial for cultivation), and public buildings. The tributes they obtained in the form of produce enabled them to boost their economy and to attract specialised craftsmen from different regions of Mesoamerica. Thus Tula became a Mecca, a region of exchange for products manufactured in Guatemala and the Maya area, as well as Zapotec and Totonaca; these were in turn exchanged for products from the Huastec region, Michua and Gran Chichimeca. Markets were held in Tula, Tulancingo, Cuernavaca, Cholula and Tultitlán every twenty days; that is, every month according to the Mesoamerican year. Further evidence confirms that the Toltecs counted their years and used the sacred calendar of 260 days, as did their successors.

Toltec palaces and houses were built from stone and mortar, and the Toltecs used the *temascal* (steam bath), which continues to exist among indigenous peoples today. Without doubt they were responsible for important changes in the architecture of Mesoamerica around the ninth century. Characteristic of these innovations are the caryatids, better known as atlantes, which consist of gigantic pillars sculpted in human form, supporting the beams or crosspieces holding up the roofing. These caryatids made possible the construction of rooms with enormous dimensions, giving rise to what research has christened "open space", consisting of large corridors or roofed spaces.

The construction system used for large buildings or palaces relied on a great quantity of stones and earth being piled up until the required size and height was reached. The structures were then decorated with sculptures and reliefs, according to the deity or person for whom the building was intended.

Structure B, or the Temple of Tlahuizcalpantecuhtli, forms the basis of our knowledge of the various characteristics of Toltec architecture. It consists of a square pyramid with five tiers giving a total height of ten metres. A central stairway is framed by borders; the tiers of the pyramid are decorated with low relief carvings depicting a procession of jaguars and coyotes along the upper part, while the middle section is decorated with eagles and vultures devouring bloody hearts and alternating with a mythical being emerging from the jaws of a serpent.

Three openings form the entrance, each framed by two columns in the shape of plumed serpents, with their heads at the bottom and their tails, or rattles, at the top, thus functioning as capitals. The temple consists of two rooms, with the roof of the first one supported by four gigantic caryatids. These represent warriors associated with Tlahuizcalpantecuhtli, The Lord of the Dawn, denoted by the decoration of red bands around their legs as well as the solar circle that appeared on their backs at waist level.

A notable construction in the form of an I is the Ball Court, where heroic feats were performed for purely ceremonial reasons. It consists of a wide corridor enclosed within walls, in the central part of which are embedded the vertical stone rings through which the rubber ball had to pass at the culmination of the game. At each end of this corridor are

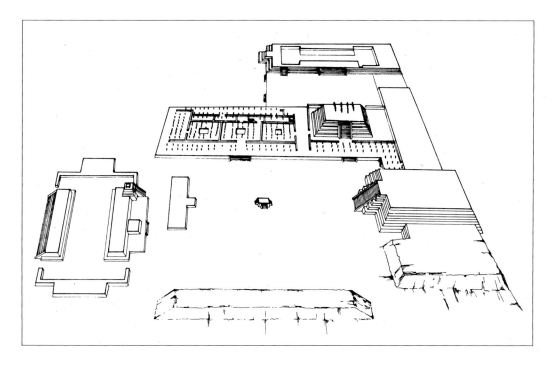

Tula played a significant role in the history of Mesoamerica. It was a densely populated urban centre and an important focus of political and economic power. Its influence extended over a large part of the centre of Mexico, parts of the Bajío, the coast of the Gulf of Mexico, Yucatán and the area of the Soconusco on the Pacific coast corresponding to Chiapas amd Guatemala. It was an extremely complex centre,with sophisticated town planning and areas with spaces dedicated to the various activities: administration, worship, trade, meetings, manufacture, residential units, different categories of neighbourhoods, streets, causeways, drainage systems etc.
In this map of the archaeological site of Tula, from left to right are: the Burnt Palace; the Temple of Tlahuizcalpantecuhtli, commonly known as the Temple of the Atlantes; Building C, possibly dedicated to Venus in its dedication of the night; a central altar where part of a sculpture known as a Chac Mool was found; and two Ball Courts.

other, shorter spaces, each placed at right-angles, mirror images of each other. In codices, this court appears as the Ball Court of the Sky, where the Lord of the Night challenges the Sun to a match, defeats him and decapitates him, burying him in the west.

Towards the north, five metres from the Pyramid of Tlahuizcalpantecuhtli, is the Coatepantli or Serpent Wall. Both sides of the wall are decorated with identical motifs in polychromatic stone relief, predominantly red, representing rattlesnakes devouring human bodies that are missing half their flesh. Above and below these figures run bands of lines, stepped or in the form of frets. The wall is topped by a series of merlons, cut in stone and painted white, displaying transverse sections of spiral shells.

The palace consists of a group of three patios enclosed by columns, with benches and altars. An open passageway separates it from the building with the four atlantes already described; together, these buildings form the north side of the plaza. Although it has been described as a palace, it is likely to have been intended not for habitation, but as an administrative building or even a market. When the excavation took place, several stone tablets were found with graphic representations of figures, which undoubtedly decorated the walls; the remains of benches decorated with warriors bearing lances and shields were also discovered; these can still be seen in situ, retaining fragments of their original paint.

At the centre of the patio is a small altar consisting of a square platform measuring approximately two metres in height, and approached by six steps on each side. A green stone plaque was found among the rubble, depicting a well-dressed figure, as well as a fragment of a Chac Mool sculpture (figure 7).

The Corral is located near the plaza of Tula Chico, approximately 1.5 kilometres north of the plaza where the Temple of Tlahuizcalpantecuhtli, or of the Atlantes, is situated. Its two superimposed tiers are characterised by being circular at the rear, with a rectangular section at the front. This type of building was generally dedicated to the god of wind known as Ehécatl.

The Tzompantli, or Wall of Skulls, backs on to the principal façade of the Corral platform, and consists of a low *talud*, with warrior reliefs bearing a panel with skulls and human crossbones. In front of this temple is a small platform, and it was here that the most beautiful ceramic piece known from this period, a burial offering, was found: known as the Coyote Head, it forms part of the collection of the National Museum of Anthropology.

Tula's large urban zone consists of residential houses of different types, according to the period in which they were built. In general terms, their rooms are rectangular in plan. Some are reminiscent of houses in Teotihuacán, while others are residential units which must have housed several families. The groundplans of these units show numerous rooms, and a number of patios with central altars; there are also buildings that must have served as residences for the ruling class and which correspond to the so-called "palaces".

The simplest construction technique used pieces of *tepetate* (stone block) with mortar consisting of mud, adobe or simply stone, sometimes erected on a low platform; only part of the wall height consisted of masonry, and sometimes perishable materials such as lime finishes were employed.

Research into the relationship and parallels between Tula and the Maya area still continues in an attempt to establish who was influenced by whom, and how the various similarities came about. The fact is that in the Yucatán, the city of Chichén Itzá also contains atlantean figures, columns in the form of plumed serpents with their tails held up to support entrance lintels and their heads on the ground, columns with warriors in low relief, a central altar, a Ball Court and a Chac Mool; there is also considerable similarity between the Temple of the Warriors in Chichén Itzá and the Temple of Tlahuizcalpantecuhtli in Tula.

The belief in life after death was a definite cult. Burials appear in ceremonial centres in the form of offerings, although the majority of these have been found in residential areas; the dead, in individual graves dug in the ground, were buried curled up and with an offering, generally consisting of ceramic pieces, although other types of materials also appear; occasionally burials have been found with the body laid out, or else curled up inside a pot. Other prevalent customs among the Toltecs included erect cranial deformation, as well as dental mutilation by filing; these customs may have reflected a particular social status.

It was important for the Toltecs to be able to exchange products or to obtain basic materials from other regions by means of trade. In some cases commercial routes that had existed since the time of Teotihuacán continued to be used; the shipments sometimes travelled far afield, and were guarded by groups of soldiers.

During the final years of the Toltec empire, internal strife arose within the political structure as well as in religious and economic terms. The Toltecs also faced serious problems from the peoples they had suppressed and from whom they demanded tributes at regular intervals.

Around this time, new Chichimeca groups from the north arrived in the Central Highlands. One of these groups, under the command of Xolotl, reached Tula which was at that point governed by Huémac, its last emperor, who fled to Chapultepec and later died.

The Mexica or Aztecs reached Tula in approximately the twelfth century, settling in the city. Mexica influence in some of the sites they controlled is negligible, as they never occupied or re-used the large structures, building their residences on top of the ruins or using alternative space, such as Ball Court Two.

Toltec impact and influence was felt in various places, such as El Pueblito, Querétaro, on the coast of Veracruz, in the Maya region and in present-day Mexico City, where México-Tenochtitlán was situated. Its presence was undoubtedly felt most strongly among the Aztecs, with whom they had a certain amount of contact. The Aztecs were to take up the cultural legacy of the Toltecs in terms of politics, religion, commerce and the arts, resulting in the creation of the great Mexica empire.

In a more widespread context, it was Tula that established such religious concepts as the influential cult of the god Quetzalcóatl, which spread across the whole of Mesoamerica; the cult eventually superseded that of earlier gods, such as Tláloc and Huehueteotl.

The study of the stars was not limited to the explanation and exploration of astrological phenomena. The people of Mesoamerica also attempted to ascertain "...the true nature of the stars, their indications, their revelations, their function as omens of divine intention".

The Prehispanic explanation of the creation of the world and its cosmography was to develop into a vigorous re-creation of mythological images, consolidating the Toltecs' cosmic vision. Magic and poetry, the fruit of both contemplation and bewilderment in the face of the inexplicable, was to inspire a particular interpretation of the structure and content of the universe, a way of thinking in which life was seen to operate on a number of different levels, and which was fundamental to Mesoamerican philosophy.

The most ancient vision divides the universe into two: sky and earth. Each contains four cardinal points or directions, and together share a single centre which joins them; this gives a total of nine regions within the universe. This concept was integrated with that of the "creator-pair", representing the creative and the receptive and manifest in the images of sky and earth. As this view of the universe developed over the centuries, a third section or level appeared in several Mesoamerican cultures: the Underworld.

An ancient myth relates how an immense monster, a type of dragon-serpent, occupied cosmic space, and was divided into several sections by the gods of creation: the head was converted into three skies, the central part into the earth and the tail into nine underworlds. All these levels occupied vertical positions: the skies were at the top, the world in the centre and the underworlds at the bottom. Thus arises a concept of sky, world and underworld, each section with four cardinal points and a common centre uniting the three different zones, giving a total of thirteen regions. Subsequently there arose a concept of the universe in which the earth, square or round according to different versions, but always horizontal, surrounded by the eternal waters, with four cardinal points and four equinoxes, was complemented by nine or thirteen celestial levels and nine underworlds. The gods occupied specific places within this structure, and had their own spheres of action. The forces of the sky and the underworld influenced the earth, creating movement, life and equilibrium. The gods and their *nahuales* or doubles, represented by certain animals, travelled throughout the thirteen regions, ensuring that divine destiny was carried out.

Man's intense study of the stars and nature taught him that the gods were constantly fighting each other. What was created and given by one of them could be annihilated by the treachery of another. The world of mythology was a world of drama, of action, of forces and powers struggling against each other. The four destructions of the world as narrated by the Mexica myth were the work of Quetzalcóatl and Tezcatlipoca, who each in turn destroyed the universe that the other had created. The sun emerges and is lost, dies and goes to the underworld, and the following morning rises again.

Vegetation may perish, but not its vital energy, which returns it to life every springtime. According to mythology, man's vital energy is equally indestructible. Man walks the earth until he dies, and after death continues to walk in another region, in the underworld where life continues under different circumstances.

One of the fundamental concepts acquired by Prehispanic man from his observation of nature was that everything that exists is subject to a constant process of transformation: "TRANSFORMATION IS ETERNITY".

6. NEW STATES, AND A NEW LANGUAGE OF FORM

Sonia Lombardo de Ruíz

During the last phase of the Classic period – between A.D. 700 and 900 – a number of the inhabitants of Mesoamerica migrated, in various directions.

The collapse of the major cultural centre of Teotihuacán in the Central Highlands left the way open for the development of states that were smaller than that of the great metropolis. These states assumed economic and political control of certain regions, and were occasionally subject, as a result, to the influence of new ethnic groups with their own distinct cultures; in some cases, these groups founded new states themselves. Xochicalco, Teotenango and Tula, each showing a certain idiosyncracy, are examples of the latter.

Xochicalco was on the edge of the area dominated by Teotihuacán during the Classic period. Towards A.D. 850, the city began to show traits suggestive of influence from the coast and the Maya area. It was around this time that Xochicalco began to enjoy a period of prosperity, which was to last until approximately A.D. 1250.

The extraordinary stone sculpture of a *guacamaya* (macaw) head, found in the Ball Court at Xochicalco, testifies to the influence of cultures from the Gulf of Mexico (plate 28). Its form is that of a big irregular prism, with two large planes creating the sides of the bird's head and converging in an arris which constitutes the beak. The bird's characteristic markings are finely incised on the surface, which as a result is slightly ridged. Three large round hollows of different shape and size represent the eyes, the nostrils and the hole for the beak. The relationship between the planes and hollow spaces within the overall volume, organised asymmetrically, shows considerable mastery of the dynamics of equilibrium.

The function of the sculpture is unknown. Some believe it to have been a ball-game marker, while others suggest that it belonged to the group of so-called "votive *hachas*" that are so characteristic of the Gulf cultures. In both cases, interpretations are related to the ball game, and iconographically the *guacamaya* – like the game – is associated with a cult of the sun. The use of sculpture and calendrical count was common in these cities, and memorable dates were often registered on stelae carved from stone, like the one shown in plate 29, which comes from Teotenango.

Here, a square prism was carved on two opposite sides with flat zoomorphic reliefs within a square frame. One side represents a jaguar weariung a bead necklace and a mask with a large eyebrow over the eye; both are symbols of Tláloc, god of water, and their association with the jaguar and the earth is a reference to the water that springs from the earth. The jaguar is represented in profile, seated in a human pose; in order to fit into the square format, it leans forward, creating a diagonal which stretches from the bottom of the relief to the upper left-hand corner through the jaguar's head. The head is the most important element in the relief, being proportionately larger than the body. At the other upper corner is a hieroglyph with the number two, the symbol of the "month of the rabbit", a date referring to the calendrical name of the person represented, who may well have been a priest or representative of the god. On the opposite side of the stela is a butterfly with the head of a bird, also wearing a bead necklace. Its body is similarly arranged in a diagonal that ascends and culminates in the animal's head, in the upper right-hand corner. In the left corner there is also a hieroglyph with the number thirteen, signifying the "month of the reptile's eye", the date of the birth of Quetzalcóatl, the "plumed serpent", god of the wind that brings rain. At the same time, the bird depicted – which seems to be a pheasant and therefore related to Xochipilli Macuilxóchitl, god of spring – has the body of a butterfly, an insect which is the symbol of the god of fire.

80

Although its exact iconographic meaning is not known, the stela is a good example of a written record using ideographic and possibly phonetic hieroglyphs, typical of the regional states during the Early Classic period. The principal function of this stela, that of communicating, means that the formal language is schematic, with the images defined only by their most basic characteristics, which are skilfully adapted to fill a frame that fits them perfectly with no room to spare. In both reliefs, maximum expression is achieved with a minimum of elements, accentuated by the dynamic balance of forms within the composition.

The manufacture of clay figurines related to cults persisted throughout the Classic period, even after the collapse of Teotihuacán. By then, Tula had begun to emerge as a leading centre of commerce, controlling numerous routes leading north and south which were used for the export of crafts bearing Tula's stylistic hallmark .

The figurine in plate 30 represents a particular type produced in Tula during the Early Classic period. It is modelled in clay, and represents a figure wearing a feather cape and a mask bearing the symbols of Tláloc – spectacles and a moustache with curled ends pointing upwards. The head is crowned by a crest of short, vertical feathers. The shape of the figure is extremely simple, consisting of a rectangle with rounded corners for the body with its feather cape, onto which is set an inverted, truncated cone that corresponds to the face and crest.

The most characteristic trait of this type of figurine is their bright colouring; here, blue and white stand out, colours distinctive of the god of water, the most popular god among the agricultural peoples.

Agriculture was extremely important for the Toltecs. They spent a great deal of attention on the development of canal systems in river basins, in order to control irrigation – an activity that had been in the hands of the priests of the Tláloc since Teotihuácan. These priests were extremely powerful because of their extensive astronomical and calendrical knowledge .

The cult of agricultural fertility embraced other concepts besides that of Tláloc, and these were represented through specific iconography. The simple elements and harmonious proportions of the female sculpture in plate 31, with a tall headdress bearing the symbols of the sun and the annual cycle, make this a fine example.

The serpent was also a symbol of the earth's fertility, expressed in many forms and associated with various deities. Its peculiar representation in the form of a throne (plate 34) gives it the appearance of a support, as the lawful protector of the dignitary who occupies the throne.

In this case, the carved serpents have moustaches curling upwards, which is the symbol of Tláloc. But at the same time, the fact that there are two serpent heads refers to a dual concept, which, in the context of Toltec culture, alludes to Quetzalcóatl; in one of his manifestations, he is represented as the planet Venus with its double: morning star and evening star.

Tlahuizcalpantecuhtli, which was the name of the deity in this form, represented a far more abstract concept than, for example, that of Tláloc, whose act of bestowing rain was far more direct and immediate. The morning star was the patron of merchants, and its cult spread along their routes through a large part of Mesoamerica.

Commerce and war were thought of as parallel and complementary in Toltec society; merchants opened the path for warriors, who later put pressure on local people in order to sustain the market, as well as to collect tributes.

The warrior group in Tula was a religious caste involved in the cult of Quetzalcóatl in his dedication as the morning star. They practised complex rituals and abstinence, as well as observing rigorous discipline.

Within the Toltec plastic arts, it is the images of warriors that best represent the art of this culture. They are known as atlantes because they were always weight-bearing, acting as columns in architecture and as supports for altars. Perhaps because of their function, they were carved as vertically elongated cylinders in hard stone, forms which were eventually to become indispensable to a large part of Toltec sculpture (see plates 31, 32 and 33). The shapes of these atlantes was solid in the extreme. In plate 32, the outer frame of the body from its feet to its shoulders has a rectangular ratio of 1:2, a robust and slightly elongated form. An almost vertical, stepped pyramid form rises from the base (although one of the sides is broken).

Within the general framework of this geometric form, ornament and clothing are depicted with only the most basic outline, consisting of a series of superimposed layers covering the body and face of the individual in an highly schematic way; for example, the toes and sandals of the feet are barely indicated on the rough shapes that represent them. The overall expression of the human figure is one of rigidity, giving it an appearance of great dignity and a certain distance from the spectator.

The figure of the standard-bearer in plate 33 is equally schematic and geometric. A strong sense of the vertical prevails, although the figure is divided in two by a powerful horizontal element represented by the arms and hands, exaggerated in size by comparison with the rest of the figure. This distortion was undoubtedly due to the figure's function as a standard-bearer, and, in contrast to the rest of the sculpture, is extraordinarily expressive. It suggests a sort of platform supporting the torso and head, and makes them appear truly monumental.

28. *GUACAMAYA* HEAD

Toltec culture. Xochicalco, Morelos. Early Post-Classic (A.D. 850-1250). Stone. Height 56.5 cm, width 43.5 cm. Toltec Hall. MNA. Cat. no. 15-950. Inv. no. 10-225799.

A cultural characteristic shared by the whole of Mesoamerican civilisation was the ball game, one of the most important ceremonies to take place in Prehispanic Mexico.

The game originated during the Pre-Classic period, around 1000 B.C., and was specifically related to the cult and custom of decapitation, in which the game formed part of a ceremonial ritual. Over the years, the game became more involved and began to require complex courts of a particular design, with specific features and finely crafted markers, aspects demanding a degree of architectural sophistication. However, this ball game was above all an eminent ritual, associated with the intricate Prehispanic religion.

The game had deep religious and symbolic meaning; its practice symbolised the daily struggle against evil, against opposite forces and against contradictory phenomena in nature, such as light and darkness or day and night.

Sixteenth-century sources and later research suggest that there were a number of variants of the game: sometimes the ball was thrown by hand; at other times a baton, stick or bat was used to hit the ball; but by far the most common and the most important practice was that of hitting the ball with the hips. In Náhuatl language, the game was known as *ullamaliztli*.

Despite the religious nature of the game, historical sources mention that betting was introduced; this was a new element clearly indicating that the game was becoming less sacred.

On an architectural level, the ball court consisted of a rectangular area with two parallel structures at either side in the form of a capital I, which could be open or closed. Similarly, the profiles and angles of these side structures might vary.

Archaeological evidence indicates that the most common type of structure in the Central Highlands was composed of *talud*, walls and benches.

Other elements associated with the ball court are niches situated diagonally opposite each other in the corners of the walls at either end, a stone disc which marked the centre of the court, and hoops known as rings which were embedded in the side walls of the central patio and through which the ball had to pass. Also notable are the remarkable markers, of which the most beautiful examples are to be found at the archaeological site of Copán; these are large stone sculptures representing a beautifully carved *guacamaya* head, almost identical to this example from Xochicalco, which was found at the centre of the Ball Court in the form of an offering. *f.s.m.*

29. STONE TABLET WITH CALENDRICAL LOW RELIEF CARVING

Toltec culture. Teotenango. Early Post-Classic (A.D. 850-1250). Stone. Height 58 cm, width 57 cm, depth 40 cm. Museo Arqueológico de Teotenango (Archaeological Museum of Teotenango). Cat. no. Pi-EI-CA-52208.

Among the ancient Mesoamerican cultures of the Early Post-Classic period was that of the Matlatzincas, who founded one of the most important archaeological sites in the Toluca valley, known as Teotenango, "In the True Place of the Rampart". As its name indicates, the city was surrounded by walls during the Prehispanic period, giving the site a particular character which made it different to other contemporary archaeological cities.

The numerous archaeological excavations that have been carried out at this and other sites in the valley of Toluca provide valuable information about these groups in terms of their politics, economics, society and religion. Here, attention centres on a sculpture found in the Serpent Building; it consists of a stone tablet of triangular section, of which the two uppermost sides have been carved in low relief.

On one side, a seated jaguar is depicted, with an open mouth out of which a speech line or volute emerges in place of a tongue; around its neck is a necklace of round beads, ending in an almost oval pectoral or medallion. This central motif is accompanied by the hieroglyph 2 *Tochtli* (Rabbit) in the upper corner, and by a double volute in the lower corner.

As a mythological animal, the jaguar was associated with night, war and the occult forces of Mictlan and death; but it also had connections with the earth through being a terrestrial animal.

On the other side of the tablet is an image of an animal with the head of a bird, legs in the form of claws and the body of a butterfly, whose wing is decorated with two circles, each with a stellar eye in the centre; around its neck hangs another bead necklace, ending in two much longer beads. The composition is completed by the hieroglyph 13, Reptile's Eye, and by two rectangles with a hollow in each centre next to the lower edge.

The creature's face represents the bird *coxcox*, or pheasant, which is characterised by its crest of five points (small circles). The pheasant is associated with the deity Xochipilli Macuilxóchitl, the lord or patron of spring, song and dance; he is accompanied by butterflies, flowers, birds and the like.

The tablet can be related to the tradition of Xochicalco partly by its style and marvellous sculptural technique, and particularly because of the presence of the hieroglyph 13, Reptile's Eye, associated with the cult of Quetzalcóatl; a close relationship with Teotihuácan is also apparent, as the city of Teotenango was founded by the Teotihuácan groups later known as the Matlatzincas, mentioned above.

The influence of these two cultural centres can be seen in the calendrical hieroglyphs, the year glyph and the stellar or Venus eyes, as well as in a certain association with the cult of Quetzalcóatl. *f.s.m.*

30. FIGURINE WITH THE ATTRIBUTES OF TLALOC

Toltec culture. Central Highlands. Early Post-Classic (A.D. 850-1250). Clay. Height 20 cm, width 12.5 cm. Toltec Hall. MNA. Cat. no. 15-68. Inv. no. 10-81700.

The cult of Tláloc, god of water, started when life became rather more sedentary for the Toltecs. Water was vital for survival, as it was for all other civilisations of the world; for the Toltecs, the forces of nature were also something to be feared, and they deified them until highly complex cults were formed.

They believed that they could request from Tláloc the amount of water that they needed for their plots of land; they manufactured different-sized vessels and bottles with the attributes of the god of water and took them as offerings to the region of Los Volcanos, associated with the god because it was so humid. The god's assistants, known as *tlaloques*, carried away the offerings and, once in the skies, hit them with a baton; the earth thus received the divine liquid. In this clay figurine, a Toltec priest is represented with a feather cape and the attributes of Tláloc, which are large earflares and a moustache. The piece has retained its colours through the ages, particularly the blue, a colour associated with the deity.   *f.s.m.*

31. SCULPTURE OF A GODDESS OF FERTILITY

Toltec culture. Central Highlands. Early Post-Classic (A.D. 850-1250). Stone. Height 142 cm, width 56 cm, depth 27 cm. Toltec Hall. MNA. Cat. no. 15-390. Inv. no. 10-229793.

After the collapse of Teotihuácan, the peoples who lived in the Central Highlands of Mexico began to display several cultural traits typical of the Gulf Coast and the southern part of the country.

The sculpture shown here, which is carved in stone, displays some of these characteristics; there was a tendency among certain Mesoamerican civilisations to show divine or anthropomorphic figures with arms crossed in front of their chests, as can be seen in this piece, the only example with this feature to have been found in the region.

Its headdress is in the shape of a triangle set on to a trapezium, which symbolises the movement of the sun's rays, thus marking the cycle of the year; this type of representation came to the Highlands from Oaxaca, and derives from the tradition known as Mixteca-Xochicalca. Its main interest lies in the fact that it depicts the deity of the annual cycle, associated primarily with the fertility of the earth.

The lives of Prehispanic peoples were directed very much according to their observation of nature; they were most interested in the movement of the stars and similarly felt a deep respect for the earth, on which they had to rely entirely for their subsistence.

The tilling of land and sowing of seeds were performed as a ritual, so that the earth's fertility and the life generated within it were given a special significance.   *f.s.m.*

32. ATLANTEAN FIGURE

Toltec culture. Mexico City. Early Post-Classic (A.D. 850-1250). Stone. Height 116 cm, width 43 cm, depth 32 cm. Toltec Hall. MNA. Cat. no. 15-196. Inv. no. 10-81767.

Tula was subject to military political rule; a hierarchical structure separated the common castes from those of high rank. As their civilisation developed, the Toltecs began to tyrannise the small settlements that surrounded them, creating a despotic system which imposed the payment of tributes.

Thanks to the sculptures that represent Toltec warriors, their form of attire is known to us. In this particular case, the standing male warrior displays a number of accoutrements: the helmet worn on the head is crowned by feathers that are possibly quetzal feathers, known as *quetzalhuitonacatl*, which was the headdress of the great lords; this one is decorated at the front with the symbol used for the butterfly pectoral. Beneath the headdress at the rear, part of a triangular cloth, which in some cases was decorated with tassels, can just be made out; it is probably a sort of protective cap similar to the ones currently used by the *danzantes* (dancers) of Oaxaca. At cheek level, in the form of a border, are large circular earflares; nose-plugs, a

celebrated feature, were used in the nose and were probably made of gold. A necklace can be distinguished below the chin, consisting of strings of cylindrical beads. Part of the piece is hidden beneath the butterfly pectoral known as *teocuitlapapalotl*, one of the most characteristic embellishments of the Toltec warriors. It was deeply symbolic, as they believed that when they died in battle they were resurrected transformed into butterflies, and accompanied the sun from their birth until they died. After dying with the sun, they were again resurrected in the form of hummingbirds. On the back of the sculpture is the divine circle, known as *tezcacuitlapilli*, from which three bands hang down; this is likely to have served as a shield in war. At the front is the *maxtlatl* or loincloth and the *maxactlachayahalli*, an elegant triangular apron whose ends are wrapped around the waist twice and tied at the front. Bands of cloth were wound around each leg and knotted at the back; the one below the knee is the *cotzehuatl*, while the other, above the ankle, is the *xoehuatl*. On the feet are half-heeled sandals known as *cactlis*; in some sculptures, the heel is decorated with the figure of a plumed serpent, identifying the warrior as belonging to the cult of Quetzalcóatl. As a weapon, the warrior carries a knife on the upper part of the left arm, of which the tip can be seen. The left hand clasps two very long darts (*ortloch*), with the tips pointing downwards, and a curved sword, an instrument similar to the Australian boomerang which could be used either for defence or offence.

The right hand clasps the spear thrower, or *atlatl*. The way in which two fingers were inserted to hold it can be clearly seen. The *atlatl* was a wooden instrument used to launch long arrows with obsidian heads. The weapon, one of the most ancient in the world, was of a functional type, suitable for use in combat.
f.s.m.

33. STANDARD-BEARER

Toltec culture. Tula, Hidalgo. Early Post-Classic (A.D. 850-1250). Stone. Height 83 cm, width 39 cm, depth 46 cm. Museo de Tula (Tula Museum). Inv. no. 10-215117.

Sculpture in Tula was generally related to architecture, as in the case of these standard-bearers, which were positioned on the upper part of the principal buildings.

Some of the standard-bearers that have been found are not anthropomorphic but take the form of animals (particularly the tiger with a hole in its back) associated with the ball game. They were generally positioned in the upper part of the ball-court building, so that when the banners of the teams who were playing were displayed there, they could be seen from every angle of the city.

These anthropomorphic standard-bearers, generally male, hold their hands out in front of them, with the fingers forming a hollow; great banners were placed in these hollows, generally made out of *amate* paper (*amate* is a species of fig tree) and decorated with molten rubber. This standard would bear symbols associated with the deity to whom the temple was dedicated; in Tula, a standard-bearer associated with the Temple of Tlahuizcalpantecuhtli, the Lord of Venus in his guise as "morning star" was found.

The standard-bearer represented here is a warrior, portrayed standing with arms held out in front of him. His clothing is very simple, but on his head he wears the *tzotzocolli*, the distinctive headdress of warriors who had accomplished their first military deed.   *f.s.m.*

34. ZOOMORPHIC THRONE

Toltec culture. Tula, Hidalgo. Early Post-Classic (A.D. 850-1250). Stone. Height 54 cm, width 91 cm, depth 42 cm. Toltec Hall. MNA. Cat. no. 15-162. Inv. no. 10-81271.

The most important of the Toltec deities was undoubtedly Quetzalcóatl, the creator of the fifth stage of humanity, who governed all aspects of their daily life. According to mythology he was the god appointed to rescue the bones of the man and woman who were in the Mictlán, or Underworld, guarded by the god Mictlantecuhtli. After overcoming a series of obstacles, Quetzalcóatl managed to get hold of the bones; in the skies, a goddess ground them into dust in her mill, while the god extracted life-giving blood from his own member. From this mixture of dust and blood was engendered the fifth humanity, which is the one that survives to the present day.

However, there was also the Toltec individual Topiltzin-Quetzalcóatl, to whom the flourishing of Tula as a city and the development achieved by the Toltecs was attributed.

His peaceful reign favoured the development of the fine arts. After several years and a number of different governments, Tula was divided by political strife, and Topiltzin-Quetzalcóatl was deceived by the worshippers of Tezcatlipoca, god of war. In great sorrow he was obliged to leave Tula; he headed towards the Gulf Coast, from where he set off towards the Maya lands; here he was given the name of Kukulcán, which has the same meaning as Quetzalcóatl: Plumed Serpent. Before leaving the Gulf area, he promised to return on a given date: Ce Acatl (One Cane); by coincidence, Hernán Cortés reached the coast of Veracruz on the same day, and was thus associated with Quetzalcóatl by its natives.

Both the god and the man were so important during this period that in most historical sources they are confused and united in the same figure; the god Quetzalcóatl also had several aspects, "duality" being one of his attributes; as is evident in this sculpture of the throne of Quetzalcóatl, generally known as the throne of two heads because of its two serpents joined together at the centre by the neck, each looking in opposite directions. The sculpture represents the duality of Quetzalcóatl among the Toltecs; this god could be Quetzalcóatl, Tláloc, god of the rain, Ehécatl, god of the wind, Xolotl, his divine twin, and Tlahuizalpantecuhtli, the god Venus in his guise as morning star.

His representative Ce Acatl Topiltzin-Quetzalcóatl, who spoke for the god, said to his people: "You will be the Toltecs, builders and inventors. Your fame will spread throughout the earth, and soon the entire population of Anáhuac will come to admire and to learn about you, the Toltec peoples."   *f.s.m.*

28. *GUACAMAYA* HEAD

29. STONE TABLET WITH CALENDRICAL LOW RELIEF CARVING

29. STONE TABLET WITH CALENDRICAL LOW RELIEF CARVING

30. FIGURINE WITH THE ATTRIBUTES OF TLALOC

90

31. SCULPTURE OF A GODDESS OF FERTILITY

32. ATLANTEAN FIGURE

32. ATLANTEAN FIGURE

32. ATLANTEAN FIGURE

32. ATLANTEAN FIGURE

33. STANDARD-BEARER

33. STANDARD-BEARER

34. ZOOMORPHIC THRONE

7. MEXICO-TENOCHTITLAN:
THE CAPITAL OF WAR AND THE JADE LAKES

Felipe Solís Olguín

It was in A.D. 1519 that the Spanish adventurers disembarked on the coasts of the Gulf of Mexico. The fever for gold and conquest had spurred them on after sailing from Cuba and travelling along the shores of Yucatán and the adjoining regions. On arrival, they asked the local inhabitants, the Totonacs, both about the precious metal which had led the Spanish there, and about the Totonaca ruler and which nation governed them. Angry and fearful, the response was unanimous: after prolonged wars they had fallen under the domination of Aztec warriors, sent by their lord Moctezuma Xocoyotzin. This was the period now known as the Late Post-Classic, which extends from the twelfth century to the sixteenth – the great age of the superiority of the Aztecs, better known as the Mexicas, founders of México-Tenochtitlán, described in the words of the poets as "the great city of jade lakes and shields of war".

This proud nation developed a mythological saga to explain its presence in these lands. They said they came from a northern region known as Aztlán, which they left towards the eleventh century A.D.; after an eventful journey with various adventures, they arrived in the Valley of Mexico.

The Mexicas began their odyssey in the year "One Flint", corresponding to A.D. 1116, stopping temporarily at different sites along the route. They finally settled at Chapultepec, the Hill of the Grasshopper, where they built both defence structures and terraces for cultivation.

Once established at this site, they came into conflict with other peoples who lived in the valley, principally the Tecpanecas, Culhuas and Xaltocamecas, who formed a coalition which defeated the Mexicas, and sent them as prisoners of war to Culhuacán. Through marriage, the Mexicas struck family and cultural links with the people of Culhuacán, who claimed to be descendants of Tula: eventually the newcomers began to consider themselves heirs of the Toltecs and their culture. They were later thrown out by the Culhuas and had to take refuge among the swamps and bullrushes of the lake. Here they found an omen decreeing that this was their rightful home: an eagle perched on a nopal devouring a serpent. It was in this spot that they founded their capital, México-Tenochtitlán, in A.D. 1325, having earlier settled in the Valley of Mexico towards the thirteenth century. The Valley of Mexico, and particularly the lakeside region in which they settled, which then covered approximately eight thousand square kilometres, was an area of great beauty, surrounded by wooded mountains and with a temperate climate.

At the time of their arrival, the great Prehispanic lake area consisted of a series of lakes and lagoons of considerable size, among the most important of which were Texcoco, Chalco, Xaltocán and Xochimilco, which had small islands in their western parts. There the Mexica built their city, Tenochtitlán, which was to turn within a short time into a powerful metropolis dominating a vast dependent state extending from the Gulf Coast to the Pacific coast, and from El Bajío to Oaxaca. Through military and commercial expansion, the Mexicas came into contact with a number of differing ecological regions in which they discovered, used and deified numerous animals. Among these the jaguar, eagle, serpent and monkey were singled out, and were represented with great realism in magnificent stone sculptures and reliefs.

Physically, this nation resembled other Mesoamerican groups: skin varying from very light to dark, and straight, black hair; baldness was rare, and the rest of their bodies were hairless; they had dark, slanting eyes, high foreheads and narrow noses. As we have seen, the average height for men was 1.60 metres, while that of women was around 1.48 metres.

8. The Mexica state and independent political groupings

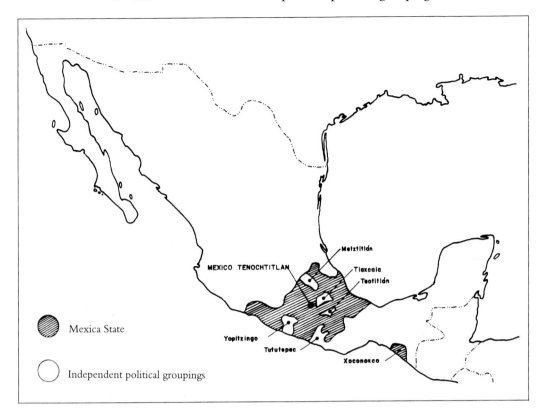

Numerous sculptural images survive from this civilisation, found in its capital city and even in distant provinces. They bear witness to a predominant pattern of idealised beauty, representing perfect citizens whose conduct was supposed to inspire the nation's youth.

Estimates concerning the population of this society vary from the sixteenth century to the present day. It is currently believed that at the time of the Spaniards' arrival, there were two million inhabitants in the Valley of Mexico, and 250,000 in Tenochtitlán. Their language was Náhuatl, part of the Yuto-Aztec linguistic family.

Tenochtitlán and its twin site Tlatelolco were island-cities which probably occupied a joint area of 13 square kilometres at this point; several generations had brought about the growth and development of the major city, extending and modifying the original landscape, and transforming it into a city of extraordinary beauty, a source of amazement to all who saw it.

From the moment of Tenochtitlán's foundation, the Mexica leaders established that at the centre of this sacred site, where the eagle had perched on the nopal in such symbolic fashion, the most sacred of all buildings would be constructed: the double pyramid dedicated to its patron deities, Huitzilipochtli, the god of both sun and war, and Tláloc, the god of rain.

Other buildings constructed in this central area were also dedicated to the gods, and were hence the most important ones. On the Spaniards' arrival, the ceremonial precinct had a quadrangular layout which measured approximately 400 metres along each side; according to the surviving descriptions, it was bordered by a defensive rampart of symbolic significance, being decorated with the serpents'-head sculptures that led to it being called the Coatepantli. This had three entrances from which the causeways linking the city to dry land emerged, running to the north, south and west. The pyramid which served as a base for the double Temple of Tláloc and Huitzilopochtli was remarkable for its size, with a double stairway flanked by broad *alfardas* (stair-rail borders).

Other temples were dedicated to different deities, principally those of the sun and of agriculture; the temple of the god of wind, a circular structure, had an entrance in the form of a serpent's head with open jaws. There were also structures such as the Ball Court and the *tzompantli*, which was built out of rows of human skulls strung together on wooden poles, macabre trophies of the sacrifice of prisoners of war.

The appearance and character of this sacred space altered as time went on; its dimensions in particular were to change. At first, the buildings reached barely a few metres in height, having been built with great effort under the direction of the first rulers. The situation changed noticeably after the war of liberation, during which the Mexicas freed themselves from Azcapotzalco domination. From this point Tenochtitlán was able to use the necessary economic resources and labour force to remodel its ceremonial precinct and probably the whole city.

Archaeological discoveries since the beginning of this century, which have taken place almost exclusively in the heart of this ceremonial space in the ancient centre of Mexico City, reveal not only this architectural expansion, but also the beauty of the ancient capital of the Mexicas. In order to complement the information we have and to reconstruct this ancient city and the art that enriched it, we must refer to historical description, whether that of the conquistadors or of the religious chroniclers and descendants of the indigenous nobility.

From the very beginning, the Mexicas conceived a rigid groundplan for their capital city, dividing it into four main districts corresponding to the four areas of the universe, and which we know as the four main areas: Atzacoalco, Cuepopán, Zoquiapán and Moyotlán. Within these four original areas were the diverse *calpullis*, quarters that had existed from the time of the initial migration. This distribution, made by the ruling group, provoked the displeasure of one sector of society, which preferred to colonise a small neighbouring island where they founded the city of Tlatelolco, eventually annexed to Tenochtitlán by force during a war of conquest led by Axayacátl, and converted into a fifth district of the Aztec capital.

Outside the ceremonial precinct were the palaces of the *Tlatoani,* or governor, and of other noblemen, as well as an open space dedicated to public ceremonies. During the rule of the second Moctezuma, the market of Tenochtitlán was concentrated in Tlatelolco, and its original area was dedicated to religious ceremonies, principally to the celebration of the game of the *voladores*. The palaces and houses diminished both in size and in the richness of their construction as they receded from the centre; craftsmen and peasants lived on the outskirts, on land reclaimed from the lake through *chinampas*, cultivated areas within the lake, which gave the city its particular character.

As has been mentioned, the islands were joined to the mainland by means of various causeways. Three of these led from Tenochtitlán: the Tlacopán causeway, which was divided along its length and had an aquaduct running down the centre which brought drinking water from Chapultepec; the Iztapalapa causeway, in two parts, joining the capital to the towns of Iztapalapa and Coyoacán; and the Tepeyac causeway. These causeways also served as dykes and, together with the *albarrón*, a stone and wood wall which ran eastward and separated fresh water from brackish water, regulated the volume of water in the lakes.

Not only did these proud inhabitants of the capitals of Tenochtitlán and Tlatelolco succumb to Spanish attack; their buildings did not survive destruction either, and their ruins served as foundations for the nascent capital of New Spain. Because of this, and due to archaeological work carried out in the centre of Mexico, remains of ancient buildings have been found, mainly decorative caracols and wall and stairway decorations in the form of wild animals, especially serpents, as can be seen in the ruins of the Templo Mayor.

The Mexicas were basically an agricultural people, complementing their diet through fishing, hunting and gathering.

The principal plants cultivated were the same as in other regions of Mesoamerica: maize, beans, chilli, pumpkin, nopal, sage seed, maguey, and such like. The lake was the source of many animals, satisfying the need for protein: frogs, *ajolotes* (amphibian animals native to Mexico), *acociles* (a type of fresh-water shrimp), fish, ducks, herons and others; there were also turkeys, deer and a special kind of indigenous dog, the *itzcuintli*, which was bred for consumption.

The Mexicas' flourishing economy was dependent on several factors: proper control of the population's labour force; intensive commerce; a system of tributes which supplied the capital with an abundance of primary materials and products needed by the ruling classes; and intensive exploitation of the surrounding environment.

Their agricultural tools were confined to a dibble stick for planting, known as a *coa*; the system of cultivation used was generally that of the *milpa* or maize field, which either relied on seasonal cycles or was irrigated by canals. In the region of the lakes, principally in the area to the south and around the lakes themselves, the predominant form of intensive cultivation took place in *chinampas*, which provided plenty of produce; the Mexicas developed advanced hydraulic technology, including canals, dykes, bridges, aquaducts and *chinampas*, among which the most notable were those intended for agricultural use. Ownership of land was communal and governed by two basic groups: the *calpulli* and the state. Despite this, a form of private property existed among some members of the nobility and high-ranking warriors, mostly affecting land that had been taken in conquest.

The Mexicas' social structure had relied from its earliest foundation on the *calpullis*, which were the basic cells of the Mexica state. The socio-economic organisation of these units was based on families; they were self-sufficient, with their own marked-out territory of communal property, cultivated by the members; they also had their own governors, wardens, priests and teachers.

Commercial activity was carried out by merchants through a formal institution, the *pochtecayotl* or merchants' guilds, who arranged trading routes that stretched from the Pacific to the Gulf of Mexico, and from the northern borders to the various points of south-east Mesoamerica. Long-distance trade satisfied the privileged class's demand for luxury objects and promoted military expansion.

The necessity of finding uninterrupted and secure methods of conducting inter-regional trade impelled the nation towards conquest, usually preceded by the imposition of payment in the form of essential materials and other products; thus the Aztecs established an efficient system of claiming tributes from the various regions. Local exchange of goods, mostly carried out by the producers themselves, took place in the markets or *tianquiztli*, where bartering was generally practised, despite the existence of trade goods that functioned like money, such as fine blankets, copper axes and especially cacao beans.

There was a pronounced class distinction within Mexica society, determined not only by the site occupied by those involved in the production of goods and services, but also by their material possessions. Two groups existed: the nobility or *pipiltin*, and the peasants or *macehualtin*. The *pipiltin* constituted the most privileged social group; they held the most important administrative posts, whether in the priesthood, politics or military service. Not only were they exempt from paying tributes and from agricultural labour, but they also received objects and foods as payment, wore fine cotton clothing and elegant sandals and were able to display their headdresses and ornaments in public. The *macehualtin*, who comprised the majority of the population, worked on communal land which could not be inherited. They were compelled to make contributions to the state and the nobility based on the produce they cultivated, and they also worked on land dedicated to the maintenance of war and the temples. They were not allowed to wear expensive garments, and even less could they own or display luxury objects.

The state kept a rigorous military record, as a result of which the *macehual* who excelled in military service could achieve a level of possessions similar to that of the nobility; in this way, the Mexica enticed their nation to grow richer through conquest.

Groups of select warriors were chosen from among the nobility, and formed associations or guilds which assumed the protection of the wild animal that was their symbol and guardian. Of these, two outstanding groups are known: the eagle warriors and the jaguar warriors, of which magnificent stone sculptures exist.

The *macehualtin* group included craftsmen, traders and *pochtecas*, who held privileged positions in society, principally through being exempt from cultivating the land; however, they paid tributes, either with their crafts or with products that they had brought from other countries.

Very low on the social scale were the *tlacotin* (slaves), who were deprived of their liberty principally because of debts or for having sold themselves. At the top of the Aztecs'

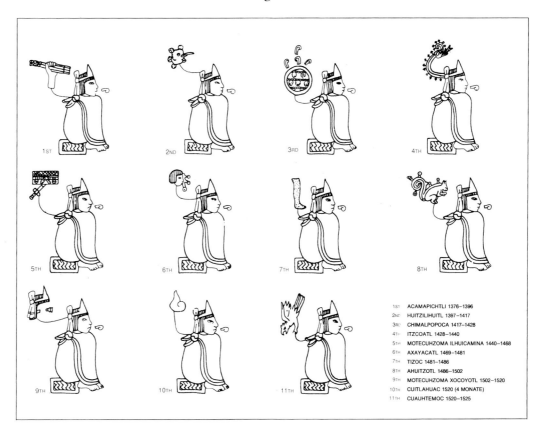

1ST ACAMAPICHTLI 1376–1396
2ND HUITZILIHUITL 1397–1417
3RD CHIMALPOPOCA 1417–1428
4TH ITZCOATL 1428–1440
5TH MOTECUHZOMA ILHUICAMINA 1440–1468
6TH AXAYACATL 1469–1481
7TH TIZOC 1481–1486
8TH AHUITZOTL 1486–1502
9TH MOTECUHZOMA XOCOYOTL 1502–1520
10TH CUITLAHUAC 1520 (4 MONATE)
11TH CUAUHTEMOC 1520–1525

political organisation was the *tlatoani* or lord, a ruler who governed for life and who was elected from among the descendants of the first ruler. He was the head of state, the army and the church, and shared his office with the *cihuacóatl*, a political dignitary who became established during the rule of Tlacaelel.

There was also a council of elders, the *tlatocan*, who intervened in decisions of major importance. On lower levels there was a multitude of functionaries and employees involved in bureaucratic work: judges, policemen, wardens of armories and others.

The Mexicas appointed their first *tlatoani* as soon as they had established themselves in México-Tenochtitlán. They chose Acamapichtli, one of the leaders from Culhuacán, who on ascending the throne allowed the Mexicas to form links with the former inhabitants of the valley. The two subsequent *tlatoanis* were Huitzilihuitl and Chimalpopoca, who governed the Mexicas while they were still subject to Azcapotzalco rule; it was during the governorship of Itzcóatl that the war liberating the Mexicas from the Tepanecas took place. After this victory, the triumphant allies Tenochtitlán, Texcoco and Tlacopán organised a political and military confederation known as the Triple Alliance, which fought the war of conquest of the lake area that lasted until 1434.

Itzcóatl's advisor was Tlacaelel, one of Prehispanic history's more striking characters, who divined Tenochtitlán's glorious destiny and decreed that measures must be taken to consolidate its prestige; he established an official history in which the Mexicas were portrayed as the chosen nation of the sun.

Following Itzcóatl came the *tlatoanis* Moctezuma Ilhuicamina, Axayacatl, Tizoc and Ahuizotl; they were responsible for extending the borders of the Mexica state through military conquest.

The character of Mexica society was transformed under the second Moctezuma, who brought about the efficient functioning of the system of paying tributes. However, his attitude to the Spanish conquistadors was passive and fatalistic, preventing his nation from defending their country.

The last Mexica lords were Cuitlahuac and Cuauhtemoc, who defended the city against European attack. When the final *tlatoani* was captured, Tenochtitlán succumbed, on the 13th of August of 1521.

Characteristic of the Mexica state was its craftsmanship, which enabled certain sectors of the population to work full-time on the production of articles for the ruling class or for trade. Production was on a family level, which obliged sons to continue the specialty of their elders. Among full-time craftsmen were stone carvers, goldsmiths, textile weavers and manufacturers of feather objects.

Metalwork evolved principally through the working of precious metals, gold, silver and copper, using techniques such as the lost-wax technique, lamination and filigree work. Only a few examples of these fine objects exist, as the majority were melted down by the conquistadors.

Crafts such as ceramics, basket weaving and the manufacture of stone objects, were not likely to have been full-time occupations, and craftsmen would probably have spent the rest of the time engaged in agricultural tasks.

Mexica pottery consisted of a variety of vessels, notable among which are those of an orange colour with black decorative motifs, given the generic title of Aztec II-IV ceramics; there was also a red ceramic with an extraordinary polish, and a polychromatic pottery brought from the Puebla-Tlaxcala region, the characteristic forms of which were two-tiered plates, mortars, cups, jars, flat pans and bowls.

Mexica attire generally consisted of *maxtlatl* (loincloths) and *tilmas* (cloaks), worn by men; and of *enredos* (wrap-around skirts), *huipiles* (a form of blouse) and *guechquemetl* (a small triangular shawl), worn by women.

When the cult of the god Huitzilopochtli spread through the various regions of the Mexica nation, sculptors, painters, goldsmiths and other craftsmen would undoubtedly have come to the city to manufacture objects with a characteristic style that would distinguish and give visual unity to the city of México-Tenochtitlán.

It is clear that the great art of this nation was monumental sculpture. We know that throughout the city, and even in its distant dependent territories, sculptured images were erected, primarily depicting the deities which governed the fate of mankind. The Great Coatlicue and the Sun Stone (now in the Museo Nacional de Antropología in Mexico City) are some of the aesthetic examples that come to mind.

Like all Mesoamerican civilisations, this group believed that the whole world was part of a magical-religious universe; they considered the entire phenomena of life to have been produced by divine forces.

Mexica religion reflected a fusion of diverse theological elements, including cults of very ancient origin, such as the cult of the god of fire; it also incorporated national tribal deities, such as Huitzilopochtli.

The origin of the world and of life was explained by different theories: the Mexica believed in a dual female-male principle, identified with the gods Ometecuhtli and Omecihuatl, the creators of everything that existed. Their image of the universe consisted of a space formed by the four cardinal points and the centre. They also thought that the world and man had been created several times, hence the myth of the five suns; they believed that they were living during the era of the fifth sun, Ollin-Tonatiuh, the sun of movement.

The principal gods, associated with the creative aspects of life, were Tezcatlipoca and Ehécatl-Quetzalcóatl, the patrons of darkness and wind respectively; the sun was Tonatiuh, the moon Meztli; the earth was conceived of as an old woman, Coatlicue, mother of all the gods and all men, or as Tlatecuhtli, a monstrous being, always ready to devour anything that died.

Huitzilopochtli was the tribal god, associated with the young sun, triumphant in the daily fight against the stars and the moon; his importance and maintenance were the justification for military expansion.

Human sacrifice was one of the characteristic traits of Mexica ritual; it was associated with the idea of sustaining the sun and life through the blood and hearts of the victims; it was also the definitive proof of the power of this nation and of its means of growth.

During the sacrifice the victim's chest was opened with a flint knife and the heart was extracted; prisoners were also burnt or drowned. Occasionally the flesh of the sacrificed victim was eaten, not as food but rather as ritualistic cannibalism, a means of communion between men and the deity, who was considered to be incarnate in the victim.

Other deities included Tláloc, patron of the rain, Chalchiuhtlicue, goddess of spring water, Centeotl, god of river water, Xochipilli Macuilxóchitl, one of the gods of flowers and springtime, Mayahuel, god of maguey, Patecatl, god of *pulque* and Xipe, god of spring and of goldsmiths.

Knowledge of astronomy was considerable, and the Mexica understood perfectly some of the stars and their position in the skies. They had a fairly advanced solar calendar, with years consisting of 365 days, composed of eighteen months, each of twenty days, and five additional days, as well as a ritual calendar of 260 days, used to forecast the destiny of man in the manner of a horoscope. A century was formed every fifty-two years, when the ceremony of the tying of the years was carried out. Writing was based on glyphs, and their numeric system was based on the number twenty.

This astonishing civilisation was completely annihilated by the Europeans; many customs and traditions of this enduring heritage, however, have survived to the present day.

8. CONCEPTUALISATION AND NATURALISM IN MEXICA ART

Sonia Lombardo de Ruíz

Prehispanic civilisation in the Highlands of Mexico was to culminate in the Mexica/Aztec culture, representing not only its own traditions but also those of numerous other Mesoamerican races: an absorption of indigenous characteristics in the process of conquest that is typical of imperialism.

Perhaps because of México-Tenochtitlán's lakeside location, the Mexicas' capital city maintained and developed to the maximum techniques of intensive agricultural production, based on the construction of *chinampas*. At the same time, they also built up a network of commerce and payment that needed war to sustain it.

The Mexica economy was thus maintained through a dependence on both war and agriculture. As a result the twin pyramids and temples of Tláloc, patron of agriculture, and Huitzilopochtli, the god of war, were next to one another in the Templo Mayor.

The surviving Mexica plastic arts are characterised by their force and monumentality. All are works of great symbolic meaning which are also extraordinarily expressive. Nothing is merely casual, lyrical or festive; everything corresponds to a strict religious symbolism. Nevertheless, a certain realism characterises Mexica art, revealing a sensitive perception and understanding of natural form. Thus, within a general aesthetic concept there are certain variations. Zoomorphic animals, despite the fact that they are symbolic and allude to fertility, being associated with the earth and water, are represented by organic forms which may be schematic but are so realistic in certain details, particularly texture, that they immediately impart a sense of reality and a high degree of sensuality. This is the case in the representations of the serpent and the caracol (plates 35 and 37).

The human figure is also given idiosyncratic treatment. Warriors (plate 36), archetypal individuals (plates 38 and 40) or goddesses in human form (plate 41) are represented with the same degree of plasticity.

Their bodies are robust rather than slim, and set on solid legs. Feet and hands are very large in comparison to the torso; faces, which are even larger, are wide, with crude features and large ears: they have big half-open mouths, in some cases showing teeth. The eyes are formed by white stone or mother-of-pearl inlays, with black stones for the pupils, which make them look not unrealistic (plate 38). The figures tend to be compact, and the surfaces smooth with a semi-ridged texture which only varies when poles with banners are held.

The figure of a hunchback (plate 39) is exceptionally realistic and, although the head corresponds to the archetype already described, the sculpture acquires freedom through the posture and the deformity of the back, creating a dynamic equilibrium that is highly expressive.

Priests are another type of sculpture frequently found in Mexica art. While deriving from the same human type, they are distinguished by bearing the attributes of the god to whose cult they were dedicated, and whom they represent. In this way, for example, the priest of Ehécatl (plate 44), who is Quetzalcóatl in his guise as the god of wind, is a naked man, covered only by a loincloth, with a mouth mask in the form of a duck's beak. Similarly, the body of the priest of the god Xipe-Totec (plate 46), "our lord the flayed one" – a title alluding to the regeneration of the earth, which annually acquired a new skin – is covered by the skin of a man, while the face wears a death mask, indicated by the closed eyes.

The Mexicas inherited the cults and iconography of many earlier gods, such as the Old God of Fire or Tláloc. In other cases – for instance, that of Coatlicue, the great goddess of the earth – they constructed their images on the basis of ancient symbols, giving them a new form and their own stylistic character.

Nevertheless, the concept behind Mexica representation was rather different to that of the Teotihuacános. The latter's gods were recognisable through a combination of symbols with vaguely human form, as in the case of Tláloc, or fantastic animals, such as Quetzalcóatl, the plumed serpent. By contrast, Mexica sculpture always involved natural representation, either animal or human, so Huitzilopochtli, the god of war and of the sun, took the form of a hummingbird; Ehécatl, the god of wind, might assume the body of a monkey, as in the extraordinary sculpture in plate 45.

In the same way, the iconography of the goddess Cihuatetéotl – a woman who died in childbirth, and who thus forms part of the sun's retinue (plate 47) – pursues the same logic of natural representation.

In this masterpiece of Mexica art, maximum expression is achieved with a minimum of means, using a method similar to that of hieroglyphs The two elements that define this deity are united: that of the woman and that of death. The kneeling woman is contained within a formal structure of three sections in the shape of a sort of Latin cross with short arms. The lower section, which represents the skirt, is a horizontal rectangle with a smooth surface and rounded angles, and with only the belt indicated. The middle section, corresponding to what would be the arms of the cross, emphasises the breasts and the monumental fists at the front. The third section is formed by the goddess's skull and hair, which are likewise of enormous proportions. The overall figure is a synthesis of Mexica plastic conception, in which only the significant elements are used and nothing is superfluous; the volume is compact, the forms are schematic but realistic, accentuating through their size what is most important and therefore what needs to stand out.

The Mexica also sculpted masks, sometimes used for funerary rituals, but on other occasions attached to statues of the gods, in which case the mask itself became the deity.

In keeping with the principle of using natural forms, deities were given human faces bearing the symbols of their identity. Techniques also varied: some were modelled in clay and painted, others carved out of stone and then also painted (plate 42), or made from wood with shell, turquoise and coloured-stone inlays, as in the extraordinary Pigorini Museum example, not exhibited here.

Finally, like other Mesoamerican civilisations, Mexica sculpture was related to their architecture. The serpents' heads bordering stairway *alfardas*, or the merlons on temple roofs, are typical. Invariably, they function as an element of identification, promoting recognition of the deity to whom the building was dedicated. Thus, for example, the Temple of Quetzalcóatl had feathered serpents along the *alfardas* (plate 48), which allude to the god's name, and merlons with cross-sections of caracol shells (plate 49), which are symbols of the wind, thus alluding to Quetzalcóatl in his role as Ehécatl.

35. SERPENT

Mexica culture. Central Highlands. Late Post-Classic (A.D. 1300-1521). Stone. Height 31 cm, length 44 cm. Mexica Hall. MNA. Cat. no. 11-3010. Inv. no. 10-220932.

From its earliest history, Mesoamerica deified the serpent, a mysterious and terrible animal which embodied not only the concept of abundance, but also all natural forces as well as the mysteries of destruction and death: all the elements of nature could be interpreted through this reptile.

One such serpent was Xiuhcóatl, the serpent of fire used by the sun both as a means of transport through the firmament and as a weapon of attack; Xiuhcóatl was visualised as being covered in tongues of red and yellow flame. Tláloc, god of water, also used the animal, either as a water serpent or in the form of a ray, illustrating the deity's beneficial influence on agriculture; not surprisingly, the earth was also believed to consist of a web or mat of serpents, and the patron deity, whom the Mexicas called Cihuacóatl, was in fact a snake woman whom they imagined as a menacing goddess, producing terrifying sounds and whistling in the night.

In this sculpture, the Prehispanic artist has captured the characteristic appearance of the serpent; its body is coiled, in a sort of oval shape, a finely polished form which emphasises the uniform texture of the almost black volcanic rock out of which it has been carved. The zoological species of the animal is immediately obvious: it is a rattlesnake and, in order to make this apparent, the sculptor has exaggerated the size of the tail with its rattles, situating it at the rear of the piece.

This serpent expresses both serenity and mystery, the movement within the knotted body suddenly ceasing in the head section; the animal rests its head on its body, displaying its enormous forked tongue, which falls in a narrow band on its breast. The eye sockets indicate that inlays, probably of shell or a similar substance, were to have been placed here, which would have heightened the realism of the sculpture.   *f.s.o.*

36. EAGLE-WARRIOR HEAD

Mexica culture. Mexico City. Late Post-Classic (A.D. 1300-1521). Stone. Height 32 cm, width 30 cm. Mexica Hall. MNA. Cat. no. 11-2759. Inv. no. 10-94.

War was such an integral aspect of the Mexica civilisation that all activities were associated with it. Thus, religion was based on the daily fight of the eagle-sun, a warrior star which stood in victory over its enemies in the celestial sphere, the moon, the stars and darkness. It should come as no surprise, therefore, that in this extremely class-conscious society, the most valiant warriors were selected from among the nobility or *pipiltin*, and formed military groups who chose for protection and patronage a wild animal, preferably the coyote, jaguar or eagle.

Here the head of an eagle warrior is represented; although the lower part of the sculpture is missing, this fragment is sufficient to indicate the importance attributed to these warriors in Mexica society. The figure is highly expressive and aesthetically pleasing, portraying a young man with virile features, whose head is completely enclosed by a helmet in the shape of an eagle's head, shown with wide-open beak and constituting the warrior's emblematic headdress. In reality, this helmet was probably made of wood covered with feathers; the bird's

characteristic features and the elaborate quality of the feathers are apparent in the fine relief.   *f.s.o.*

37. CARACOL

Mexica culture. Templo Mayor. Late Post-Classic (A.D. 1300-1521). Stone. Height 105 cm, width 75.5 cm, depth 48 cm. In store. MNA. Cat. no. 11-5410. Inv. no. 10-213080.

Numerous creatures associated with water belonged to the symbolic and sacred ensemble with which the Mexicas accompanied the offerings in the Templo Mayor, temple of Tláloc and one of the two buildings located in the sacred centre of México-Tenochtitlán. This large sculpture, representing a sea shell, is just such a piece.

The sculptor took advantage of the basalt rock's own formation to define the caracol using finely incised line to exaggerate the striation of its corrugated surface, which is so particular to this zoological species; the animal's genus, according to specialists, is the strombus. Three of these monumental marine caracol sculptures were discovered during the most recent excavations at the Templo Mayor, found in an east-west alignment at the back of the pyramid of Tláloc.   *f.s.o.*

38. TORSO

Mexica culture. Puebla-Tlaxcala Valley. Late Post-Classic (A.D. 1300-1521). Stone. Height 33 cm, width 20 cm. Mexica Hall. MNA. Cat. no. 11-2918. Inv. no. 10-40607.

Monumental sculpture carved out of volcanic stone is probably the sculptural form that is most clearly identified with Mexica civilisation. Such sculptures were to be found not only in the capital city of México-Tenochtitlán, but even in distant regions dominated by the Mexicas, where craftsmen imitated the metropolitan style in local materials.

As regards sculpture of the human figure, aesthetic patterns clearly played a part in capturing in stone not only the popular elements of beauty but also the attributes of the model citizen. In this torso, which alas is incomplete, the artist achieved a vitality that is unique among this group of anthropomorphic figures, enhancing the naturalistic qualities of the anatomy with great realism and focusing attention on the facial features.

The piece presents a young Mexica man, with a face free of the wrinkles that herald old age. It portrays a real person, a man of strength, as was required by this society; the lifelike expression is accentuated by the shell inlays of the eyes. The eye-catching rectangular cavity at the centre of the chest is known (from contemporary records) to have housed a small piece of jade, especially a bead symbolising life; the placing of jade in this cavity, which was then covered with stucco, indicated that the figure had the necessary lifeforce to survive in the universe.*f.s.o.*

39. HUNCHBACK

Mexica culture. Central Highlands. Late Post-Classic (A.D. 1300-1521). Stone. Height 33 cm, width 17 cm. Mexica Hall. MNA. Cat. no. 11-3421. Inv. no. 10-97.

According to ancient Mexica mythology, the present universe, that of the Fifth Sun, had been created in Teotihuacán through the efforts of a deity called Nanahuatzin, which could be translated as *El Bubocita* (Little Tumour), the deformed deity. He was probably a hunchback with crooked arms and legs, whose body was smothered in sores, which have been interpreted as external evidence of syphilis.

Although difficult to believe, it appears that this deformed character, one of the manifestations of the ancient creator Quetzalcóatl, played a crucial role in the formation of the fifth era. Myth suggests that Nanahuatzin, in spite of his deformity, undertook the huge task of building the Pyramid of the Sun in Teotihuacán, placing in front of it an enormous fire into which he threw himself, setting himself alight and thus being transformed into the star king. Because of this, anyone born into Mexica society with a deformity, particularly dwarves, albinos, Siamese twins and hunchbacks, were thought to be children of the sun who had supernatural qualities; they were kept out of sight, in special houses where they were cared for until there was an eclipse of the sun, when they were sacrificed in the belief that the star was exercising his primary rights on them.

This sculpture represents one of these deformed people with a realism that might be termed sarcastic, and which displays both the characteristic hunchback of the spine and a projection on the thorax. The individual is shown seated, resting on his right thigh and clothed only in the traditional *maxtlatl*. The singular hairstyle has something akin to a strand of hair hanging down at the right side. In Mexica society, all male individuals who wanted to make their mark through their activities as warriors had to capture one or more live prisoners and take them first to their own military encampment and then to the capital, where they would be sacrificed to the gods. Only then was the warrior's hair cut (it had previously been combed in a long pony tail) creating the strand that indicated his bravery and skill. The fact that this characteristic warrior hairstyle is apparent in this deformed man substantiates the interpretation of the hunchback as one chosen by the sun, the fighter who triumphs over his enemies and combs his hair in the style of a victorious warrior.   *f.s.o.*

40. SCULPTURE IN RITUALISTIC POSTURE

Mexica culture. Central Highlands. Late Post-Classic (A.D. 1300-1521). Stone. Height 80 cm, width 28 cm. Mexica Hall. MNA. Cat. no. 11-3362. Inv. no. 10-220926.

This is the most complete and best-preserved male sculpture bequeathed by the former inhabitants of the Mexican capital. The figure is evidently complete, and any deterioration is imperceptible. The proud Mexica youth displays his virility, strength and determined attitude in the face of life. Without any detrimental effect, the figure is completely naked, with his sex chastely covered by the *maxtlatl*, that passes between the legs, covering and protecting the youth's virility; this cloth was wrapped around the waist, and tied and knotted at the front, with the ends hanging down between the legs.

The physical characteristics of the Mexicas can be clearly seen in the face; short, straight hair, slightly slanting eyes, a broad nose, clearly defined cheekbones and the complete absence of facial hair, either as a beard or as a moustache.

The figure is upright, in a definitely ritualistic pose: his right hand is placed on his chest while the left arm is bent upwards,

pointing forwards, with the hand forming a cavity, which has led to the association of this figure with the standard-bearer group.

Either seated or upright, these anthropomorphic sculptures were placed outside temples, holding banners in their hands, announcing the presence of the deity inside and bearing the emblems of their god. Several centuries had elapsed since the earliest civilised inhabitants of the central valleys of Mexico had tried to capture in stone the physical features of man. Undoubtedly a masterpiece of Pre-Columbian sculpture and of world art, this piece shows to what extent artistic perfection had been achieved by the native population when the Spanish conquistadors arrived in the sixteenth century.   *f.s.o.*

41. TETEOINAN, GODDESS OF THE EARTH

Mexica culture. Tlalmanalco, State of Mexico. Late Post-Classic (A.D. 1300-1521). Stone. Height 107 cm, width 41 cm. Mexica Hall. MNA. Cat. no. 11-3701. Inv. no. 10-1077.

Tlalmanalco is a small settlement in the state of Mexico, sitting on one of the slopes of the volcano Popocatépetl, a region lying between the temperate lands of the central valleys and the hot region of the southern valleys.

Surviving sculpture indicates that there was a notable workshop of stone carvers or artists in this region, of which the Goddess of the Earth shown here is one of the clearest examples.

This is an image of a robust and demure adult woman, standing firmly upright; both arms hang at her sides, held in to the body. The woman is barefoot, but wears the traditional woman's clothing still worn today in some regions of Mexico. The medium-length skirt covering the lower part of the body is tied with a large belt or sash, which is knotted at the front and has ends hanging down in the form of tassels, opening in the middle to reveal a low-relief design on the skirt. This image, contained within a rectangular frame, reaches down to the hemline of the skirt, and shows a monkey that seems to be dancing, accompanied by three circles; a zoomorphic design that can be interpreted as the calendrical date "Three Monkeys".

The *quechqemetl* (*guechquemetl*) is the striking garment covering the torso and hanging down in a point in an inverted triangle at the front and back; this elegant garment has enormous tassels along its border as a graceful decoration, which in reality must have been made from cotton. The figure represents the goddess Teteoinan, patron of the earth: this iconographic identification is based partly on the calendrical element, which is the deity's name, but also on the headdress, the symbol of the goddess; it consists of a band of white cotton cords girdling the head, behind which can be seen the paper crest that distinguished the woman's nobility. The realism of the face was accentuated by the shell inlays that are still visible in the eyes.   *f.s.m.*

42. MASK, GODDESS OF WATER

Mexica culture. Mexico City. Late Post-Classic (A.D. 1300-1521). Stone. Height 37 cm, width 17.5 cm. Mexica Hall. MNA. Cat. no. 11-5220. Inv. no. 10-15717.

The Mexica inherited an extremely rich culture from the civilisations that preceded them; traditions ranging from those of the Olmecs to those of the Toltecs can be perceived in the use of ceremonial masks, which either had a funerary connotation or identified the gods. This example, sculpted out of very dense, black volcanic rock, to which its high quality is partly due, is associated with a specific cult, that of the goddess of water, whom the Mexicas called Chalchiuhtlicue, "she of the jade skirts". The sculpture takes the form of an elongated oval, the elongation being accentuated towards the top; one of the elements identifying this goddess is the elegant headdress formed by a band with four stripes and decorated borders at top and bottom, above which rises a crest of undulating feathers.

Physically the anatomical features of the goddess are almost perfect, but two shallow squares which have been scraped out on the cheeks contrast strongly in texture because of their rough surface. They were left like this by the sculptor so that he could fix the inlay or paint that was applied to the mask in the form of ritualistic make-up more firmly, just like the make-up worn by the goddess herself. At the rear of the piece is a fine inscription of the date, "Eight Mallinali", which is the calendrical name by which this deity was also known. At both sides of the face are the holes that were used to tie the mask to the image or sculpture of the water goddess.   *f.s.o.*

43. EHECATL, THE GOD OF WIND

Mexica culture. Provenance unknown. Late Post-Classic (A.D. 1300-1521). Stone. Height 60 cm, width 45 cm. Mexica Hall. MNA. Cat. no. 11-5197. Inv. no. 10-229760.

Using military power, the Mexicas took over much of ancient Mexico, imposing their language and their religion, and their artistic style; thus, monumental stone sculptures representing the traditional deities and religious cults of Tenochtitlán have been found in distant regions. Naturally, if ancient civilisations with their own forms of artistic expression existed in the conquered territories, a cultural fusion took place, resulting in hybrid works in which two stylistic currents are united.

Such is the case with this figure, which represents one of the most important gods worshipped by the Mexicas: Ehécatl-Quetzalcóatl, the deity that produced the wind in all its magnanimous and destructive power. Here, the god is represented as an obese figure, seated in a ritualistic pose very similar to the oriental "half lotus" position: he sits supported on his left leg, sharply bent at the knee and lying flat on the ground with the heel held against the sexual organs; the right leg is raised, bent at the knee and held against the front of the body; in each hand, the god grasps a serpent, whose bodies intertwine behind his back; in holding them his arms are bent at different levels, which produces an internal rhythm within the figure.

The head is remarkable in its unusual shape, with a bulbous deformity most apparent in the deity's elongated profile. The lower half of the face consists of a characteristic half-mask in the form of a bird's beak, which identifies the "maker of wind". The skull formation and the obesity, particularly accentuated in the stomach, imply that the figure was produced in a coastal region, probably one inhabited by the speakers of the Huastec language, such as Castillo de Teayo, Veracruz. This was a region which had been invaded and colonised by Mexica armies, where Huastec-Aztec figures are known to have been sculpted.   *f.s.o.*

44. EHECATL

Mexica culture. Calixtlahuaca, Mexico. Late Post-Classic (A.D. 1300-1521). Stone. Height 176 cm, width 56 cm, depth 50 cm. Museo de Antropología e Historia , State of Mexico. Cat. no. A-98011. Inv. no. 10-109262.

This example is undoubtedly one of the most extraordinary and best-proportioned sculptures of the Mexica period, discovered at the site of Calixtlahuaca. The Matlatzincas had lived in the valleys of Toluca since the earliest times, and their most important capital was Tecaxic. Principally known for its fishing activities, this civilisation also acted as the commercial link with the distant regions of Western Mexico; this was one of the reasons why it was conquered by Mexica armies. However, the conquest did not survive long, as the unruly Matlatzincas used every opportunity to rebel. The Tenochtitlán governors therefore decided to set up a military colony next to Tecaxic, and thus begins the history of the city of Calixtlahuaca .

This military colony was designed and constructed in the architectural style of the Mexica capital, and although it was largely destroyed during the Spanish conquest in the sixteenth century, some of the remaining buildings constitute the finest examples of architecture to survive from the Mexica era. The circular building dedicated to the god of wind at Calixtlahuaca drew the attention of archaeologists in the first decades of this century, and excavation work was carried out which established the different stages of construction of the characteristic architectural configuration, where a quadrangle lay in front of a platform which has a circular layout. It was during this excavation that this fine example of sculpture was discovered, representing the sturdy image of the god of wind Ehécatl-Quetzalcóatl, to whom the building was dedicated; the figure had been destroyed by the inhabitants themselves, because just as they sacrificed human victims in honour of the gods, so they also "killed" their effigies with blows. Only when the sculpture had been completely restored was this impressive figure truly appreciated. It is portrayed almost life-sized, with magnificent proportions, albeit in a hieratic pose, and could be described as the indigenous sculpture that most nearly approaches classical canons.

The artist's skill is clearly visible, capturing a sense of masculine force and solidity which is projected through the form; the hands and arms convey a certain tension in their readiness to hold something – probably banners, weapons or some other emblem. The naked body can be seen almost in its entirety: only the sexual organs are covered, by the *maxtlatl*, the loincloth that covered the sex organ and was tied at the waist; in this case, the two ends of the garment are tied in a knot hanging down at the front. The figure wears a spectacular mask in the form of a bird's beak (a reference to the deity already mentioned) which probably derives fom a duck's bill, and still retains some of its original red pigment.   *f.s.o.*

45. MONKEY

Mexica culture. Huastec Potosí. Late Post-Classic (A.D. 1300-1521). Stone. Height 33 cm, width 20 cm. In store. MNA. Cat. no. 11-3063. Inv. no. 10-220157.

According to indian beliefs, the principal animal representing Ehécatl-Quetzalcóatl, the patron god of wind, was the monkey, and the god was able to transform himself into this animal. The identification of this small mammal with the wind was probably due to the monkey being one of the most unpredictable animals in terms of character: while it can be extremely tame and amusing, it also becomes easily enraged and its aggression can turn into direct and violent attack. The same can be said of the wind, which on the one hand can be gentle and pleasant, but on the other, one of the most destructive elements of nature.

The Mexicas left behind several images of this animal, of which this is one of the most interesting; it is evident that the sculptor took advantage of an existing stone tablet, or thin plaque, on which to outline the monkey's profile, showing the body and its extremities in profile and depicting the head viewed from the front and from above. With regard to its original location, the figure may have been lying down, perhaps attached to the floor, so that the head and body formed a single horizontal line; equally, however, the animal may have been placed with the head facing upwards, thus imbued with an artistic and symbolic meaning of ancestral significance, linked with the traditions of the Olmecs, who considered monkeys to be observers of the stars and who depicted them holding their head in their hands, just as in this sculpture.

The wind, as an element of nature, is intimately connected with movement, and there is evident movement in three directions in this sculpture: the positions of the arms and legs suggest a helix formation, while the tail at the rear is coiled in the form of a spiral, and the head marks a line that divides the whole sculpture in two. The monkey wears bead bracelets as decorations on both arms, together with a pectoral in the form of a caracol section on its chest; this was the symbol of the god of wind, Ehécatl, the element of nature with whom the animal was directly associated.   *f.s.o.*

46. XIPE-TOTEC, GOD OF GOLDSMITHS

Mexica culture. Tepexi El Viejo, Puebla. Late Post-Classic (A.D. 1300-1521). Clay. Height 97 cm, width 35 cm, depth 24 cm. Museo Regional de Puebla. Inv. no. 10-203061.

Probably the most impressive festival celebrated by the ancient Mexicans during their eighteen-month year (each month twenty days long) was held during the second month, known as Tlacaxipehualiztli, "the flaying of men in honour of Xipe".
The festival involved the sacrifice of young warriors captured in battle, who had been kept prisoner specially for this occasion. Each of the victims was arrayed with white bird feathers covering his body and head, given a mock weapon, and tied by the waist to a circular stone called *temalacatl*, facing five elegantly dressed Mexica warriors, either eagle warriors or jaguar warriors. Naturally, the latter had real arms with obsidian blades. The confrontation between the captured warriors and the Mexicas, which took place in public, was planned by Tenochtitlán leaders to arouse pride in their nation's military might. Because the festival had the characteristics of a public fight, Spanish chronicles described it as "the gladiatory sacrifice", as it reminded them of the fights celebrated in the Coliseum of ancient Rome. The most impressive part of the festival was its finale, as the warrior prisoner was sacrificed through the extraction of his heart and the corpse was carefully flayed. A mask was made from the skin of the face, and a gory suit made from the skin of the victim's torso, arms and legs; these spoils were used to identify the deity and were worn by Xipe's priests or by others who had made a promise to the god to wear them. The figure shown here, made from fired clay, shows one of these individuals wearing Xipe's ritualistic attire. The face appears to show the stretched skin of the mask, and is painted yellow with a special facial make-up in the form of red vertical bands over the eyes and cheeks. The suit, or skin of the flayed warrior, can be seen in the textured surface that covers the trunk and part of the arms and legs and indicates that, in real life, those who wore the skin turned it inside out, with the fatty and bloody part on the outside. The individual wears elegant sandals, indicating that he belonged to the *pipiltin* social class, the equivalent of the European nobility: sandals were used exclusively by this group.

The figure displays the considerable mastery of the indigenous pre-Columbian craftsmen who executed such realistic clay sculptures. This magnificent piece was found during archaeological excavations at the site of Tepexi El Viejo, in the present-day state of Puebla, a region lying between the Mixtecs and those who spoke the Popoloca language. Defensive ramparts were found there, as was also one of the circular stones that played a part in the gladiatory sacrifice. This find, undoubtedly the first of its kind, has made it possible to relate the cult of Xipe to the *temalacatl* and to effigies representing the deity.   *f.s.o.*

47. CIHUATETEO, THE DEAD WOMAN

Mexica culture. Mexico City. Late Post-Classic (A.D. 1300-1521). Stone. Height 83 cm, diameter 56 cm. Mexica Hall. MNA. Cat. no. 11-3282. Inv. no. 10-1145.

As well as being companion and wife, the woman in Prehispanic Mexico, on whose maternal nature the continuity of mankind relied, was associated with all the fertility cults that had been developed by the peoples of ancient Mexico since its earliest history. During the Late Post-Classic, which extends from the twelfth to the sixteenth centuries, women who died in childbirth were deified in the belief that, just as the warrior offered his life on the battlefield, the woman who died at the moment of giving birth also symbolically gave her life to the gods while trying to bring a being into the world. These women-gods were given the name of Cihuateteo, which effectively had this meaning, and also Tzitzinime, which can be translated as "ghost" or "spectre", because according to tradition, on their death, these women became transformed into fantastical beings that were equivalent to living-death.

Several of these sculptural figures were discovered during the construction of a typical nineteenth-century building in the historical centre of Mexico City, where there had probably been a sanctuary dedicated to the Cihuateteos. All the figures follow a similar formal pattern: they are represented kneeling and resting their weight on their legs, with both arms raised and held up in front of them; instead of hands, they have enormous eagle claws or jaguar paws. Each wears a plain skirt, tied with a band knotted at the front, and her breasts are bare, alluding to her maternal character. The face is the most impressive part, being totally devoid of flesh, but the eyes protude in such a way that the suggestion of living-death acquires exceptional realism. Historical records note that these goddesses are known to have had different calendrical identities; in this case, the goddess is Cihuateteo, "One Monkey"; the inscription is on the upper part of the head, in the middle of the tangled hair that is characteristic of the dead.

f.s.o.

48. ARCHITECTURAL ELEMENT: SERPENT

Mexica culture. Mexico City. Late Post-Classic (A.D. 1300-1521). Stone. Height 54 cm, length 54 cm. Mexica Hall. MNA. Cat. no. 11-3481. Inv. no. 10-81558.

In the historic centre of Mexico City sits the Palace of Government, on the east side of the Plaza Mayor. At present, the visitor sees a building of elegant baroque European character, with a third floor that was added in the twentieth century. Beneath this construction, however, and acting as its foundations, are the remains of the former Palace of Moctezuma, which amazed the Spanish conquistadors with its vast number of rooms and patios. Unfortunately, this building was virtually destroyed during the military siege of the Mexica city, and was later built over by colonial buildings; available information about the palace is thus very limited. Several sculptures, such as this serpent's head, provide an impression of the magnificent nature of the palace decorations.

This sculptural piece probably formed part of an architectural unit, either the crest of an *alfarda* at the top or bottom of a stairway, or as part of the sculptural ornamentation of a wall. It consists of what archaeologists call an architectural stud, that is, a figurative element which has a peg to embed it into the wall; although the peg is broken, the animal's head is preserved in perfect condition. The design is based on a cube, each side presenting an independent design, so that the viewer would perceive a different image depending on whether the piece is seen in profile or from the front. From the side, we see the profile of a serpent opening its jawsd, with an enormous curved fang, a large eye, protuberances on the nose and elegant curving feathers at the rear of the head in the form of a mane of hair. From the front, four curved coiled bands are apparent, two above and two below, with four teeth in a row – more teeth than it has in reality, indicating that the sculptor wanted to emphasise the terrorising aspect of the serpent.

The sculpture retains some of the original polychromy that coloured the layer of stucco covering the entire head.

f.s.o.

49. MERLON IN THE FORM OF A CARACOL SECTION

Mexica culture. Historical Centre of Mexico City. Late Post-Classic (A.D.1300-1521). Clay. Height 190 cm, width 112 cm. Mexica Hall. MNA. Cat. no. 11-5346. Inv. no. 10-228054.

The architects of Pre-Columbian Mexico decorated the upper part of their temple roofs with ornaments in the form of crests or merlons, carved out of stone or made of baked clay. Archaeological evidence of this tradition dates back to at least A.D. 300, especially in the palaces and temples of the ancient city of Teotihuacán.

At the Templo Mayor in México-Tenochtitlán, the double pyramid that served as a platform for the sacred buildings of Huitzilopochtli (god of sun and war) and Tláloc (patron of rain) are known to have been differentiated and to have been identified from afar by their colour and their merlons; it is very probable that this merlon belonged to the temple of Tláloc, as drawings made of the temple during the centuries following the Conquest depict it with just such an element.

Its relief design is based on a circular motif, starting coiled in a spiral band at the centre which unfurls and extends upwards, to end in a hook-like tip. On each side of the spiral are three lobes. This was the typical native representation of the caracol, which in turn is the symbolic image of the wind, because the Mexicas used the marine caracol to blow into, producing sounds similar to those of a trumpet.

The piece is notable for its size; an enormous mould must have been used to produce it, and the ovens in which it was fired must also have been colossal.

The merlon was discovered in the 1940s, broken into numerous fragments, during excavations carried out at the rear of Mexico City Cathedral. It was then carefully reconstructed to give the public an idea of the artistic quality of the sacred buildings of the Mexica.

f.s.o.

35. SERPENT

36. EAGLE-WARRIOR HEAD

36. EAGLE-WARRIOR HEAD

37. CARACOL

116

38. TORSO

39. HUNCHBACK

39. HUNCHBACK

39. HUNCHBACK

40. SCULPTURE IN RITUALISTIC POSTURE

41. TETEOINAN, GODDESS OF THE EARTH

41. TETEOINAN, GODDESS OF THE EARTH

41. TETEOINAN, GODDESS OF THE EARTH

42. MASK, GODDESS OF WATER

43. EHECATL, THE GOD OF WIND

43. EHECATL, THE GOD OF WIND

44. EHECATL

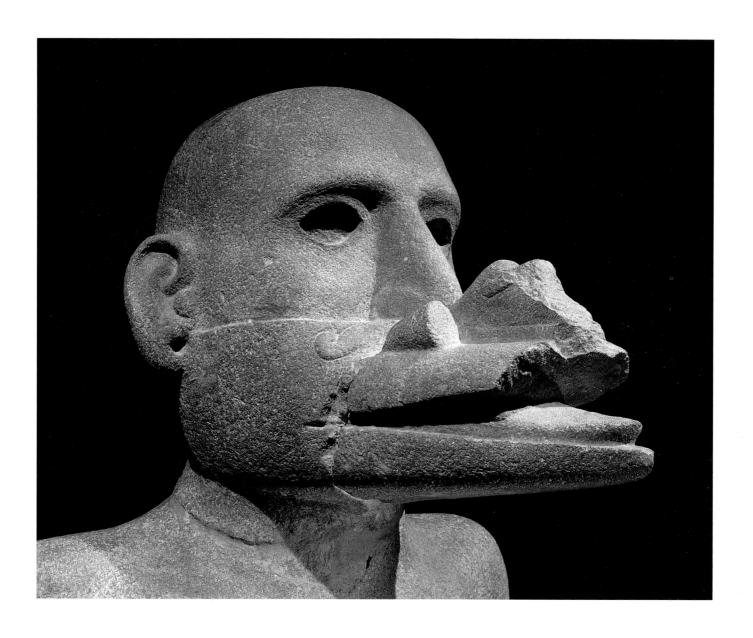

44. EHECATL

45. MONKEY

45. MONKEY

46. XIPE-TOTEC, GOD OF GOLDSMITHS

47. CIHUATETEO, THE DEAD WOMAN

48. ARCHITECTURAL ELEMENT: SERPENT

49. MERLON IN THE FORM OF A CARACOL SECTION

9. OAXACA: "LAND OF TOMBS, URNS AND GOLD"

Felipe Solís Olguín
Martha Carmona Macías

Oaxaca is a state of considerable geographical diversity. Its shores are washed by the Pacific Ocean, and it is a tropical region with a hot, dry climate, 17° north of the Equator. It is rich in tradition, and there are a great many ethnic groups: the sixteen linguistic groups still present today probably already coexisted there at the time of the Conquest.

The state can be divided into seven large regions: the central valleys, the Mixteca, the coast, the mountain range, the isthmus, the Cañada and the region of Tuxtepec or the Papaloapan.

Three of these regions – the valleys, the Mixteca Alta (High Mixteca) and the Cañada – have been widely studied; neighbouring each other, they are semi-arid, and correspond to what are known as the Oaxacan Highlands.

The valley of Oaxaca, formed by three sub-valleys, was the seat of the Zapotec civilisation; the Mixtecs, who dominated several vast regions, reached this area at a relatively late date. Among the best-known archaeological sites are Monte Albán, Mitla, Lambityeco, Zaachila, Yagul, Dainzú and San José Mogote. From these sites it is clear that this region, from its earliest history right up to the present, has been the home of the greatest socio-cultural developments; today, the capital is also located there.

The Mixtec region is the Mixteca Alta, formed by numerous small valleys in a mountainous area; Monte Negro, Huamelulpan, Yacuila and Yucundahui, are among the sites that have been explored.

The Cañada is the hottest and driest region, situated between the Oaxacan valley and the valley of Tehuacán in Puebla. Because of the local environment, settlements were concentrated near rivers at the bottom of the ravine and in the few places where there were springs. The region was inhabited by the Cuicatecos; several archaeological sites exist there, such as Rancho Dolores Ortíz and Llano Perdido.

The early presence of man in Oaxaca is dated around 9000 B.C., and is proved by the evidence of stone artefacts in San Juan Guelavía, in the valley of Tlacolula, some twenty kilometres to the south-east of the contemporary city of Oaxaca. These artefacts were used by hunting groups which hunted animals that are now extinct.

There were also several settlements of hunting-gathering groups in the area around Mitla and in the Mixteca Alta, dating from around 7000 B.C., when agriculture and plant cultivation began at the site of Guilá Naquitz. Changes began to appear all over Mesoamerica from this date – man, the appropriator of the environment, became the producer of food -and certain cultural changes evidently brought with them a sedentary way of life.

Between 1500 and 1400 B.C., permanent village settlements began to appear, forming small communities that produced ceramics and practised agriculture: this was the start of the period known as Pre-Classic or Formative.

The first villages appeared in the lower part of the Oaxaca valley, located to the north-west of the capital of the State, between the Atoyac River and its tributaries. This site attracted the first groups of farmers, who took advantage of the mountain foothills and of the alluvial plain, where it was possible to obtain water at a depth of no more than three metres, and to irrigate the cultivated fields using wells. At the same time, they settled on the lower mountain slopes, through which flowed permanent or semi-permanent streams which enabled them to channel water to the *milpas* or maize fields.

The initial phase of the Early Pre-Classic was called Tierras Largas (1500-1150 B.C.), and evidence of the first agricultural settlements in the valley of Etla date from this period. A series of dwellings were excavated at the site of Tierras Largas, comprising approximately

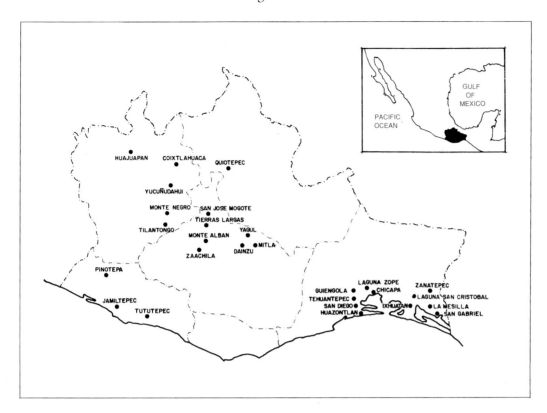

ten houses which were grouped next to the cultivated fields, forming a small village of approximately 60 inhabitants; the houses were rectangular in layout, and measured between 18 and 24 metres square. Evidence of domestic activity was found in some of these dwellings, such as objects and tools made out of stone, bone implements, and basketwork; holes were dug within the settlement's territory for the storage of grain. There is no evidence of differentiated social classes, nor of economic specialisation. Burials took place in an area outside the village.

The site of San José Mogote, located in the central valley, is typical of the next phase, known as San José (1150-900 B.C.) a time when village growth was to increase. Different types of residential patterns were discovered in this settlement, an area of mud huts with numerous grinding stones and crude ceramics that testify to the economic activities associated with an agricultural group. In another part of the same site, houses built of the same material were found, with very elaborate ceramics and countless fragments of magnetite, haematite, mica and green quartz, as well as marine shells from the Gulf of Mexico and perforators used to bore shell, proof of the existence of a group of craftsmen. A tiered rectangular platform, two metres high, was found in the same part of the settlement, constructed from blocks of stone and a very light, porous volcanic stone, both of which were used to form a *talud* at the front of the structure.

Village communities continued to develop during the Middle Pre-Classic, and greater social stratification is evident; thus during the Guadalupe phase (900-600 B.C.) the dominant class of the groups inhabiting the valley of Oaxaca established the trading of luxury objects with the Olmec groups of the Gulf Coast. Six villages dating from this phase have been located in the valley of Etla, but small communities evidently continued to develop in other parts of the valley as well, as the first occupation of Mitla dates from this phase.

At Barrios de Rosario Huitzo a series of platform-like structures were erected around patios, residential patterns that are indicative of a differentiation of status and of social organisation during the Late Pre-Classic period.

The first monuments bearing hieroglyphic inscriptions in the valley of Oaxaca appeared between the years 600 and 200 B.C.; a series of regional political groups already existed, possibly as rivals. At the end of this phase, most of these disintegrated and the population of the valley was united under a new type of political organisation, the city-state of Monte Albán, which became the Zapotec capital and dominated the valley from this time onwards.

The construction of this great civil and political centre began during the phase Monte Albán I (500 to 200 years B.C.), The site chosen was a high-altitude area formed by five interconnecting hills, rising on average 400 metres above the level of the valley. The community of Monte Albán was initially divided into three separate residential areas, and it has been suggested that the layout of both the main plaza and the rest of the city was the result of the possible union of two of the valley's previous rival political groups, forming a sort of Zapotec confederation. There is evidence of an increase in ceremonial and funerary activity by this time, as well as of a centralisation of power and greater social stratification. The population increased and expanded to over 40 localities, and agricultural activity was intensified through the construction of the first irrigation channels for cultivated fields. It seems that the defensive potential of the Monte Albán location was the determining factor in attracting the first settlers here, as the city itself was erected on the summit of an isolated hill in the valley, where there are no springs or water sources, where the hillside soil is inappropriate for agriculture, and where there are no natural resources. In other words, there is no possibility that this site might have been chosen in order to establish a large centre of trade and production. Evidently the choice of location was based on the impressive potential for the centralisation of power that was to make possible the existence of this great civil and political centre here in the valley, which perhaps relied on tributes for its existence.

The inhabitants of the site began the construction of the Main Plaza during this period, levelling the earth to allow for the siting of the different architectural units, which had both civil-religious and domestic functions.

One of the earliest public buildings at the site is the so-called Building L, in the south-west corner of the Main Plaza. This structure is also known as The Danzantes, as stone tablets carved with low-relief human figures were found on its walls; initially these figures were christened "*danzantes*" (dancers), "swimmers" or "deformed beings", as they are naked, adopt peculiar postures, and have closed or swollen eyes. The images are currently identified as sacrificed prisoners, as one of the conventional motifs found throughout Mesoamerican iconography in general is the representation of prisoners or captives naked and in positions of subjugation.

Two reliefs known as Stela 12 and Stela 13 are associated with Building L, and portray one of the most ancient hieroglyphic texts known in Monte Albán. Calendrical and non-calendrical glyphs are found in the inscriptions, signs of an original system of Zapotec writing. The majority of the hieroglyphs at Monte Albán were developed between the years 500 B.C. and A.D. 700, and provide complementary information about the rise and fall of the Zapotec state.

Eleven calendrical glyphs are known from phase I of Monte Albán, probably related to the calendrical ritual of 260 days called *piye*, which was divided into four units of 65 days called *pitáo,* meaning "lightning flashes" or "great spirits". Each period of 65 days was in turn divided into five periods (*cocii*) of 13 days (*chij*).

During phase II of Monte Albán (200 B.C.-A.D. 100), the Zapotec state extended its political, economic and military influence, not only in the valley of Oaxaca, but also spreading to previously autonomous territories. The layout of the Main Plaza was finalised during this period, as was its levelling. The architectural element most characteristic of Monte Albán continued to be the pyramidal base with constructions on the upper part, generally consisting of two rooms, some of which were destined to be the residences of those of a high social standing, while others were dedicated to temples and administrative buildings. The system of construction, in the case of the *taluds*, consisted of staggered stone tablets covered in plaster; rooms were built out of adobe, with stone floors. Notable among the public buildings erected on the Main Plaza is Structure J, in the form of an arrowhead. It has been suggested that this building might have been an astronomical observatory due to its peculiar form and alignment; however, this continues to be only an attractive theory.

The Zapotec nobility maintained the cultural traditions of the preceding period; the development of religious ideas and the cult of ancestors meant that the tombs built were larger, and as well as the flat-roofed tombs of the previous epoch, roofs were made of stone tablets that formed a sort of rudimentary vault. Some tombs have small antechambers and wall niches, and are decorated with mural paintings of which unfortunately only a few traces remain.

The site grew enormously in the periods following Monte Albán II, becoming an urban complex over six kilometres square. Constructions occupied all the adjacent hills, principally El Gallo, Atzompa and Monte Albán Chico; thus, the Main Plaza became the administrative and religious centre of the whole urban site, and one of the great Mesoamerican capitals. During the phase Monte Albán III (A.D. 100-600), the cultural tradition was to crystallise in what has been defined as the Classic Zapotec epoch. This phase did not suddenly happen, however, but was preceded by a transitional phase called Monte Albán II-III, in which Monte Albán II elements persisted alongside new cultural elements from the metropolis of Teotihuacán, located five hundred kilometres to the north, in the Valley of Mexico.

During phase III of Monte Albán, the population grew to approximately 30,000. The five centuries of this stage are divided into two archaeological sub-phases, IIIA and IIIB. The settlement reached its greatest territorial expansion during the second sub-phase, but then decreased, possibly due to the fact that it was competing in economic terms with Teotihuacán, which by this time occupied an area of twenty-five square kilometres with a population of approximately 100,000.

It was principally during this phase that an artistic style known to many authors as Zapotec developed in Monte Albán, a style which reflects the increasing power of the new Oaxacan metropolis; as the city's power became increasingly centralised, so its size and monumentality increased. Its architecture in particular emphasises this fact, and its importance is most clearly illustrated by the so-called "scapular" panel.

Relations between Teotihuacán and Monte Albán are believed to have been peaceful, and it is possible that commercial incentives spurred on the visit of Teotihuacán dignitaries to the "Hill of the Jaguar".

The sub-phase Monte Albán IIIB (A.D. 650-900) represents the climax of the Classic Zapotec civilisation, which developed a flourishing and distinctive artistic style that achieved its maximum expression at this time; the so-called "funerary urns" that are characteristic of this civilisation are particularly noteworthy.

The planning and building of the Zapotec capital reveals the nation's remarkable zeal for construction. During the Classic period, the Zapotecs created one of the most extraordinary architectural units of Mesoamerica, featuring a large plaza consisting of temples, palaces, ball courts, minor plazas, sunken patios and platforms, all harmoniously amalgamated to create an extraordinary architectural-sculptural whole.

There was a noticeable increase in funerary ritual from sub-phase IIIA onwards. The development of the system of tomb construction is symptomatic of this change, in that tombs became veritable architectural structures, some with a cruciform layout and wall niches.

Various tombs contain elaborate mural paintings, especially tombs 103 and 104, which date from the transition Monte Albán IIIA – IIIB, and in which representations of deities or priests can be seen on the walls, as well as symbolic elements and glyphs painted in beautiful colours. The murals from phase IIIA are similar to the frescoes of the Teotihuacán palaces, although their style is clearly Zapotec.

The phase Monte Albán IV (A.D. 700) signified the collapse of the great Zapotec city, and its gradual abandonment. Most of the civil-religious centre was probably in ruins by the year A.D. 900, as only a certain number of burials within the destroyed buildings date from this period. Today, the cause of this decline is still unknown; several hypotheses, however, have been put forward. One theory is based on the rapid increase in population during phase Monte Albán IIIB, and demographic distribution through areas of low agricultural yield, which must have provoked a series of conflicts and disputes concerning ownership of land, either among small domestic units or larger territorial units. This could

140

well have caused the socio-political disintegration of Monte Albán as the ruling centre of the central valleys of Oaxaca. During this period, Monte Albán's urban population was gradually integrated with other centres in the area, such as Zaachila, Lambityeco, Cuilapan and Mitla. These had existed as rivals since the foundation of Monte Albán, but only at this point did they reach their full development and expansion.

Well into the Post-Classic period, towards the year A.D. 1350, the last phase of occupation began, called Monte Albán V, which has been identified with the arrival of groups from the Mixteca; however, the metropolis remained uninhabited. Phase V has been established by the presence of Mixtec burials at Monte Albán, as the Mixtecs re-used the Zapotec tombs to bury their chiefs. Possibly one of the most extraordinary finds in twentieth-century Mesoamerican archaeology is the famous tomb 7 of Monte Albán, typically Zapotec in its architecture, inside which a series of outstanding gold, jade, turquoise, rock crystal, onyx, shell, coral and pearl objects were deposited, representing the funerary dowry of a Mixtec prince. During this era, only one section of the North Platform of Monte Albán was reinhabited by the Mixtec invaders, while the rest of the city remained in ruins.

The fall of Monte Albán created instability and a vacuum in the socio-political control of the valley of Oaxaca; the Zapotec groups withdrew into small principalities or *cacicazgos* (groups led by a chieftain), whose over-riding priority was to repel foreign invaders, principally the Mixtecs and the Aztecs, who gradually occupied areas of the central valleys. The separation of Mitla and Zacchila, the former into the principal religious centre and the latter into a political centre, is a clear example of the fragmentation of the great Zapotec culture.

With regard to the other important cultural group – the Mixtecs – several legends exist, according to which they were guided by their titular gods to the mountainous region of Oaxaca, entering it through Coixtlahuaca, then passing through Apoala and finally establishing themselves at Achiutla and Tilantongo. Here the earliest dynasties mentioned in historical records emerged, described as "Mixtec reigns". From the eleventh century, Tilantongo became the region's most important centre, and, together with the other sites mentioned, forced the neighbouring towns into submission, establishing its first *cacicazgos*.

The socio-political organisation of the Mixtecs was recorded in their codices, in which a series of dynasties of the lords who governed the "Mixtec reigns" were registered. Like other Mesoamerican groups, this nation traced its royalty back to a divine origin; Quetzalcóatl, Xolotl and Tonatiuh were its ancestral gods, and Eight-Deer-Tiger's Claw is mentioned as one of the most important lords.

In spite of the evidence provided by the central valleys, the Mixteca archaeological sequence is incomplete, as research has taken place principally in the Mixteca Alta, so that the cultural evolution is interrupted between one phase and the next. Today, it is still not known whether the Mixtec culture stems directly from several components of the Classic period, of which evidence has been found in the Mixteca Alta, or whether it owes its origins to elements and traditions from other cultural areas. However, in either case, it is obvious that this civilisation reached its heyday during the sixteenth century, in the Post-Classic epoch, and continued to flourish until the Spanish conquest.

The Post-Classic period was characterised by militarism, and the Mixtecs were no exception, being absolutely typical of the warrior groups of this period. Around the fourteenth century, the Mixtecs conquered the city of Zaachila and extended their domination over the valley of Oaxaca, principally towards the western region, where the political capital was Cuilapan.

The Mixtecs were only unified in ethnic and cultural terms, and, in contrast to the Zapotecs, were not organised as a great political state entity, but instead formed small political groupings that were generally independent, governed fundamentally by militarism. It is not known whether there were professional soldiers, but recruitment took place throughout each city, as all citizens were obliged to participate in combat. The captains and leaders may have belonged to a higher social class, and in turn acted as priests, from which it may be assumed that the Mixtecs were ruled by a military theocracy.

This group's mastery of the handling of precious metals was exceptional; fantastic works of art were created out of gold, silver and copper. Similarly, they produced magnificent examples of ceramic work, which shared the tradition of the Cholula area, famous for its polychromy, giving form to images of deities, glyphs and geometric and fantastic motifs.

Mitla stands out during this period for the importance and richness of its architecture; various groups of buildings exist, of which the best preserved is the so-called "group of the columns". Mitla's distinctive feature was its ornamentation, in which thousands of small fragments of stone figures were assembled to form different mosaic panels whose predominant decorative motif was the stepped fret, placed in distinct alignments and positions; through this ornamentation, walls acquired an extraordinary sense of movement and an effect of light and shade that had never before been achieved in the Oaxaca region. The use of this design spread throughout distinct regions of Mesoamerica, principally in the area to the north of Yucatán. During the phase of Mixtec domination, very colourful polychromatic ceramics were also produced, related to those manufactured in Cholula. The most important form of artistic expression during the Mixtec era, however, was metallurgy. The principal metals used were gold, copper and silver, and beating and melting of the metals were employed to produce extraordinarily beautiful necklaces, rings, pectorals and diadems, of which the most impressive example consists of the fabulous funerary jaguar found by Alfonso Caso in Tomb 7 at Monte Albán.

One other aspect of the Mixtec nation affirms their genius: their books and codices, documents folded like a screen, whose smooth sheets of deerskin were covered with a thin layer of stucco and then painted in detail with Mixtec history and mythology.

The first Mexica invaders of Oaxacan territory were led by Moctezuma Ilhuicamina towards A.D. 1456; Coixtlahuaca was captured, and several colonies and settlements were established in the area, one of which was Huaxyacac, which has developed into the present-day Oaxaca.

Later, the Mexicas penetrated further into the region, conquering Mazateca and Chinanteca territory, where they took over the prosperous city of Usila.

Under the leadership of the new Mexica *tlatoani* Axayácatl, the Mexicas successfully got as far as Tehuantepec, and seized control of the lands of the Huaves, destroying Teotitlán del Camino, which had rebelled against them. Similarly, Yanhuitlán was re-conquered by Tizoc.

During the reigns of the last governors of Tenochtitlán, Ahuízotl and Moctezuma Xocoyotzin, Oaxacan territory was the scene of bloody battles. From the mid-fifteenth century until the arrival of the Spaniards, there was continual fighting between the Mixtecs and the Mexicas, a fact which made conquest easier for the new invaders.

10. THE DIVERSITY OF OAXACA'S CLAY PRODUCTION

Sonia Lombardo de Ruíz

The civilisations of the valley of Oaxaca, in their Pre-Classic and Classic phases, are represented in this exhibition by pieces created by Zapotec groups. They were fundamentally agricultural peoples, and they settled in lands with rich alluvial soils, so clay was one of the principal media for sculpture.

Fertility and abundance are ideally expressed through fullness of form, and this is perfectly evident, for instance, in the tripod dish with mammiform supports illustrated in plate 50.

Three forms like swollen breasts, smooth and sensually rounded, are symmetrically placed as supports for the dish which, crown-like, completes this work. The projecting border, curved slightly downwards, sends the dynamics of the form back to the earth in a natural manner, simultaneously framing the ample vessel. This simple work captures the sentiment of the Pre-Classic village cultures dedicated to agriculture, whose principal concerns were subsistence and reproduction, and breasts are the symbol that most harmonises with nature.

By contrast, the cylindrical tube from Atzompa (plate 51) testifies to the process followed by the Zapotecs in the Classic period in establishing a system of symbols of religious character, as well as in the development of writing and numeration as forms of expression. The conception of this object is diametrically opposed to that of the previous one. Sensuality is absent here and, by contrast, intellect prevails. It is a closed geometric form, in which expression is given by the aggressively ridged texture, produced by low relief, where a series of abstract symbolic forms are incised, among which several numbers can be recognised, ordered within a symmetrical composition.

During the Classic period, in parallel with the development of religion and the corresponding array of gods, a priestly system was set up, the members of which established themselves as the ruling caste. The representatives of the different gods commissioned models of themselves in ceramic objects, especially sculptures (plate 53) and funerary urns destined to be placed in the tombs of worthy individuals (plates 52 and 54).

The different styles of these objects can be attributed to groups of craftsmen from diferent sites, or to the iconographies of the diverse gods. However, there are certain elements that do not change, such as the naturalistic expression of the face, the use of right-angles in the composition and the horizontality accentuated in the headdress. The proportions of the body tend to be almost square; hence their strong sense of solidity and stillness.

The extraordinary sculpture in plate 54, which represents the seated god Xipe, grasps a baton in one hand while the other holds the head of the sacrificed victim whose skin he was to wear. The part corresponding to the body is inscribed within a square; the face or mask sits centred on the top of this square and appears as the principal element, both in terms of its position and because of its size, which is relatively large, and it is further emphasised by being surrounded by the enormous headdress which frames it like a halo.

Lesser elements with smooth surfaces (legs and mask), hollow forms (the bells on the skirt), appliquéd circular forms (the beads on the pectoral) and small flat and elongated surfaces (in the headdress) function as counterpoints in this baroque work, which was originally polychromatic. A wide range of textures and vibrant chiaroscuro is thus formed, so that the piece becomes dynamic and graceful; however, its expressive impact relies on the contrast between the internal energy and the external stillness of the form and, even more, on the crudity of the ritual, which is represented – to our eyes – with a lively ingenuity, and which was the product of a deep religious conviction.

During the Post-Classic period that folowed, the Mixtecs were known for promoting cultural development in the territory of Oaxaca. They were natives of the harsher regions of the sierra, and organised themselves in small political groupings which, through numerous matrimionial alliances, managed to constitute a regional state, invading Zapotec land, conquering their ceremonial centres and even re-using their tombs for the burial of their dignitaries.

Mixtec craft production was distinguished by its fine quality; the Mixtecs were skilled in jewellery production, using several metals and stones. Their ceramics, which were equally sophisticated, were widely distributed as commercial objects, and in some cases their designs influenced other civilisations, such as that of the Caribbean coast of the Yucatán peninsula. There is evidence that in México-Tenochtitlán they were used for ritualistic purposes because of their beauty and high-quality finish.

The polychromatic ceramics in Mixtec style are notable for their decoration, and are among the finest and most elaborately decorated ceramics in the whole of Mesoamerica.

The stepped fret was a highly typical decorative motif among both Zapotec and Mixtec cultures; it was used in stone mosaics in their architecture, in their painting and in their ceramics. The Mixtec tripod cup in plate 57 is a fine example, where frets follow a geometric formation originating from a straight horizontal line, and are decorated with yellow and white beads on a red background; the border and base have bands filled with the same beads alternating with larger ones.

An interesting element of this style is the concept of space, in which no blank is left undecorated. The interstices left between the stepped fret and the matching complementary inverted fret are also occupied by different motifs, such as interlaced volutes, circles or smaller frets, and different types of human heads or masks with a variety of zoomorphic headdresses.

The decoration is entirely symbolic, and the constantly repeated motifs, although as yet undeciphered, seem to register a certain type of prayer or litany, an adjunct to the ritual to which the vessel was dedicated.

Other elegant forms (plate 56) were produced as variants of the same style in several regions of Oaxaca, all featuring the same intensive decoration because of the Mixtec "horror of emptiness".

Also of Mixtec manufacture is the expressive vessel from Zaachila with the figure of Coqui Bexelao, the god of the underworld and of death (plate 58), who is represented by a skeleton clutching a type of fan in the form of a heart or flint knives with handles. In both cases, the god's association with human sacrifice is evident; Mixtec codices inform us that these sacrifices were probably dedicated to the sun.

Stone carving was another craft in which the Mixtecs developed great skill. In contrast to the capricious forms they produced in clay, the inherent resistence of stone preconditioned a more sober style, in which expression is created by the simplicity and beauty of the proportions, as can be seen in the tetrapod vessel in plate 59.

Seen as a whole, the collection from the area of Oaxaca shown here displays the variety of style and expression produced in different periods and in the various regions.

50. MAMMIFORM TRIPOD DISH

Zapotec culture. Monte Albán. Oaxaca. Late Pre-Classic (800 B.C.-A.D. 250). Clay. Height 26 cm, diameter 27 cm. Oaxaca Hall. MNA. Cat. no. 6-39. Inv. no. 10-61322.

This type of vessel is characteristic of the Late Pre-Classic (400-200 B.C.) period known as Monte Albán I. The principal ceremonial area of the site, known as the Main Plaza, was established during this period. Among the more important discoveries were not only the Danzantes structure with its low-relief sculpted panels, but also the entombments containing ceramic offerings that included vessels like this dish modelled in clay, which was located in the patio of Building B and formed part of a rich funerary offering. Most remarkable about this vessel are the three beautiful extended "mammiform" supports which are delicately modelled in clay; the outside surface of each one has been decorated with incised geometric motifs.

These types of vessels were very common during this period; in later years they were decorated with paint on top of a thin layer of stucco.   *m.c.m.*

51. CYLINDER WITH HIEROGLYPHS

Zapotec culture. Atzompa. Oaxaca. Classic (A.D. 200-900). Clay. Height 53 cm, diameter 23.2 cm. Oaxaca Hall. MNA. Cat. no. 6-2123. Inv. no. 10-13608.

Modelled in clay, this cylinder has incised hieroglyphs all over the outer surface. This piece was found during excavations at the archaeological site of Atzompa and corresponds to the Zapotec culture of the Classic period (A.D. 200-900).

Atzompa was a settlement dating from the end of the Classic period, near the great Zapotec capital of Monte Albán; it was a residential complex linked to the capital as a civil-administrative-religious centre inhabited by a prestigious and powerful population.

The use of hieroglyphs dates from Oaxaca's earliest history, becoming apparent around 600 B.C. During Monte Albán I (400 B.C.-A.D. 100), stelae were erected with calendrical glyphs or dates that conform to a particular structure; most of the signs have calendrical associations.   *m.c.m.*

52. ANTHROPOMORPHIC URN

Zapotec culture. Monte Albán, Oaxaca. Classic (A.D. 200-900). Clay. Height 81.5 cm, width 66 cm. Oaxaca Hall. MNA. Cat. no. 6-5801. Inv. no. 10-61343.

This is probably one of the most beautiful of the many varied objects found by archaeologists at Monte Albán. It is a ceremonial urn, made especially by Zapotec potters as a recipient for placing an offering in the royal tombs of the ancient Oaxacan metropolis. As Tomb 77 was excavated, archaeologists were surprised to catch a glimpse of this individual's features among the rubble and earth. The figure is probably the priest of the cult of the God Cosijo, who appears in the central motif of the piece.

The artist clearly gave free reign to his imagination, initially employing a cylinder of grey clay, to which he added, one by one, the elements that constitute the urn. At the centre, he placed the face of an adult whose physical features were represented with great naturalism. The cranial deformation is an additional element that enables the clear line of the forehead to stand out, and the priest wears a sort of chest protector in the shape of a semi-circle that frames him. In the upper part of the urn, in the form of a headdress or emblem, is the stylised head of an animal, whose protuberant nose is believed to be the symbolic element of the God Cosijo, the Zapotecs' patron of rain; it could also be interpreted as a bat.   *m.c.m.*

53. FIGURE

Zapotec culture. Monte Albán, Oaxaca. Classic (A.D. 200-900). Clay. Height 34 cm, width 27.7 cm. Oaxaca Hall. MNA. Cat. no. 6-55. Inv. no. 10-6195.

Urns are frequently called "funerary urns" as they generally play a part in offerings in tombs and burials; they are characteristic of the Zapotec civilisation.

These urns are definitely sculptures in clay; their basic form was established during Monte Albán I (400-200 B.C.), and consists of a cylindrical vessel with a figure on the front, and with the vessel itself usually being open at the top. The size of these urns varies, and they continued to be manufactured until Monte Albán IV (A.D. 900-1350). During Monte Albán III (A.D. 200-900), symbolic elements in the headdresses were accentuated and they became the central and dominating aspects of the design, while the size of the human figures represented was correspondingly reduced. Moulds were introduced to form the basic elements of the urns, which were generally painted in a variety of colours such as red, white, black, yellow and green. The characteristic posture of the human representations is that of a seated figure with crossed legs and hands resting on the knees.

Deities have been positively identified on these urns, and priests or important men or women who, for some reason, merited being portrayed on an urn, could also be represented, with different degrees of splendour. In addition, zoomorphic representations were produced for the same purpose.

In this light brown clay urn in the form of a female figure, the depiction of the typical *huipil* and *quesquemitl* (*guechquemetl*) can be seen; the figure is represented upright, wearing the typical headdress of Yalalteca, a necklace of alternating round and elongated beads, simple circular earflares and *huaraches*, or sandals, that are knotted at the front. The garments display the same degree of detail as can be admired even today in similar clothing from this region.   *m.c.m.*

54. URN REPRESENTING THE GOD XIPE

Zapotec culture. Monte Albán, Oaxaca. Classic (A.D. 200-900). Clay. Height 50.8 cm, width 44.8 cm, depth 34.9 cm. Oaxaca Hall. MNA. Cat. no. 6-6439. Inv. no. 10-3284.

The great Zapotec capital which became known as Monte Albán after the Spanish Conquest was undoubtedly the principal residential, political, economic and religious centre of the central Oaxacan valleys. Its history began long before the Christian era, and thanks to the efforts of numerous generations of masons, sculptors, ceramicists, peasants and others, it had become, by the sixteenth century A.D., one of the most beautiful metropolitan centres of Mesoamerica.

Virtually the entire archaeological history of the site is known due to excavations directed for many years by Don Alfonso Caso with considerable skill; his team explored and restored most of the architectural monuments that can be seen today, and carefully excavated, one by one, over one hundred tombs located at Monte Albán. This magnificent urn comes from Tomb 103, and portrays one of the Mesoamerican deities associated with a ritual in which the victim was sacrificed and flayed. This was the deity known as Xipe Totec, who was principally the patron of goldwork, but was also associated with the process of natural renewal that occurs year after year with the arrival of spring.

The figure represented here is probably not the god himself but the priest, who played a colourful part in the ritual; his attire is most striking, dominated by a beautiful headdress of large feathers and a necklace with a pectoral consisting of a rectangular element and a disc. He also wears a short skirt with enormous bells that were intended to accompany his dance rhythms. In his right hand is a sceptre, and in his left, the head of the decapitated victim, held by its hair and displayed by the priest as an impressive trophy, the result of the ritual.

The identification of the deity and his cult was made possible by the central figure's mask, which is known to have been made with the flayed skin of the sacrificed victim's face, and symbolises the renewal of the surface of the earth.   *m.c.m.*

55. JAGUAR VESSEL

Zapotec culture. Atzompa, Oaxaca. Classic (A.D. 200-900). Clay. Height 30.5 cm, length 36.5 cm, width 30.9 cm. Oaxaca Hall. MNA. Cat. no. 6-4853. Inv. no. 10-61341.

This extraordinary vessel, modelled in clay, was discovered in Tomb I during archaeological excavations carried out at the site of Atzompa in one of the central Oaxacan valleys. It represents an endearing feline animal, undoubtedly a representation of a jaguar. The animal stands on all four legs, with its head turned to one side; the eyes and mouth have been bored, as a precaution against damage during the firing process. As a distinguishing feature, the feline wears a necklace, an intertwined cord from which hangs an elongated object, probably a pectoral or bell. This wild animal was deified by nearly all the indigenous civilisations of ancient Mexico, but for the Zapotecs of Oaxaca in particular it represented the symbol of power; the original Prehispanic name of the ancient city of Monte Albán appears to have been "Hill of the Tiger or Jaguar".   *m.c.m.*

56. CUP

Mixtec-Puebla culture. Chinantla region. Oaxaca. Late Post-Classic (A.D. 1300-1521). Clay. Height 18 cm, diameter 17 cm. Museo de Antropología e Historia del Estado de México. Inv. no. A-36393.

Mixtec potters, who inherited the tradition of polychromatic ceramics, doubtless acquired this art form from the inhabitants of the Puebla-Tlaxcala valleys and, more specifically, from the ancient city of Cholula and the region it dominated.

Here we see an elegant example of a cup. The vessel, whose profile combines curved lines with straight, is set on an annular base in the form of a truncated cone. Mixtec artists had a clay of excellent quality close at hand which they decanted until a homogenous substance was obtained. With this they manufactured very thin-walled vessels of mimimum weight; in spite of the thinness of the walls, the material was surprisingly resistant once fired.

The most remarkable feature of this cup is its tri-partite decoration, . The motif on the upper and lower parts of the vessel is repeated, consisting of a stepped fret known as *xicalcoliuhqui* in Nahuatl, which represents the movement of serpents in a schematic and stylised way, and in essence also represented the deified serpent Quetzalcóatl. The design on the central part of the vessel consists of three highly stylised eagle heads; the bird has been schematised to a minimum: the head is shown in profile, and the feathers and huge beak are also recognisable. The contrast of red lines on a cream background is the strongest feature of this vessel, and is enhanced by the polished finish of the layer covering the surface, which is known as *engobe*.

The exact provenance of this object is unknown, but there can be no doubt that a cup of such elegance and quality could only have been produced for use in the ceremonies of the Mixtec nobility, and that it was eventually placed as an offering or treasure in the tomb of one of its owners.   *f.s.o.*

57. TRIPOD VESSEL

Mixtec culture. Zaachila, Oaxaca. Late Post-Classic (A.D. 1300-1521). Clay. Height 18 cm, diameter 17 cm. Oaxaca Hall. MNA. Cat. no. 7-2667. Inv. no. 10-79143.

The Mixtecs stand out among the various indigenous groups that developed important cultures in the Oaxacan region. Several of the rulers who governed the region's main sites were to make numerous attempts to form a Mixtec state, in particular a brave warrior known by his calendrical name, Eight-Deer-Tiger's Claw. In spite of the fact that such a state never actually existed, in cultural terms the Mixtecs excelled themselves in the creation of beautiful objects, making it feasible to speak of a characteristic Mixtec style.

Polychromatic ceramics are one of the distinctive elements of this style, and the piece shown here is among the finest examples owned by the Museo Nacional de Antropología in Mexico. A tripod vessel with a composite silhouette, its supports are in the shape of serpents' heads with open jaws and menacing fangs; the polychromatic decoration consists principally of the indigenous *xicalcoliuhqui* (stepped fret) design; the interior is filled with small circles, and in the gaps between the frets richly-attired human heads are depicted in profile, together with other stylised zoomorphic motifs.   *f.s.o.*

58. VESSEL WITH THE REPRESENTATION OF COQUI BEXELAO, GOD OF DEATH

Mixtec culture, Zaachila, Oaxaca. Late Post-Classic (A.D. 1300-1521). Clay. Height 32.5 cm, diameter 17 cm. Oaxaca Hall. MNA. Cat. no. 7-2345. Inv. no. 10-78270.

Zaachila was an important city to the south of the present-day city of Oaxaca, and its name signifies "Place of the Government". Reliefs with representations of death and animals intimately associated with it, such as the owl, have been found inside one of its tombs.

The Mixtecs in particular left splendid examples of the cult of death. Among the objects excavated from Tomb 7 at Monte Albán is a gold pectoral depicting a figure wearing a mask that is devoid of flesh. Similarly, the tombs explored in Zaachila brought to light magnificent materials, among which this fine tripod vessel modelled in a reddish-brown clay stands out; attached to it is the realistic figure of a skeleton, which represents the god Coqui Bexelaxo, Lord of the Underworld. Known as Mictlantecutli by Nahuatl groups, he was the patron deity to whom the city of Mitla was dedicated. The Zapotec name for the city was Yoopaa: in both languages, the meaning is "City of the Dead" or "place of death" and, in both the Classical and the Post-Classic periods, it was the home of high priests and the cemetery of the rulers.

On the vessel that comes from this site, a thin layer of stucco can be seen, which still preserves some red colouring; red also appears on the inside, close to the border, and is reminiscent of blood, thereby signifying life. In this way, within the effigy-vessel a duality is created, commonly represented in Prehispanic Mexico in masks, ceramics, codices and legends, and which constantly refers to the profound philosophy of life and death among the ancient Mesoamericans.

The skeleton attached to the body of the tripod vase has a free-standing skull. The bones of the arms and legs are hollow, while the hands and feet appear to belong to a living person. In the right hand the skeleton holds an elongated object, which some researchers have identified as a baton of authority, raised to the level of the skull; the left arm hangs down, and in the hand, which rests on one leg, is a knife used in sacrifice. Except for the half-bent legs, the skeleton is attached to the vessel.

The deity of death appears in Mixtec codices associated with sacrifices, armed with flint axes or knives, devouring victims or hearts, seated in temples or on thrones with mortuary glyphs. Associated with the colour red, which represents life, its cardinal point is the East, the place of the birth and resurrection of the sun; it is represented devoid of flesh with four red points. One day of the year has the same name, and the Mixtecs also called the sun Yca Caa Maha, Lord One Death.   *f.s.o.*

59. TETRAPOD VESSEL

Zapotec culture. Oaxaca Valleys. Late Post-Classic (A.D. 1300-1521). Stone. Height 18.3 cm, diameter 22.5 cm. Oaxaca Hall. MNA. Cat. no. 6-4856. Inv. no. 10-61344.

Work in stone was common from the time of the Prehispanic hunters, who used the different types of stone found locally as primary material; the first weapons and tools to be used by man were made of obsidian, flint, rock crystal, basalt and other kinds of rock.

Stone was also used from early times to manufacture vessels, the most ancient ones in Mesoamerica dating from 2300 B.C., preceding forms modelled out of clay.

Different kinds of stone were to continue in use to an extent, especially for the manufacture of weapons and tools. However, the Monte Albán III phase (A.D. 200-900) witnessed a rise in the popularity of stone as a material. Animals and anthropomorphic figures were represented, crudely carved out of greenstone, and earflares and necklaces were also produced. Some of these ornaments formed part of luxurious funerary offerings. This was the period of Teotihuacán influence, which had decreased by the time of the sub-phase Monte Albán IIIB.

During the period Monte Albán IIIB and IV (A.D. 750-1350), vessels with jaguar paws for supports were produced in the valleys of Oaxaca. These pieces are generally polychromatic and are exceptionally beautiful.

This vessel constitutes a fine example of stone carving, made out of a single block and coloured red. The vessel was polished twice, once when the carving was completed and again when the pigment was applied, thus giving the impression of a delicate tetrapod vessel modelled out of black clay.

The basalt block out of which this dish with its slender legs was created was sculpted using beating, eroding and polishing techniques; the toes of an animal were incised with vertical lines, and may represent the extremities of a jaguar, as the supernumerary toe that the animal usually develops at the rear of the leg can be seen. The piece reveals strong Mixtec influence.   *f.s.o.*

50. MAMMIFORM TRIPOD DISH

51. CYLINDER WITH HIEROGLYPHS

150

52. ANTHROPOMORPHIC URN

52. ANTHROPOMORPHIC URN

152

52. ANTHROPOMORPHIC URN

53. FIGURE

154

53. FIGURE

54. URN REPRESENTING THE GOD XIPE

55. JAGUAR VESSEL

56. CUP

57. TRIPOD VESSEL

58. VESSEL WITH THE REPRESENTATION OF COQUI BEXELAO, GOD OF DEATH

59. TETRAPOD VESSEL

11. THE GULF COAST, SITE OF BIRTH AND REGENERATION

Marcia Castro Leal

Three civilisations existed in the Gulf Coast area: in the north there was the Olmec civilisation, then came the Centre of Veracruz, and in the south were the Huastecs. The developments of the latter two occurred over a very long period, extending from long before Christianity to the arrival of the Spaniards in the sixteenth century. However, whereas the development of the first civilisation occurred mainly before the birth of Christ, the peak of each of the three cultures occurred at different times. The Olmecs reached their zenith during the Pre-Classic period (1200-100 B.C.), the Centre of Veracruz during the Classic period (A.D. 200-900), and the Huastecs during the Post-Classic period (900-1521).

In spite of pronounced differences, these Gulf Coast civilisations had many elements in common, enabling them to be thought of as a single entity. The first of these common elements was a shared geographical environment; the second was the way in which various people adapted themselves to this environment.

The narrow plain known as the Gulf Coastal plain extends from the south of Tamaulipas to Campeche. Its height above sea-level is less than 800 metres, and it forms the boundary line between temperate and hot country.

The area can be considered an ecological unit (as was the case during the Prehispanic epoch), as it has a series of common characteristics: a natural vegetation of tropical forest with tremendous powers of regeneration, in which up to two harvests per year could be obtained, with the exception of a semi-arid area in the Centre of Veracruz. For the most part, the annual rainfall is in excess of 1000 millimetres. Although the rainfall is fairly high, it varies considerably from one place to another. Maximum rainfall occurs more frequently in temperate lands than in hot lands, but in general the amount of rain increases towards the south. The region has numerous streams, a river system with large river basins and extensive fluvial plains, and lakes and reservoirs: all these elements provide both food and transport.

There are four river systems in the area, which are among the most important in Mexico; the Pánuco-Tamesí, the Papaloapan, the Coatzacoalcos and the Grijalva-Usumacinta, with their four river basins formed by low-lying land and their rich, wide alluvial plains.

A large part of the lowland plains consist of water-logged savannahs, swamps and lakes. However, the expanse of plain that extends from the Pánuco River to the Papaloapan River is an area of rolling hills and well-drained countryside. The Chiconquiaco Sierra at the centre of the region breaks the monotony, representing an advance of the Eastern Sierra Madre that reaches almost up to the sea.

Naturally, the vegetation changes according to the amount of rainfall, and thus the region south of the Cotaxtla River is almost entirely covered by tropical forests, except for the alluvial plains flooded by the Coatzacoalcos and Papaloapan River basins. The rainfall diminishes in the Centre of Veracruz, and most of the vegetation consists of low brushwood, cacti and grassy savannahs, interrupted along the rivers by areas of tropical forest. The hills to the north of Totonacapan are also forested; it is difficult to reconstruct the vegetation of the Pánuco River basin even further north during this period as it has been completely altered by agriculture and cattle-raising following the arrival of the Spaniards; it was probably also an area of tropical forest. Although much agricultural land could not be used as it was permanently flooded, there were also extremely fertile lands, such as the well-drained alluvial plains and the hill area. Highly productive meadowland areas are found in the Pánucao-Tamesí River basin and in the centre of Veracruz, although here they are combined with savannah vegetation and semi-arid conditions.

This geographical environment determined the distribution of the population in small groups, in villages, small towns or, infrequently, in large nuclei of population with ceremonial centres. However, although there was a relatively high number of these centres, they were rarely highly populated, nor did they achieve the size or effect of the centres in the Central Highlands. From the Classic period onwards, the groups seem to have been organised in small political groups, but they never formed large states based on conquest, as did other civilisations of ancient Mexico. This difference may have been the result of the agricultural system, as, unlike other areas of Mesoamerica, it was not necessary to have collective work requiring more than the extended family; and there was no need for the state, or the dominant group, to have as one of its principal functions the increase of agricultural potential. There was a better distribution of population than in the Central Highlands, with a lower density.

Very early on, the Gulf Coast groups established commercial relations with other regions of Mesoamerica, trading, for instance, their valuable primary materials, such as cacao, cotton, feathers and merchandise, and thus converting these into a symbol of wealth among the peoples of other Mesoamerican civilisations.

The Olmecs

The word Olmec means "inhabitant of the region of rubber". In the history of Mesoamerica, various Olmec groups existed during different periods; we shall refer to the most ancient, the group that lived on the Gulf Coast in the south of Veracruz and part of Tabasco during the Pre-Classic period, and in particular during the Middle Pre-Classic (1200-600 B.C.).

The area occupied by this civilisation is limited in the north by the Gulf of Mexico, in the south by the first foothills of the Sierra, in the west by the River Papaloapan and in the east by the Blasillo-Tonalá River basin. The whole area is irrigated by a vast hydraulic network of rivers, springs, lakes and swamps, which give it its particular character.

From an environmental point of view, the area is characterised by tropical rain-forest, with annual rainfalls in excess of 1500 millimetres. and temperatures that are occasionally high enough to exceed 40°. A large part of the area is permanently covered by water and mud, which imposed certain restraints on the group's adaptation to the terrain. Water was a dominant factor, and was feared more for its excess than for its scarcity. The dense, impenetrable tropical forest vegetation obliged the inhabitants to make use of the rivers and lakes as the best routes of trade and communication.

Most of the area is low-lying, interrupted only by the mountainous Tuxtlas massif, around 500 metres high, from which the Olmecs quarried most of the stone for their sculpture.

Food was provided by hunting, fishing or gathering the rich and varied fauna. However, while animals represented food, they were also frequently threatening, since poisonous reptiles and insects or such terrifying animals as the crocodile and the jaguar imposed their presence and became symbols of the forces of nature.

The Olmecs' physical appearance can be reconstructed on the basis of sculptures and figurines. Cranial deformation seems to have been a generalised practice, as was the modification of the form of the teeth, known as dental mutilation; both practices were related to the Olmecs' religious theories. Individuals were represented as being obese, with short legs and neck, bulbous cheeks and wide noses, as in the Gulf Coast colossal heads or in the clay and jade figurines. Another distinct type of character also appears, of a greater height, slimmer, and with an aquiline nose; the use of the beard stands out above everything else. Occasionally, both types are represented together, as in the Alvarado stela.

It is not known precisely what language the Olmecs spoke, as there is no written record, but linguists have strongly suggested that they must have spoken a language pertaining to the Zoque-Mixe family. The indigenous peoples currently inhabiting the region occupied by the Olmecs 3000 years ago speak Popoluca, a language that is part of this family.

The Olmecs had a very complete knowledge of the carving of hard stones, such as basalt, serpentine or jade; most of their work tools were made out of stone, both the ones necessary for sculptural, domestic, agricultural or hunting tasks and those used to produce ornaments such as earflares, necklaces or concave pyrite mirrors. Knowledge of stone carving techniques was not widespread, and everything seems to indicate that it was controlled by the ruling class. The fact that the material used for the large sculptures had to be transported from a distance of several hundred kilometres and that materials such as jade and jadeite for small sculptures were brought from even greater distances reinforces the idea that supervision must have been necessary to direct this type of undertaking, which became very complex because of the political and social organisation.

The Olmecs were among the first to attach great importance to jade. In Mesoamerica, this green stone came to symbolise that which was most valued, and always retained a relationship with the cult of fertility.

One of the Olmecs' greatest technological achievements was the construction of the first system of water control in Prehispanic Mexico. San Lorenzo in the state of Veracruz has a network of drainage or drying out canals flowing throughout the site; the main artery is 1764 metres long, while the three secondary canals measure only 294 metres. All the canals are made out of perfectly cut and assembled stone slabs, and incorporate the necessary incline for water to flow out.

The transport and cutting of the thirty tons of basalt from which the stone slabs were made, as well as the knowledge implied in the calculation of the system, implies that this is the work of specialists. By comparison with stone carving, which seems to have been largely dedicated to ceremonial usage, ceramics can be considered to be a popular craftwork; vessels were produced not only as offerings to the deceased, but also as objects for everyday usage. Olmec ceramics are fairly simple, modelled out of a creamy clay that is typical of the Gulf Coast and usually has little decoration. Some of the vessels that appear in different places in Mesoamerica are associated with the Olmec culture because of certain distinguishing features, such as ceramic ware with straight walls and flat bottoms, or decorations consisting principally of jaguar elements distributed within the body of the vessel.

The size of the Olmecs' ceremonial centres lead us to assume that they took over several neighbouring villages or settlements, integrating them into the larger centre. This represented a new form of social and political organisation, concentrating power and knowledge in one group – undoubtedly the one that lived in these centres.

The environment did not permit the growth of very large settlements; recent excavations, however, have modified the idea that Olmec sites were exclusively ceremonial, as their population seems to have been far larger than originally calculated. It was broken down into a hierarchy of social classes, some of them with specific privileges such as access to a particular bank of knowledge, or holding certain powerful offices, such as those exercised by priests, artists, craftsmen and merchants.

The best-known sites are La Venta in Tabasco and Tres Zapotes, San Lorenzo-Tenochtitlan and Laguna de los Cerros in Veracruz, where for the first time in Mesoamerica planned ceremonial centres were built according to a concept of orientation in the buildings. Pyramidal bases were of a distinct shape, either rectangular or rounded, and were constructed around open spaces serving as ceremonial plazas; these became the axis of Mesoamerican religious architecture. Their buildings were made from earth or clay, and never reached the monumental proportions of those built during the Classic period by other Mesoamerican civilisations.

There was also a type of stone architecture: examples include the tomb constructed with basalt columns in La Venta, Tabasco; the walls formed by the same type of columns in Tres Zapotes, Veracruz; and the floors made of serpentine fragments found inside the pyramidal bases at various Olmec sites. The Olmecs, however, were sculptors rather than architects; their spirit found its greatest expression through stone sculptures which reflect their religious ideas, their explanation of the world and their artistic ability. Hundreds of monumental sculptures are currently known, most from the sites just mentioned; they are made from very hard volcanic stone such as basalt and andesite. Although some are more ancient than others, all of them reflect what can be termed a single style.

Their sculptures can be divided into human figures, animals, ceremonial objects and work tools. Of these, human figure sculptures are the most common; they come in the form of colossal heads, altars, stelae or statues. The exact symbolism of the huge heads, which are unique in Mesoamerica, is unknown; however, they may portray leaders or players that were decapitated in the ball game; in the altars, the Olmecs gave visible expression to their ideas about their own history. As well as monumental sculpture, they also produced a variety of smaller sculptures in greenstone, such as jade or jadeite, dedicated to ceremonial ends or used as ornament.

At the opposite extreme of Mexican territory, in the State of Guerrero, the paintings of Juxtlahuaca and Oxtotitlán are to be found, on the walls of rocky caves. Through the attire, ornament and certain symbolic elements the scenes and characters represented give us a clear idea of the Olmec world. It is possible that both caves formed a sort of sanctuary for Olmec merchants who reached Guerrero in search of jade, one of the factors that determined various commercial routes.

Writing and the use of the calendar were one of the major achievements of the Prehispanic civilisations of Mesoamerica. Knowledge of the calendar implied, firstly, observation of the stars over long periods in order to discover their cycles of movement. Their knowledge enabled the Olmecs to measure time, and, later, to place the stars within a chart formed by numerals and figures representing the different units, either the days or months of a cycle, both lunar and solar.

The Olmec civilisation was the first to record a calendrical system on stone, as appears on Stela C of Tres Zapotes, which bears the most ancient date in Mesoamerica known at present: 31 years B.C. But the Olmecs went beyond the simple charting of a calendrical system, because they discovered a method of ascribing a different value to the same numeral according to its position: numerals were given a prescribed value depending on their position within a vertical column. This discovery enabled calculations based on extremely high numbers to be carried out.

After the Olmec civilisation, the calendrical system, and possibly writing as well, spread throughout Mesoamerica, particularly among the Mayas, to whom they passed on the mathematical knowledge mentioned above.

The Olmec religion was organised around a cult of fertility symbolised by the jaguar and the serpent who represented the principal deities, and by certain ceremonies which were depicted in some of their sculptures. The importance attributed to the babe-in-arms suggests some form of sacrifice which may be related to those carried out by the Mayas at a later period. The Olmecs developed a complete and complex social structure, the principal elements of which served as the foundation for Mesoamerican civilisation.

The Centre of Veracruz

The groups that lived in this area during the Prehispanic era created a different culture to the one found among the Olmecs, or among the Huastecs, who occupied the northern part of the Coast. Their territory extended from the Cazones River in the north and the Papaloapan River in the south, to the eastern side of the Sierra Madre mountain range, including small parts of the present-day states of Puebla and Oaxaca. During the Prehispanic epoch, this region possessed a variety of local cultures which expressed themselves through specific artistic styles, although they shared general traits. The name "Centre of Veracruz" is somewhat vague, and only explains their geographical location; however, in some publications they are described as Central Veracruz cultures, and a third name, El Tajín, is used to describe the particular style emanating from one principal centre.

Their economy was based principally on the farming of maize, beans, chilli, cultivated and gathered fruits, and was complemented in some places by the hunting of animals such as deer, armadillo and rabbit, as well as by fishing and the gathering of molluscs from lakes, rivers, springs and the sea.

The languages spoken during the Prehispanic period were Popoluca from the Zoque-Mixe family in the southern part, and, in a large part of the remaining area, Nahuatl. Around the year A.D. 800 to A.D. 1000, Totonacan-speaking groups arrived in Veracruz, settling principally in the regions of Papantla and Misantla. The indigenous groups today continue to speak these three languages.

During the Pre-Classic period, the economy of the groups settled along the coast was fundamentally based on fishing and the gathering of molluscs; a little later, when they began to practise agriculture, they settled in inland areas, although they established their villages close to rivers or springs to ensure the supply of water.

Important relations existed between all the Gulf Coast civilisations during this period, as is apparent from the similarities of their ceramics; it was also, however, the time when individual characteristics distinguishing the Olmecs and the Huastecs from their neighbours developed.

At the beginning of the first century A.D., certain centres of cultural development from the Pre-Classic period were still in existence, enriched by new elements. Thus, sites such as Tres Zapotes and Cerro de las Mesas, which already had a distinct culture, continued to thrive in the Olmec area, preserving their Olmec heritage, which was to survive until very much later. During the Classic period, Veracruz was home not to one homogenous culture but, on the contrary, to a number of diverse centres which influenced a wide area. Reference can be made to several of these, each with different characteristics but showing close links with each other. The southernmost centre, where former Olmec sites had existed, consisted of sites such as Cerro de las Mesas, Tres Zapotes, Catemaco, Alvarado, Cocuite, Nopiloa and Los Cerros, where important stone carvings and later high-quality clay sculptures were produced. Another centre included the region of Tenenexpan, in Remojadas, where artistic emphasis was focused on clay products such as "smiling face" figurines. The third centre, further to the north, manifested its architectural and sculptural style in the site of El Tajín.

During the early part of the Classic period, the relationship between the Gulf Coast and Teotihuacán was extremely important, and exemplified in a certain type of clay figurine, as well as in the cult of gods such as Xipe or the Old God of Fire; the influence, however, was reciprocal, as the presence of coastal traits in Teotihuacán painting and sculpture is widespread and significant. This relationship must have had both a commercial and a religious nature; an example of shared iconography is the cacao palm, a tree that grows in hot regions, which is painted on the walls of Teothuacán palaces and which also clearly appears at coastal sites such as Cerro de las Mesas, Matacapan, Remojadas, El Tejar and Paso de Ovejas, among many others.

Around the years A.D. 600 to 900, Veracruz intensified its relations with the Maya and several Central Highlands cultures, as can be seen in the stelae in a notably Veracruz style at Cholula, Puebla, or in the "Bebedores" or "Drinkers" mural paintings in the same city, which are similar in style to the paintings at Las Higueras, Veracruz.

The separate groups occupying the coast from Tamaulipas to Yucatán were particular keen to promote maritime contacts, and as a result, Maya elements appear in different parts of Veracruz. Clay figurines from Nopilos and Los Cerros display a strong similarity with those of Jonuta and Jaina from the Maya culture. The same influence appears in architecture, as in the Maya corbel vault, or false arch, found in Building A and in the altars at the centre of the stairways in the Pyramid of the Niches, both found at El Tajín.

Towards the year A.D. 800, after the fall of Teotihuacán, the group of Nahuatl-speaking immigrants arrived in Veracruz who were described as *pipiles* in written sources: that is, noblemen or sons of princes. These people brought their culture with them, established themselves for a while in the coastal region, acquired the cultural traits of the region and shortly afterwards set off towards Central America. Sculptures such as *yugos, hachas* and *palmas*, as well as clay figures in the form of small animals with wheels, musical instruments and, above all, a complicated ceremony that revolved around the ball game, accompanied by human sacrifice, are some of the features of the region extending from the coast towards places such as the coast of Chiapas and Santa Lucía Cotzumalhuapa in Guatemala and Quelepa and Chalchuapa in El Salvador.

Ceremonial architecture was introduced during the Pre-Classic period, once the religious cult and the priestly class had been established; it brought with it certain changes, such as the use of stone instead of the earth, either tamped down or burnt, that had previously been the predominant construction material. However, in some places earth continued to be used for walls and floors, but was covered with stucco and painted. The outer wall of the bases was constructed with boulders and, in some cases, with thin stone slabs enabling niches and frets to be formed, decorating the exteriors and *alfardas* of buildings.

The most important site in the northern part of the Gulf Coast was undoubtedly El Tajín, both because of its size and because of the quality and number of its buildings: around 200 constructions were built, forming small plazas. Not all of them date from the same period, as the site was occupied for a very long time, from A.D. 300 to 1100. The architecture of El Tajín takes elements used at Teotihuacán, such as the *talud* and *tablero*, but adds others such as the cornice, niches and frets, which unite in an original style.

In other parts of the coast earth construction persisted, and incorporated large earth sculptures, as can be seen at the site of El Zapotal.

Like all the other Gulf Coast arts, the sculpture reveals a well-defined style. The materials used were stone and clay; clay sculptures are basically anthropomorphic, executed in a realistic style with sensual outlines. They represent an enormous advance in technical terms. The exceptionally large hollow Mixtequilla sculptures (some 170 centimetres tall) are typical examples: although certain long-standing decorative techniques are evident, including appliqué and the use of *chapopote* (tar), other, new elements appeared, such as the use of moulds for figurines or for details.

These clay figurines depended for their subject-matter on the array of gods or individuals related to religious festivals, ceremonies or cults. However, the gods of this region were not supernatural, but human; for example, Tlazoltéotl, the goddess of fertility, was personified by a woman whose only ritualistic attribute is her small mouth mask, sometimes indicated only by a simple black mark; the Cihuateteo, women-warriors associated with death during childbirth, have a belt in the form of a serpent, or a shield on their arms as ornament; the long-nosed gods, associated with the sun, have no identifying religious element. Other figurines represent participants in festivals, either dancers or

musicians, whose joyful spirit is expressed by laughing or smiling, or with a posture suggesting dancing or acting, with arms raised in the air. The "smiling face" figurines belong to this type.

The most important sculptural features of Classic period Veracruz are the *yugos, hachas* and *palmas*; shapes and decorative elements are found in these that are unique in Mesoamerica, with complicated patterns of interlacing and volutes accompanying animals and sacrificial scenes. As yet the function of the horseshoe-shaped *yugos* has not been ascertained; they generally depict animals, such as toads, tigers and birds, associated with certain mythological beliefs that are in turn related to the cult of the dead and the ball game.

Hachas and *palmas* are also unexplained, but like the *yugos*, their decorative elements, which are similar, express the same sorts of concepts.

Mural painting reached its height during the Classic period (A.D. 300-900). The region's most important mural paintings are found in the north of Veracruz, close to the coast. Las Higueras is a site with a number of buildings: in the so-called Pyramid I, paintings were found displaying varied styles and motifs that undoubtedly correspond to different periods of time and to the different artists who took part. The themes are religious and ceremonial, with representations of gods such as Xipe, Tlazoltéotl, the Hurricane and the Sun. The ball game and a scene depicting the investiture of a new lord, accompanied by dancers and musicians, complete the repertoire. All the figures are depicted with great clarity. A basically religious aspect underlies the use of colour, hence the predominance of red above all other colours, which include blue-green, white, brown and orange. The themes of the paintings relate them to El Tajín, Aparicio and to the Ball Court at Chichén-Itzá, while the style has its own hallmark.

The Prehispanic society of the Gulf Coast saw major changes during the Post-Classic era, among them the arrival of the Totonacs, a group that built its capital at Cempoala. According to written evidence, the Totonacs came from Chicomoztoc, the mythical home of several of the Post-Classic groups who played an important political role in the fourteenth, fifteenth and sixteenth centuries. However, Torquemada also mentions the Totonacs as taking part in the construction of the city of Teotihuacán.

The oldest Totonac settlements are found in the Puebla Sierra, from where the Totonacs gradually spread towards the coast, concentrating in various centres such as Cempoala, Misantla, Papantla, Naolingo, Perote and Zacatlán. During the sixteenth century, 764,000 Totonacs inhabited an area extending from the Cazones River in the north to the Antigua River in the south, and westwards to the Puebla and Hidalgo Sierra.

The Totonacs undoubtedly had contact with Toltec groups during their early development, as they displayed certain Toltec traits, though these have been interpreted by certain authors as Mexica; Chac Mool sculpture is one of these features, as are the representations of certain animals as decorative elements; also characteristic are buildings with mixed layouts as well as the cult of Ehécatl-Quetzalcóatl, god of wind. All these traits are evident in the Totonac capital Cempoala and in other sites in Mesoamerica.

The architecture of this date shows characteristics that relate to a period of frequent fighting, as a result of which defence became one of the main concerns of society. Settlements were established in high areas and protected by ramparts; paved streets also increased, as did the general usage of sewers and cisterns for the storage of water. However, the quality of construction diminished and the outline of buildings was simplified, although the buildings themselves became more impressive. Sculpture, particularly in stone, declined in quality, though fine stone such as alabaster was used for several sorts of vessel, many in the shape of animals such as monkeys, lizards and rabbits.

The ceramics of the Isla de Sacrificios represent the final manifestation of a type of decoration that characterised Veracruz during the Classic period. In spite of the similarity of its forms with those of Mixtec-Puebla ceramics, its decoration, based on frets, volutes and interlacing, show all the grace and fluency of the Veracruz style.

The Mexica empire began to extend towards the coast in two distinct directions, establishing military garrisons at key points to ensure the supply of basic materials brought from the coast. By the end of the fifteenth century and the beginning of the sixteenth, many Totonacs had fallen under Mexica domination. By 1519, when the Spaniards arrived, there had already been an attempt at rebellion: the Totonacs were tired of paying the high taxes that the Mexicas demanded in the way of products such as cotton, jaguar pelts, chilli, salt, liquidambar (an aromatic balsam), rabbits, wild turkeys, and also slaves. So when Cortés presented himself in Cempoala, the Totonac ruler received him kindly, thinking that in now he would find allies in the fight against México-Tenochtitlán.

The Huastecs
The Huastecs inhabited the northern part of the Gulf Coast, where they still live today. The geographical area they occupied included the present-day states of Veracruz, San Luís

Potosí, Hidalgo and Tamaulipas, as well as small portions of Puebla and Querétaro, although now they are to be found only in small parts of Veracruz and San Luís Potosí. They inhabited an area that included a wide variety of climates and natural landscapes, from the hot and inhospitable coastline and coastal plain to the lower parts of the eastern Sierra Madre, the Potosí Highlands and the sheer mountain range of Tamaulipas.

Along the coast, the area was defined by the Tuxpan River in the south and by the Soto la Marina River in the north; inland, the eastern slopes of the Sierra Madre served as the Huastec boundary. As well as the rivers mentioned above, the Tamesí and Pánuco Rivers played an important role in the development of Huastec culture, as the first villages appeared near the banks of the Pánuco River. Numerous springs and lakes, as well as the sea, provided an extensive range of fish, molluscs and aquatic birds, enabling numerous groups to subsist in water-side locations from very early times.

The Huastec language forms part of the Maya language family, from which it became separated approximately 3500 years ago as a result of the infiltration of different groups with their own languages. The Huastec language continues to be spoken today by some 40,000 indigenous people from Veracruz, San Luís Potosí and Hidalgo.

The Huastecs did not remain in the same region throughout their evolution; like all the Mesoamerican groups, they migrated at different times. During the Pre-Classic period they were settled principally along the coastline, on the coastal plain and in the Sierra foothills. Later they spread northwards to Tamaulipas, and towards the coastal plain of Veracruz. It was only in the Classic era that they reached the Potosí Highlands, the Hidalgo sierra and part of Querétaro.

During the Post-Classic period they inhabited a noticeably smaller area; groups in the Tamaulipas sierra were left outside the sphere of Huastec culture, as were groups in the Potosí highlands. However, some of the groups extended towards the northern sierra of Puebla.

By the time of the Spaniards arrival, the Huastecs were occupying a territory that extended from the Tuxpan River to the Pánuco River along the coast, and inland, towards the northern part of Puebla, the low lands of the Hidalgo Sierra and the Potosí coastal plain, up to the Huayalejo-Tamesí Rivers.

From the records left by Fray Bernardino de Sahagún, various Huastec practices are known, such as cranial deformation and dental mutilation (modifying the form of the upper and lower front teeth), customs that were shared by other coastal groups. In appearance they were slim and of average height, occasionally decorating themselves with tattoos and scarification, as well as with ornaments such as earflares, necklaces and bracelets; they made holes in the tip of the nose for nose-plugs.

Huastec economy was founded principally on maize agriculture; however, where possible, there was a great deal of fishing and mollusc gathering. At first, their ceramics were similar to those of the Centre of Veracruz, the Maya area and even the initial phases of Monte Albán. This similarity highlights the relationships that existed between the coastal civilisations and several civilisations in the south of Mesoamerica.

Huastec ceramics acquired their definitive characteristics in the Classic period (A.D. 300-900), and vessels began to be manufactured using a creamy, fine-paste clay; pumpkins, animals and female figures were among the forms that occurred most frequently. Later, during the Post-Classic period (A.D. 900-1519), ceramics showed a greater affinity with those of the rest of Mesoamerica, but without losing their distinctive touch; however, certain similarities can be found with ceramics such as those from Cholula. Their more advanced technique allowed the creation of a greater diversity of forms, including that of the female with bare breasts, as well as simple bowls with handles or dishes of varying sizes. Decorative elements were similar to those found in stone sculpture, generally depicted in black and scarlet on a light background.

There are notable differences between Huastec architecture and that of other Mesoamerican groups; these include not only shape but also materials and systems of construction. The predominant shape from the beginning was circular; later this was substituted by a rectangular or square layout with rounded corners. During the earlier period, Huastec sites were unplanned, as in other parts of Mesoamerica. In general, architecture was fairly modest, with small dimensions. Earth was the most commonly used material for the construction of the bases, although occasionally boulders or limestone slabs tamped down with clay are found. In the region near the coast a mixture of oyster shell and sand was used to fill in bases or for floors. Tancanhuiz, Cuatlamayán and Tamposoque in San Luís Potosí are some of the sites that date from this period. Funerary architecture also came into being, with the construction of tombs such as those of Huichapa and Vinasco.

During this Early Post-Classic period (A.D. 900-1250), Mesoamerican influence introduced the concept of planning in the ceremonial centres, as well as the use of *alfardas* and stucco and, as a result, of mural painting, as can be seen in sites such as Tamuín. The impact of the El Tajín style in the use of stone slabs for the construction of tiered bases is also important, as seen at Cebadilla and Ozuluama.

In the Late Post-Classic period (A.D. 1250-1519), settlements were established in areas that were easy to defend, and several fortresses were built, as at Metlaltoyuca.

Like the other groups that occupied the coast, the Huastecs were great sculptors. The style of their works was completely original, and characterised by the use of geometric planes to create slightly hieratic self-contained figures, representations which seem to have originated as a form of low relief, acquiring volume little by little. Some of the figures never became fully independent from the stone block and their legs were only crudely carved. Huastec sculpture reached its peak after the years A.D. 900-100; there were three principal subjects: female representations with bare breasts, hands on stomach and ornaments on the head, which are images of the goddess of fertility; male representations that are naked, including several adolescent figures as well as priests with ritualistic attire; and sculptures of elderly hunchbacked figures holding a *coa* or dibble stick in their hands. The finest examples of stone sculpture are undoubtedly those in the style of the region of Tamuín, San Luís Potosí, where the technique acquires a degree of perfection not seen in other works. Surviving Prehispanic sculptures still play a part in certain rituals performed in traditional festivals of indigenous groups that still occupy the Huastec region today.

Mural painting is scarce; up to the present, only one example has been found: on a round altar at the site of Tamuín, San Luís Potosí. A series of individuals (both gods and priests) were painted in scarlet on a white background. The brushstrokes used to depict them recall the shell-work technique in which the Huastecs excelled.

Shells were cut vertically for use as pectorals by priests dedicated to the cult of the god of wind Ehécatl-Quetzalcóatl, for whom the shell was his insignia. Religious or mythological scenes were engraved on the shells, rivalling the scenes depicted in the codices of other Mesoamerican civilisations. These were drawn by a fine, well-defined incised line, depicting scenes including one or several figures. In some cases the subject was embossed, while the surrounding area was delicately cut back; in other cases, the pectoral consists of fretwork.

Metallurgy was practised in the Huasteca and several examples survive, but in general it was fairly modest, and in comparison to the shell work lacks original style. The coastal civilisations retained maritime contacts with one another; this was undoubtedly based on a rudimentary knowledge of navigation techniques which nevertheless allowed them to establish commercial relations with fairly distant groups. Sixteenth-century chronicles speak of the trading of salt between the Mayas and the Huastecs through merchant-navigators, corroborating this contact among the inhabitants settled along the coast. According to the recorded mythological origins of the Huastecs, tradition narrates that peoples who had come by sea disembarked in Panutla, another name for the Huasteca.

Relatively little is known about the social and political organisation of the Huastecs. The Huastec area appears to have been divided into various independent political groupings or polities, which occasionally united against a common enemy, as when they fought against the Mexicas. Tziuhcóac, Tuxpan, Pánuco, Huejutla and Tampache among others are mentioned as polities. In terms of social organisation, the scant existing data indicates that there were totemic clans with a supreme chief; in some places there was a council of elders which was charged with meting out justice.

The Huastecs lived in small spread-out villages, consisting of a few houses made from clay and branches, and generally oval in shape. Later they built platforms on which to set both domestic dwellings and temples, in order to raise them above the damp.

The Huastecs influenced groups in the Central Highlands, such as the Toltecs, through the cult of certain gods that were long-established in the coastal areas, such as Tlazoltéotl and Ehécatl-Quetzalcóatl, who were to be absorbed into the Mexica religion.

The Mexica empire launched its offensive against this region towards the year 1458, when it got as far as Tziuhcóac, establishing power over one of the routes leading towards the coast and forming the frontier between the Huastecs and the Totonacs. In order to ensure supplies from the coastal region, the Mexica also created a military garrison at Castillo de Teayo, leaving their mark on its architecture and sculpture. Between the years 1486 and 1502, when Ahuízotl ruled the Mexica, they dominated the area up to Tuxpan, that is, up to the sea. Towards 1517 several Huastec communities rebelled, and many of them became independent, with the exception of Castillo de Teayo; in 1519, when the Spaniards arrived, the Huasteca as a region had already freed itself from the yoke of the Mexica empire.

12. MONUMENTALITY, EXPRESSIONISM AND SENSUALITY IN THE ART OF THE GULF COAST

Sonia Lombardo de Ruíz

Few civilisations can boast such vigorous sculptural forms as the Olmecs from the Centre of Veracruz. If the sculptures had to be defined by some characteristic, it could well be their affinity with the earth: their symbolism, their volume and their massive size.

The cylindrical vessel from Cerro de las Mesas (plate 60) is an extraordinary example of Olmec aesthetic conception. Its proportions are in the ratio of 1:0.8, almost square, the horizontal measurement being only slightly larger than the vertical. Sitting solidly on a flat base, with straight sides that diverge slightly, and decorated with bands of grooves which accentuate its horizontal nature, it is made out of black clay, which gives it weight. All these factors combine to make the vessel tectonic, immobile, monumental and expressive, in spite of its small size.

The Middle Pre-Classic period was the time when, in iconographic terms, various Mesoamerican deities began to take shape, and men identified themselves with totemic animals. It was during this time that the concept of cosmic forces materialised, and that the jaguar acquired its complex divine identity among the Olmecs, though retaining its essential earth-bound nature. The birth of a priestly lineage is also evident in humanised jaguars (plate 64) or in jaguar-men (plate 65). The animals transmitted their supernatural forces to these men, who monopolised power and ruled their society.

It was also the period when particular types of greenstone were to find a permanent place in Mesoamerican ceremony, perhaps because among the agricultural peoples the colour of the stone evoked the colour of germination, and in their magical and religious ideas it became synonymous with fertility.

Thus, a series of representations of human figures emerged in Olmec art, carved in stone of differing shades of green, ranging from light to dark. Generally this stone was very hard, and the superb quality of the polished finish could only have been obtained through a high degree of specialisation and the development of great technical skill.

The Olmecs established a physical pattern that was followed and diffused throughout a very wide area, which explains Olmec presence in many Mesoamerican sites. Whether the sculptures represent balanced figures sitting in a lotus position at complete rest, with crossed legs and arms resting on their knees or the floor as if in a ritualistic posture, or upright figures, asexual and naked, they always have very large, broad faces, with chubby cheeks, broad noses and half-open mouths with down-turned lips. They often show cranial deformation or a wedge-shaped depression in the occipital bone of the skull associated with the formation of the jaguar skull. These bold faces give the impression of being distant, as if in ecstasy (plate 61), with the implication that they represent men dedicated to worship.

Another recurring motif in Olmec art is that of very young children, known as "baby faces". They are represented in different postures, and among them the figure shown in plate 63 is exceptional. The texture achieved by the artist in moulding the plump body and chubby face in clay transmits the sensation of tender young flesh with an extraordinary naturalism. Furthermore, the symmetrical composition of the open arms and legs in the form of the flexible arms of a cross gives the sculpture a dynamism that is perfectly balanced. The contrast between form and solemnity lends the face an expression that is contradictory, as it is both joyful and extremely dignified.

During the Pre-Classic period, the Olmecs created a unified and widespread aesthetic, which established many of the fundamental aspects that were to be consolidated by Mesoamerican culture. By contrast, in cultural terms, during the following Classic phase the Gulf Coast was inhabited by a number of peoples that were rather independent of each other, and although they shared common traits, they displayed their own particular styles, especially in their sculpture. As a result, Classic-period art in this region is expressed in a formal language that is extremely rich.

Of the many elements inherited from the Olmec culture, the jaguar continued to be one of the most frequently represented motifs, and its symbolic association with the earth seems to have persisted. The two examples of the jaguar in this exhibition clearly reveal the characteristics of Veracruz art.

One of them, carved in stone (plate 67), represents only the head of the animal. This is constructed on the basis of rounded masses of different sizes, as if a series of conventional scrolls had been fused together to form eyebrows, ears, nose and maw. However, they are organised symmetrically to produce a violently effective chiaroscuro, and the unity of the piece is achieved by the similarity of the carefully placed forms. Shell and dark stones have been added to the baroque head to indicate the eyes and fangs, details which concentrate the ferocious expression of the animal.

The other jaguar (plate 68), modelled in clay, expresses a completely different feeling because of the malleability of the material. Seated with its rear legs folded and resting on its front legs – which are in a slightly human posture - it displays its sexual organs, and raises its head. The head is accentuated, being proportionately larger than the body, and within it, emphasis lies on the enormous open mouth, brimming with teeth and great fangs. These fangs are similar in form to the claws on the four powerful paws which, as a whole, impart a sense of strength, power and aggression.

The fantastic lizard-serpent head alluding to the earth and its fertility (plate 66) is equally expressive and vigorous, with attributes very similar to those of the jaguar. Displaying a dynamic linear diagonal form, it is also made of clay, and opens its enormous jaw to reveal its forked tongue.

In formal terms a great sense of freedom is apparent in these three works, with an expressive force achieved by the deliberate accentuation and deformation of some elements. In contrast, the figure of the owl carved on the *yugo* in plate 69 is completely the opposite. Its style is reminiscent of Teotihuacán culture, with which the peoples of the Centre of Veracruz maintained close ties. In the carving, the bird is completely constrained by and adapted to the *yugo*'s functional and closed form, very much in line with the intellectualised, rigorous and geometrical perceptions of Teotihuacán art. The head and feathers within the body are only superficially indicated by fine lines in low relief.

Together with the *yugos*, the ceremonial *palmas* and *hachas* form a characteristic group within the Classic culture of the Gulf of Mexico that are apparently associated with the ball game, human sacrifice and funerary practises, although their true function remains unknown. It was these three types of object that inspired the Gulf nations to create their masterpieces in carved stone.

The *palmas* have a vertically elongated form, with a gently rounded upper edge. They are sometimes decorated with zoomorphic motifs like the crocodile in plate 70, whose tail has been ingeniously bent round to adapt it to the curve of the *palma* itself; or else they are left unadorned (plate 71), assuming a quality that suggests affinities with the modern sensibility of abstract art and in which the uneven surface texture softly distributes the light over the elementary form.

The *hachas* have a flat, irregular shape, and often represent human heads, as in plate 72, as a result of which it has been suggested that they are related to sacrifice by decapitation.

Also distinctive of the Classic Gulf civilisations are the upright female figures with open arms modelled in clay. These embody a rich variety of expression, some of them dramatic (plate 73), others serene (plate 74) while the most remarkable ones are smiling (plate 76). Their clothes, which are richly decorated, are made from sculpted panels, and textile designs are indicated by means of colours or incised line; headdresses of various forms crown the deformed heads, which always emphasise the horizontal.

The most important goddess in Veracruz culture was Tlazolteotl, the goddess of fertility, sustenance, dance, music and love, in her principal manifestations. Almost all the female figures represent her or her priestesses. In the sculpture in plate 75 she has been modelled with great naturalism in the figure of a mature woman, seated with crossed legs covered by a skirt fastened by a belt of serpents. The only ornament on the naked torso is a band knotted at the middle of the chest. Her hair falls across her shoulders and on her head she wears a type of helmet. The sculpture is solemn and magnificent, constructed within a pyramidal form above the solid base, comprised by the legs and large feet. The facial expression, with lowered gaze and half-open mouth, suggests that she is in a trance or meditating.

No other work in Gulf Coast Prehispanic art can refer to philosophical dilemmas with greater intensity than the head known as The Duality (plate 77). Originating in an iconographic tradition that is recurrent in this region, representing half-living and half-dead faces, this piece is extremely impressive. Although the living half is a little schematic and lacking in detail, the artist achieves an exceptional effect of fleshiness, while leaving the area corresponding to the dead part rounded and unformed; this makes it much more suggestive, as it broadens the field for reflection. Life and death, being and non-being are concepts that have a great affinity with modern thought, which makes this work exceptionally attractive.

One of the most outstanding artistic manifestations of the Huastec civilisation that developed on the Gulf Coast during the Pre-Classic period is sculpture. Fertility, of which various iconographical types can be found, was undoubtedly the most important subject-matter.

The figures of women modelled in clay, in some cases holding children in their arms (plate 79), are characterised by their large thighs and long, narrow waists and necks. The heads are large in comparison to the bodies, and earflares and headdresses are worn. Facial features are clearly delineated and the eyes are incised, the pupil being indicated with a graver.

Elderly figures (plate 80) are also associated with fertility and, because of their age, it is likely that they acted as priests; they are represented upright, with arms stretched out holding the *coa* or dibble stick, in a ritual to protect the sown seeds. Their iconography is stereotyped and all of them are sculpted in the same posture, the only variation being the degree of expression in the details. The elderly figure leans forward, forming a diagonal which is paralleled by the *coa*, with a rectangular gap left between the two. The figure thus expresses great movement while at the same time maintaining a tense equilibrium within the sculpture.

Phallic sculptures are another sculptural type associated with fertility rites. The example in plate 81, of monumental dimensions and ornamented with beads, was worshipped and used during agricultural festivals.

However, possibly the most interesting and varied representations in Huastec sculpture are those of the female figure which, expressing numerous sentiments, represent goddesses of fertility, though constituting a very rigid iconographical type – upright, with bare breasts, hands held together on the stomach and with a conical headdress with a type of semi-circular crest or fan.

Two of these are shown in plates 82 and 83. The first has finer proportions, with a small face in comparison to the headdress; this consists of a short horizontal rectangle and a tall vertical cone, with an undulating or fluted crest; over all it is a fine and graceful figure. In contrast, the second sculpture has a rectangular skirt, inordinately crude hands, broad shoulders and arms that are widely separated from the body, leaving large gaps between them. The face is comparatively larger, the rectangle of the headdress has a more horizontal emphasis and the cone is shorter, with a smooth crest which has well-defined straight and curved edges. This sculpture transmits above all an expression of strength, and the exaggeration of the hands takes it to the limit of dramatic expression.

Chicomecoatl is also the goddess of fertility (plate 85), though represented with a different iconography. Totally geometrical, the sculpture is stylistically apart from the sensual Huastec forms, indicating influence from the centre of Mexico. It is sculpted in a prismatic block in which the lower third constitutes the feet and skirt of a woman, and the other two thirds the rest of the body and the headdress, which surrounds the face as if it were a temple structure. The face and the feet are the only naturalistic elements that have not been geometricised, although they have suffered a certain degree of schematisation.

But it is the rich tradition of male figures in Huastec sculpture that has brought the greatest sculptural fame to this region. The images of upright adolescents are famous, combining sensually stylised naturalistic forms with elements symbolising deities, principally the sun. In spite of being merely a fragment, the El Consuelo head (plate 84) indicates the sculptural quality achieved by Huastec artists.

The soft sandstone used enabled smooth surfaces to be carved, delineating the face of a young man with large eyes and fine eyebrows. Unfortunately, the nose is broken, but what remains indicates that it had a nose-plug, possibly in the form of a horizontal tube, as was customary among the Huastecs. The half-open mouth, with thin lips, displays teeth filed down into points, as was customary among high-ranking personages in this society; the head is crowned by the typical conical Huastec headdress with a semi-circular crest.

The piece has a graceful elegance, as on one plane its conical mass is horizontally divided into three parts, of which the head occupies the lower part, while the remainder is occupied by the tall, vertical headdress. On a second plane, the rounded form of the semi-circular crest balances the vertical elements and frames the figure, endowing it with great dignity.

The El Naranjo Priest (plate 86) is an upright male figure, like those traditionally sculpted by the Huastecs, even if its execution is cruder than most. The body is inscribed within the form of a large vertical rectangle, on which rests the small head surmounted by a tall conical headdress. Two powerful short, solid legs, clothed with a short skirt held up by a large belt from which a row of hearts is suspended, form the lower third of the sculpture. The central section consists of a broad thorax with an enormous pectoral, and in the lower area the ribs are indicated, allowing the heart to be seen at the centre. The head, displaying earflares, has a headdress with a skeleton as the principal ornament.

The sculpture is a strange combination, integrating elements of the living person with others, such as the ribs and heart, that are characteristic of representations of sacrificed victims. During the Post-Classic period, the Huastecs had close ties with the Aztecs, as a result of which the religious practice involving human sacrifice that was endemic in the Mexica area also became associated with the Gulf region. In this imposing figure, the priest and the ritual he performs (the extraction of the heart as an offering to the god) are simultaneously represented.

60. VESSEL

Olmec culture. Cerro de las Mesas, Veracruz. Middle Pre-Classic (1200-800 B.C.). Clay. Height 21 cm, diameter 27.5 cm. In store. MNA. Cat. no. 13-648. Inv. no. 10-223652.

Though expressing complex religious concepts in their decoration, the Olmecs' earliest clay products were extremely simple in form, at the same time as being objects of great beauty. Such is the cylindrical vessel with a flat base seen here. Its almost straight walls provide an inviting field for the development of the decorative motif running round the vessel, which is basically formed by a rhythmical repetition of various elements.

Black polished ceramics constitute one of the most interesting types of ceramic ware from Cerro de las Mesas, Veracruz, as the decoration does not appear on any other type of vessel. The elements are predominantly geometric, consisting of triangles, dots and especially curved or parallel lines, and were executed after the vessel had been fired, producing sharp, rigid lines that are very different to those of ceramics that have not been fired, or that have been left to dry so that the clay is still soft.

The decoration of certain objects was produced by scraping part of the surface, as in this case where the central motif, consisting of two thick, twisting lines emanating from a central rectangle, is framed above and below by a series of parallel grooves.

The vessel is unique in terms of its size, decorative design and proportions, and was found during the excavations of 1941, when the finest archaeological material at the site was discovered, pertaining to the Olmec culture of the Pre-Classic period (600-200 B.C.). *m.c.l.*

61. FIGURE

Olmec culture. El Tejar, Veracruz. Middle Pre-Classic (1200-800 B.C.). Stone. Height 15 cm, width 8.5 cm, depth 6.5 cm. Mesoamerica Hall. MNA. Cat. no. 13-437. Inv. no. 10-228060.

The carving of semi-precious hard stones was the work of true specialists. These craftsmen probably formed part of the priestly caste, as knowledge of the technique seems to have been restricted, and controlled by the ruling group, as were other forms of knowledge which included the calendar, writing and architecture.

The Olmecs were the first in Mesoamerica to employ high-quality stone to produce ritualistic objects dedicated to their gods, using basalt for large sculptures and greenstone such as jade, jadeite and pyrite for the smaller ones.

The tools used to produce these works must have been the same as the ones used to produce other, ordinary pieces, but as the sculptors had higher aspirations, the process was much longer and more enterprising.

After cutting the stone down to the required size, it had to be bored in some cases, and the design produced by incision or by smoothing down part of the surface, afterwards polishing it by rubbing with sand or dust from volcanic stone to give it the desired form and shine. As well as needing certain the tools for production, these small sculptures were the result of combined determination, effort and artistic genius.

The various types of stone figurine include several figures whose posture and dignified appearance indicate that they represent high-ranking figures believed to be priests, as in the figure exhibited here. *m.c.l.*

62. FIGURE

Olmec culture. Gulf Coast. Middle Pre-Classic (1200-800 B.C.). Stone. Height 14.5 cm, width 7 cm. In store. MNA. Cat. no. 13-814. Inv. no. 10-223637.

Numerous stone figurines, generally green or greenish in colour, represent Olmec man in all his simplicity, without ornamentation or clothing. Through these figures, certain Olmec customs are known, such as the modifying of the shape of the skull by using cotton strips to put pressure on the heads of new-born babies; the skull thus developed in a manner that either seemed beautiful to the Olmecs, or had a ritualistic meaning. To display this type of deformation, the Olmecs shaved off their hair and left their heads bare of any ornament.

The facial features of these stone sculptures recall those of the clay figurines, with almond-shaped eyes, small noses (and occasionally snub-noses), chubby cheeks and the mouth with down-turned lips known as the "Olmec mouth", with an appearance similar to a jaguar's jaw. Do these characteristics reveal the Olmecs' true appearance, or did they correspond to an ideal beauty, or a specific cult?

These questions are difficult to answer for the simple reason that there are few Olmec skeletal remains, and it is impossible to reconstruct their physical appearance on this .However, a skull with this type of deformation has recently been found in Chiapas at a site that clearly displays Olmec influence, corroborating the evidence of the stone figurines. *m.c.l.*

63. SEATED BABY-FACE FIGURE

Olmec culture. Gulf Coast. Middle Pre-Classic (1200-800 B.C.). Clay. Height 25.4 cm, width 28.5 cm. In store. MNA. Cat. no. 13-150. Inv. no. 10-220867.

The representation of new-born babies is one of the recurring themes of Olmec art. They have the same characteristics in both stone and clay: babies only a few months old, completely naked and without any kind of adornment, with no indication of their sex, and with a cranial deformation that is immediately apparent because in most cases they have no hair. When they are made out of clay, the figures are hollow, seated, with plump bodies, fat arms and legs and chubby cheeks; their arms are usually raised or bent, as is typical of babies of this age.

Clay sculptures of this type were made in all the sites influenced by the Olmecs during the Pre-Classic period, including the Valley of Mexico, Puebla and Morelos. In some cases slight differences are perceptible as a result of local characteristics becoming fused with Olmec traits. *m.c.l.*

64. HUMANISED JAGUAR

Olmec culture. San Lorenzo, Veracruz. Middle Pre-Classic (1200-800 B.C.). Stone. Height 90 cm, width 35 cm. Olmec Hall. MNA. Cat. no. 13-617. Inv. no. 10-81268.

The Olmecs frequently combined jaguar features with the human form because of the religious concept that saw the jaguar as the ancestor of man. The jaguar represented the fertile depths of the underworld, the region out of which every living thing emerged, and thus symbolised the earth itself. In this series of sculptures, jaguar features are apparent in the eyes, nose and mouth, which sometimes has the upper lip raised to such a degree that it becomes confused with the flattened snub nose; as well as the facial features, the limbs are bent into a position that can only be achieved by animals.

This sculpture, found at a depth of 140 centimetres, was buried at one end of the main sequence of irrigation canals found in San Lorenzo, a fact that reaffirms its association with the idea of fertility. The piece probably served as a crest, but was also used as a water fount.

Found during excavations carried out in the years 1966-68, the figure wears a headdress composed of a frontal band surmounted by a rectangular helmet, which is split in two by a deep central incision, possibly related to the fontanelle of recently born babies or to the occipital depression in feline skulls; many Olmec sculptures show the same traits. The helmet is decorated with designs associated with the rain; at each side of the face hang two corrugated bands, reminiscent of the ornamentation of the Mexica god Tláloc.

A flattened nose and a jaw with half-open lips displaying toothless gums and fangs hanging down are grafted onto the human face, along with the perfect almond-shaped eyes of the animal. On the figure's chest hangs a rectangle with the San Andrés cross, which represents jaguar markings.

This piece forms part of a series of works in which the features of the humanised jaguar are very clear; it has been interpreted as an Olmec god of water, with which the frequently found stone and clay sculptures of babies are associated.   *m.c.l.*

65. DIGNITARY

Olmec culture. La Venta, Tabasco. Middle Pre-Classic (1200-800 B.C.). Stone. Height 119 cm, width 93 cm, depth 64 cm. Museo de Antropología "Carlos Pellicer". Villahermosa, Tabasco. Cat. no. A-0027 (1414).

This sculpture forms part of the group of figures in which man and jaguar are united. In this case, both the body and the posture are completely human; by contrast, elements of the deity are concentrated in the face and hands. The seated posture with crossed legs is similar to other pieces, but the position of the arms, hanging down at either side of the body, differs from that of other sculptures, where they are placed in front of the legs; the torso is also different, as here it is completely upright, whereas in other figures it slants forward. Another feature is the belt adorning part of the thorax.

The head is covered with a helmet, similar to those worn by the colossal head sculptures of San Lorenzo. It is the eyes, nose and mouth that establish the relationship with the mythical jaguar figure; the eyes, in the form of a hook-shaped groove, are found in many other representations and are characteristic of the so-called God I. The nose has almost disappeared, but must have been snub and flattened; the mouth, in the form of a jaguar's maw, has a raised upper lip and the remains of fangs.

The piece comes from La Venta, Tabasco, one of the most important Olmec centres. Unfortunately, during the 1940s it was removed from its original site and taken to the city of Villahermosa, where it can be seen today.   *m.c.l.*

66. SERPENT'S HEAD

Centre of Veracruz culture. Gulf Coast. Post-Classic (A.D. 900-1521). Clay. Height 78 cm, width 51.8 cm, depth 46 cm. In store. MNA. Cat. no. 4-1252. Inv. no. 10-76640.

Although the exact provenance of this piece is not known, it has all the characteristics of the Gulf Coast sculptural style. The only people to produce sculpture of this size were the Veracruz artists of the Prehispanic period; the freedom of line, executed with few resources, are also typical of this group. In the hands of Gulf Coast sculptors, clay acquired a life of its own, expressed in sensuality of form and simplicity of decoration. The serpent was one of the animals to be represented by the coastal communities from very early Pre-Classic times (1200-200 B.C.) until the sixteenth century. In some cases, as here, crocodile elements were combined with those of the serpent; like the latter, the crocodile was associated with the earth.

The Gulf Coast Olmecs were the first of the vast majority of Mesoamerican civilisations to represent this deified reptile, which in their eyes had links not only with the earth but also, and especially, with the figure of the mother goddess as the guardian of providence.

The artist exaggerated the serpent's attributes, transforming it into a most impressive figure with a huge mouth displaying fangs. This piece may have formed part of the decoration of a temple; its size would have enabled it to be seen by people watching the ceremonies from the main plazas.   *m.c.l.*

67. JAGUAR

Centre of Veracruz culture. Gulf Coast. Classic (A.D. 200-900). Stone. Height 25.4 cm, width 17.9 cm, depth 4.5 cm. In store. MNA. Cat. no. 4-2225. Inv. no. 10-757012.

The recurrent theme of the jaguar symbolised the energy that lay within the earth and as such was a form of Olmec expression 1000 years B.C.; 1500 years later, when the Spaniards arrived, the jaguar still had a sacred role as the god of the caves, connecting the visible world with the underworld.

This piece combines a theme that was omnipresent in Prehispanic Mexico with the Gulf Coast groups' skill in stone carving. Shells and a darker stone are superimposed on the dark grey, almost black volcanic stone to create the eyes. The concave shape of the rear of the piece suggest that the piece was a type of mask. Prehispanic ceremonies with stone jaguar masks are not known, but indigenous groups today still perform dances in which tigers are the protagonists. One particular dance is still performed by the Popolucas of Veracruz: several dancers wear tiger masks and are accompanied by musicians, women and others. The aim of the dance, a form of fertility ritual, is to request a good harvest and sufficient rain for the maize.   *m.c.l.*

68. JAGUAR

Centre of Veracruz culture. Gulf Coast. Classic (A.D. 200-900). Clay. Height 43.9 cm, width 33 cm, depth 40.8 cm. In store. MNA. Cat. no. 4-3012. Inv. no. 10-222228.

Out of Prehispanic man's broad knowledge and observation of nature came his assumption that several animals merited being transformed into gods. The jaguar was one animal that was viewed as possessing the same overwhelming strength and energy as seemed to exist in the depths of the earth, causing not only the growth of plants but also earthquakes. From very early on, the jaguar was represented as one of the deities that participated in the religious complexities of earth-darkness-fertility rites, which were so important on the Gulf Coast.

In the piece shown here, the clay was used to present the jaguar with a certain candour, counterbalanced by the wide-open jaws displaying fangs. The use of black paint on the eyes and nose was characteristic of coastal groups, who used tar, *chapopote*, to decorate their sculptures. The sexual organ is pronounced in this piece, not only because of a desire to be realistic, but also because the jaguar had links with the energy of life, of which sexual manifestations were a part. It is worth mentioning that even today, among the Popolucas from southern Veracruz, the word used to designate the tiger also refers to the female sex.   *m.c.l.*

69. *YUGO* FROM A FUNERARY OFFERING

Centre of Veracruz culture. Gulf Coast. Classic (A.D. 200-900). Stone. Height 14 cm, length 49 cm, width 42.5 cm. Gulf Hall. MNA. Cat. no. 4-987. Inv. no. 10-79901.

The basic function of the *yugo*, whose horseshoe-shaped form was fundamental and evidently crucial to its meaning, remains unknown, but like the *palmas* and *hachas*, these votive objects were produced in spite of great technical difficulty. The interpretation of the *yugo* has been the subject of discussion since 1880, and various theories have been proposed; archaeological discoveries have verified that it is associated with the ball game and with the cult of the dead, as well as with the rites associated with them. One theory, now totally discredited, held that the *yugos* were stone copies of the belts (made of a totally different material) used by the ball-game players.

The theory that, according to the Mesoamerican concept, *yugos* were associated with the underworld, is corroborated firstly by the fact that they have been discovered in burials, and secondly because most of them are carved with the image of a toad, an animal that represented the earth in nearly all Mesoamerican cultures. This *yugo* is exceptional, as its ends meet, which is a very rare phenomenon; there are only two or three *yugos* of this type in existence. However, the owl that is carved on it corresponds to the symbolism of the *yugos*, as it represents the world of darkness and death, as well as sacrifice. Among other creatures carved on *yugos*, apart from the toad, which is the most frequent, are the jaguar, the quetzal and the eagle. *m.c.l.*

70. *PALMA* REPRESENTING A CROCODILE

Centre of Veracruz culture. Gulf Coast. Classic (A.D. 200-900). Stone. Height 52.5 cm, width 22.5 cm, depth 14 cm. Gulf Hall. MNA. Cat. no. 4-976. Inv. no. 10-9823.

Thoroughly at home in the Gulf Coast environment, the crocodile inhabited, and continues to inhabit, the banks of rivers and the edges of swamps, where the civilisation of this region evolved. It is for this reason that it is associated with all the Gulf Coast groups, who depicted it in stone or clay, either showing it in its entirety or using just its head as a headdress for

figures modelled in clay. Linked with the concepts of earth and water, the crocodile stood out among other animals because of its amphibian nature, which ensured it a special place among Mesoamerican deities. The crocodile form was used as one of the hieroglyphs of the days of the calendar, with the name of *cipactli*.

In this piece, the artist took advantage of the shape of the *palma* to carve the animal's tail curled round on the upper part. In other examples, the *palmas* are decorated with the interlacing and scrolls that define the so-called El Tajín style of the Classic period of Veracruz. This *palma* shows all the traits characteristic of these objects at the time of their greatest popularity (A.D. 600-900); later, they were reduced in size and became broader. Occasionally, they were combined with elements of the *hachas* to create hybrid objects.   *m.c.l.*

71. *PALMA*

Centre of Veracruz culture. Gulf Coast. Classic (A.D. 200-900). Stone. Height 75 cm, width 20 cm, depth 15 cm. Gulf Hall. MNA. Cat. no. 4-1882. Inv. no. 10-3050.

This piece forms part of the series of sculptures from the coast of the Gulf of Mexico associated with the ball game and the cult of the dead.

The name *palma* suggests the form of a palm leaf; that is, narrower at the bottom and broadening out towards the top. The sculptures are generally between 50 and 80 centimetres in height, although later they became shorter; however, they retained their bases, which were intended to hold them upright. Some *palmas* have decorative elements associated with human sacrifice; others show only the motifs that are found on nearly all the *yugos*, *hachas* and *palmas*. There is a faint similarity between the form of the *palmas* and the ornaments of certain ball-game players, for instance those represented in the Ball Court at Chichén Itzá or on the Aparicio Stela, Veracruz. They were probably included in the paraphernalia that was used by the participants of the ceremony of which the ball-game was a part. By the time this palma was produced, fairly late on, the meaning of the elements that were supposed to decorate this type of object had probably been lost. The shape remained, but the association with the cult of the dead and with all the concepts associated with the game are likely to have been forgotten.   *m.c.l.*

72. VOTIVE *HACHA*

Centre of Veracruz culture. Gulf Coast. Classic (A.D. 200-900). Stone. Height 37.5 cm, width 21.5 cm, depth 4.8 cm. In store. MNA. Cat. no. 4-2054. Inv. no. 10-222305.

Votive *hachas* formed part of the *yugo-hacha-palma* trilogy mentioned above. The *hacha* is a stone sculpture whose form is deeply significant but not yet understood. It generally consists of a thin stone, with an average height of 20 to 30 centimetres and a width that is always less than its height, with the same figure carved on both sides. All known *hachas* have been carved so that they can be placed upright and viewed from both sides; they seem to have been made to be embedded, forming part of an architectural unit. Might they have been ball-game markers, like the famous *guacamaya* heads in the Ball Court at Copán?

Human and animal heads predominate, undoubtedly as a result of a certain type of head cult which required expression through a particular form and style, not practised by any other Mesoamerican culture. The facial features correspond to real physical types, and may well portray actual individuals, accompanied by decorative elements. Here, the head bears a simple headdress which shows off the polish of the stone. *m.c.l.*

73. PRIESTESS

Centre of Veracruz culture. Tlaltixcoyan, Veracruz. Classic (A.D. 200-900). Clay. Height 49.5 cm, width 45 cm. In store. MNA. Cat. no. 4-2004. Inv. no. 10-70586.

Clay was a malleable material obedient to the whim of the Veracruz artist, allowing, for instance, the grace of the female figure and the sensual lines of clothing to be modelled in representations of women. This hollow piece represents a priestess or, more probably, the goddess herself, with a wide headdress and a full dress, or *huipil*, decorated with wide horizontal bands. Small dots of black paint decorate the eyes and mouth, confirming that this piece was connected with a particular goddess whose mouth was stained with black and who was extremely important in Veracruz: this female figure was undoubtedly dressed for a ceremony dedicated to the goddess of providence and mother of the gods. As part of the ritual, women danced and sang, and one woman, who represented the goddess herself, was finally decapitated. Her sacrifice served to provide new forces for the regeneration of all forms of life.

All the Mesoamerican cultures had goddesses equivalent to the ones represented on the Gulf Coast, but no other region attributed the same importance to them. The quality and size of these Classic clay sculptures remained unsurpassed by those of any other culture of later years. *m.c.l.*

74. PRIESTESS

Centre of Veracruz culture. El Faisán, Veracruz. Classic (A.D. 200-900). Clay. Height 34.5 cm, width 29.1 cm. In store. MNA. Cat. no. 4-3468. Inv. no. 10-228045.

This sculpture was produced from a mould, and is hollow at the back. Sculptures of this type generally consist of whistles or whistle-bells, as in this case. The cream-coloured clay has been decorated with red and black paint; black paint was frequently employed by the coastal groups to decorate clay sculpture, and was dedicated in particular to the goddess Tlazoltéotl. Eyes, hair, necklaces and teeth were all painted black; the decoration of teeth with black paint was still customary in the sixteenth century, as recorded in Spanish chronicles. Priestesses were richly attired, and their bodies painted all over. Their clothing consisted of a skirt with geometric decorations of triangles, stepped frets and parallel lines, while the garment covering the breast and upper part of the body was decorated with symbols. The head of the statuette, which has a deformed skull, is decorated with black paint, and the symbol of movement is painted in red and black on the cheeks. The style and technique firmly indicate that the work dates from the last years of the Classic period, by which time the volume of a sculpture was no longer considered important. *m.c.l.*

75. SCULPTURE ASSOCIATED WITH TLAZOLTÉOTL, GODDESS OF FERTILITY

Centre of Veracruz culture. Gulf Coast. Classic (A.D. 200-900). Clay. Height 90 cm, width 53 cm. In store. MNA. Cat. no. 4-3113. Inv. no. 10-221983.

In Veracruz, certain exceptional pieces were modelled in clay that have no parallel in any other Mesoamerican culture. The size of the pieces, which reach a height of up to 1.6 metres, represents a technical advance in terms of both the modelling and their excellent firing, although the type of oven used remains an enigma. The perfection with which they were manufactured demonstrates that they were not one-off pieces, but rather the work of specialists with the weight of tradition behind them, who showed great skill. The female figure is one of the subjects best represented in clay; woman in various roles, as mother, priestess, warrior or goddess, is a recurring theme which is expressed in some of the most versatile and significant sculptures of the Gulf Coast peoples during the Prehispanic era. The dark staining around the mouth indicates that this hollow piece represents the goddess Tlazoltéotl, one of the livelier and more colourful of the Gulf Coast deities. When she is represented as the mother who died during childbirth, she carries a shield and a belt of serpents that convert her into a warrior; in that case, she is recompensed by the honour of accompanying the sun on its departure at the end of the day. Although this beautiful sculpture wears the serpent belt, she is believed to be a priestess rather than a woman-warrior. *m.c.l.*

76. PRIESTESS

Centre of Veracruz culture. Gulf Coast. Classic (A.D. 200-900). Clay. Height 50 cm, width 31 cm, depth 21 cm. Museo de Antropología de la Universidad Veracruzana . Jalapa, Veracruz. Inv. no. 10-1028.

Throughout history, world art has frequently shown us the expression of human happiness through figures smiling or laughing. The clay figures of smiling men and women of the Classic period in Veracruz (A.D. 200-900), commonly called "smiling-face figurines", are exceptional for this very characteristic, both in terms of their extremely human sentiment and because of their beauty. Hollow figures representing smiling men, women and children began being made at the beginning of the Christian era in the southern-central region of Veracruz, between the Blanco and Papaloapan Rivers. Sculptures of this type were left as offerings to the dead for at least 900 years. In general, they were made from moulds, with heads and bodies made separately and then joined together; some are whistles or bells, and all are closely associated with music and dance. Men are represented with loincloths and a band on the chest, ornaments in the ears, necklaces in the form of bells, and bells around their ankles; they often hold musical instruments in their raised hands. The women wear skirts decorated with rich, geometric patterns in relief; the most common are stepped frets, combinations of angles, and scrolls, spirals, criss-cross patterns, rattlesnakes and serpent heads. On their breasts they wear a band or the triangular garment known as a *quechquemitl* (*quechquemetl*), or else they are bare-breasted. They wear earflares, necklaces and occasionally bracelets.

All these figures have deformed heads and, on what appears to be a cap, they have a figure that is either a monkey, a serpent, a heron, a stepped fret or simple crossed angles at the centre in the form of an adornment. Some of them have half-open mouths displaying teeth that have been filed down into points. The Mesoamerican custom of mutilating teeth must have been in existence for around 1000 years before the Christian era, and continued in practise until the sixteenth century, especially among the coastal peoples. Most of the figures have their arms stretched out at the sides of the body, or raised to the level of their heads, in a clear posture of dance; occasionally they hold one hand to the mouth in the gesture of making a noise. In other rare examples, the arms are mobile, joined to the body by means of a cord, and are reminiscent of the Teotihuacán figures known as "puppets". They are probably related to the rites and ceremonies of the cult of the goddess Tlazoltéotl, who symbolised vital energy, celebrated through dance, laughter, music and drunkenness all emphasising the regeneration of life. She was also associated with the mystical meaning of music and dance represented by the monkey.   *m.c.l.*

77. REPRESENTATION OF DUALITY

Totonac culture. Port of Veracruz. Post-Classic (A.D. 900-1521). Stone. Height 44.5 cm, width 22.5 cm. Museo de Antropología de la Universidad Veracruzana. Jalapa, Veracruz. Cat. no. PJ.3975. Inv. no. 10-3975.

At the crux of Mesoamerican religion was the concept of duality, first manifested in masks representing life and death in the form of a face of which one half was without flesh. This idea is repeated continuously throughout all the civilisations in Prehispanic Mexico, although it is not always expressed in the same way. Here, the artist has left half of the head without any detail. The presence of death no longer appears, nor do any of the other elements that were associated with the other part of the duality, such as life-death, light-darkness, sky-earth. Had the meaning represented by duality been abandoned, or was the artist seeking a more abstract solution than other, earlier sculptors had been able to find?
Executed shortly before the arrival of the Spaniards, this piece, though it may lack the mastery of earlier times, retains the meaning that had been expressed since the Pre-Classic period, some 600 years before the Christian era.   *m.c.l.*

78. MURAL FRAGMENT FROM LAS HIGUERAS, VERACRUZ

Gulf Coast culture. Las Higueras, Veracruz. Classic (A.D. 200-900). Clay, stucco and paint. Height 50 cm, width 60 cm, depth 8 cm. Museo de Antropología de la Universidad Veracruzana. Jalapa, Veracruz. Cat. no. 4883.

As well as having an aesthetic value, the paintings of Las Higueras provide a great deal of information about Prehispanic life in the Gulf Coast region. The subject matter of these murals has been carefully studied, as the themes indicate what was considered important by these coastal peoples; the same gods appear in these murals as are represented in low reliefs and sculptures, although here they are dressed differently and are associated with specific colours. Thus, the sun is painted in the form of a man whose torso has become a circle with four rays; the moon is a woman wearing a richly decorated garment; the maize plant is turquoise in colour because of its high religious

value. Other gods who appear are Xipe, the god of springtime, the Hurricane and the lizard, who was considered to be the monster of the earth. Accompanying the gods are priests, who wear quetzal-feather crests, carrying batons in their hands and bags for the *copal* or incense that they burned in the temples. Musicians with large trumpets who took part in the ceremonies, blowing into caracols during the processions, also appear; next to them come women holding banners.
Subject-matter that is both political and religious, such as the investiture of authority, is evident in various scenes. Decapitated ball-game players were painted in contrasting colours, showing how their blood was transformed into seven serpents — a motif also represented in other works in the same region.   *m.c.l.*

79. FIGURINE WITH CHILD

Huastec culture. Gulf Coast. Classic (A.D. 200-900). Clay. Height 30 cm, width 9.5 cm. Gulf Hall. MNA. Cat. no. 3-412. Inv. no. 10-223605.

Whatever the medium used, Huastec art displayed particularly well-defined characteristics, giving rise to a singular style that contrasts with those of other Mesoamerican societies. The Huastecs' cultural manifestations of the Classic period (A.D. 200-900) reached a level of development that represented the culmination of a long-standing tradition. In ceramics, clay figurines with slender, graceful lines began to appear, in which the female body is portrayed naked, with slim hips, large thighs and erect breasts on a long, stem-like body, surmounted by a small head wearing a tall headdress. This physical type (undoubtedly an ideal, as Huastec women were, and still are, short) would have been a ritualistic representation of the essence of woman.
These Classic figurines were modelled by hand in a cream-coloured clay, decorated with white, and occasionally black, paint (tar that is still found on the surface of this petoleum-producing region, the use of which was characteristic of Gulf-Coast ceramics in Prehispanic Mexico).
In some cases, the headdress is formed by a diadem surmounted by a feather crest; in others, the hair is rolled up in a tall chignon, increasing the height of the individual. The figurines' ornamentation, rendered in an appliqué technique, consist of necklaces, bracelets and earflares, although occasionally they have narrow waists which has led to the assumption that they might be female ball-game players. The female as a source of nourishment is emphasised in this figurine by the presence of a small child sucking at the mother's breast.   *m.c.l.*

80. SCULPTURE ASSOCIATED WITH FERTILITY

Huastec culture. Gulf Coast. Post-Classic (A.D. 900-1521). Stone. Height 57 cm, width 17 cm, depth 32 cm. In store. MNA. Cat. no. 3-657. Inv. no. 10-222230.

One of the principal themes of Huastec sculpture was that of the elderly figure holding a *coa* or dibble stick. These are highly original works, expressing the long-established Mesoamerican concept of duality, in which opposites come into contact and are fused together. The representation of man in the final stages of his life, when he is hunchbacked and covered in wrinkles, toothless and with legs bent almost double by old age, is transformed into a symbol of vitality and filled with a sexual force that makes him the supreme progenitor; the rod in his hands represents the wooden instrument used to make a hole in the earth to take the seed that ensures the continuous regeneration of life. The elderly man, close to death, is also the initiator of new life; thus are combined the extremities of the lifespan of all beings in the world. Sculptures of this type began to be made towards the end of the Classic period (A.D. 800), and were modelled at different times and by different hands; they are more-or-less realistic, with extremely accurate stone-working and all sorts of ornamentation; the flower on the shoulder of this sculpture indicates that the figure represents the eternal vitality of nature. By contrast, other figures are barely schematic representations, in which the broken silhouette of a stone was used to delicately suggest the hunchback; however, the face and the hands holding the rod are generally well-worked, and are the fundamental attributes of this figure. *m.c.l.*

81. PHALLIC SCULPTURE

Huastec culture. Gulf Coast. Post-Classic (A.D. 900-1521). Stone. Height 156 cm, width 80 cm. In store. MNA. Cat. no. 3-742. Inv. no. 10-229763.

The cult of the phallus was extremely important among the Huastecs; they were not the only Mesoamerican peoples to practise it, but they were the only ones to express it in a significant number of works of art in stone. A large number of sculptures representing males clearly display their sexual attributes; many of these figures were destroyed in the sixteenth century by the Spanish friars who came to America to convert the indigenous population to Christianity, and for whom the cult of fertility expressed through sexuality appeared to be the work of the devil.

According to Mexica traditions of the Late Post-Classic period, the Huastecs were both lascivious and shameless: the nudity of heroes and others associated with this culture is mentioned in various episodes as improper conduct typical of the group. The ritualistic codices of the period, such as the *Codex Borbonicus*, record that in the ceremony of the mother-goddess Toci, the dancers wore large, artificial phalluses.

This sculpture was discovered around 1890 in the plaza of a small town in the State of Hidalgo called Yahualica, in a region currently known as the Hidalgo Huasteca. It was sent to the Museo Nacional de Antropología in Mexico City this year. In Yahualica at sowing time, the sculpture was traditionally hung with floral garlands while the inhabitants danced around it to request fertility for their fields. *m.c.l.*

82. GODDESS OF FERTILITY

Huastec culture. Tampico, Tamaulipas. Post-Classic (A.D. 900-1521). Stone. Height 116 cm, width 47 cm, depth 15 cm. Museo Regional de San Luis Potosí. Cat. no. M.R.SLP 2-6. Inv. no. 10-336136.

Like all the groups that inhabited the Gulf Coast, the Huastecs were obsessed with giving form to the forces of nature and the continuity of life. These ideas were embodied by woman, and for this reason she was continually represented in both stone and clay. The Huastec goddesses had similar characteristics to each other, although their attributes are very clear. Here, the

sculpture is carved using simple, soft lines, probably in response to the type of stone from which it was made.

The large headdress consists of three parts, the conical cap, a rectangular section and, at the rear, the upright feather "ruff" that stretches from one shoulder to the other. The earflares, which consist of a circular bead and a second element hanging from it, also appear on certain other goddesses.

The figure's chest is bare, with the finely indicated breasts that are a fundamental feature of these sculptures, as are the hands on the stomach; in this example, the fingers are shown in an unusual interlocking position. The lower part of the body is suggested by a skirt that has been left plain. The face has an expression of great tranquility, and the facial features are beautifully indicated. The artist appears to have been particularly concerned with giving a perfect finish to those parts that were crucial for understanding the symbolism of the deity, and did not detail other parts that were less important. The sculpture is from the Prehispanic site known as Las Flores, which is in the city of Tampico. *m.c.l.*

83. GODDESS OF FERTILITY

Huastec culture. Tampico, Tamaulipas. Post-Classic (A.D. 900-1521). Stone. Height 117 cm, width 41 cm, depth 12 cm. Gulf Hall. MNA. Cat. no. 3-1. Inv. no. 10-81365.

This piece comes from an area surrounding the city of Tampico, an important commercial port in the north of the Gulf of Mexico, and a region where there are many Huastec archaeological remains. This work corresponds to a group of female representations in which the ornamentation that was particular to the goddess, that is, conical cap, a rectangular section and a fan-shaped crest, are presented schematically. Her face, which appears to be that of a corpse, has closed eyes and a rigid expression not seen in other goddesses. The crudely-carved hands are placed on the stomach in the same position as most of the female representations. The lower part of the body is covered by a skirt with a simple decoration at the front.

The Huastecs were deeply concerned with the human body, both female and male; when sexual attributes were shown they were sculpted in a naturalistic manner. As a general rule, women are portrayed naked from the waist upwards, and men are completely nude. A particularly important role was attributed to this goddess, whose hands on her stomach indicate the source of the vital energy which produces life and its eternal regeneration.

Huastec stone sculptures revolve around a religious lunar concept, consisting of elements of fertility, rain, woman, serpent and death, as well as periodical regeneration. This rich mythological concept produced very different representations, as each of its aspects responded to a specific deity, but all of them are related to one another. *m.c.l.*

84. PRIEST'S HEAD

Huastec culture. El Consuelo, San Luis Potosí. Post-Classic (A.D. 900-1521). Stone. Height 42 cm, width 25 cm, depth 12 cm. Casa de la Cultura, San Luis Potosí. Inv. no. DB-CCP-4/IV/71-1RMA.

The Huastecs of the Post-Classic period (A.D. 900-1521) built houses and tombs and executed paintings in Tamuín and the surrounding area, in the State of San Luis Potosí. From these buildings come some of their best sculptures, especially the sculpture known as The Adolescent, which has been called the masterpiece of Huastec art.

This head, which is all that remains of the original piece, comes from the same place. The stone has been carved with a rare softness and delicacy, the facial features finely traced, eyelids well-defined by a thin line and irises that resemble buttons. The nose is broken, but there is evidence to show that there was a nose-plug, an ornament frequently used by the Huastecs. Thin, half-open lips reveal the purposely mutilated teeth; scarification of the cheeks also appears.

The headdress is formed by a wide band at the front of the forehead, a conical cap and, at the rear, a fan-shape. The remaining earflare is in two parts, similar to those of many other stone sculptures.

In spite of the quality of the craftsmanship, a certain decadence is evident in this piece: the symbolic elementsb have been reduced to an excessive simplicity, implying a corresponding decline in their importance, and the possibility that they had become purely decorative elements.   *m.c.l.*

85. CHICOMECOATL, GODDESS OF FERTILITY

Huastec culture. Castillo de Teayo, Veracruz. Post-Classic (A.D. 900-1521). Stone. Height 150 cm, width 42 cm, depth 26 cm. In front of the Gulf Hall. MNA. Cat. no. 3-734. Inv. no. 10-157014.

This piece comes from Castillo de Teayo, Veracruz, a Huastec site until the end of the fifteenth century, when external religious, political and aesthetic ideas were introduced by the Mexica empire through conquest. The sculpture clearly expresses this influence, as it has all the formal characteristics of the Mexica culture and is particularly related to the goddesses of Mexica codices dating from the Late Post-Classic period.

The sculpture has been identified both with the goddess of maize and the goddess of fertility, but in any case there can be no doubt that it belongs to the group of images related to agriculture and the provision of food.

The figure is framed by the block of stone, which constrains it within rigid vertical lines descending from the head to the hips, becoming slightly less pronounced in the skirt, legs and feet. The front of the tall headdress displays the glyph representing the year, a triangle with a trapezium, a common element among sculptures of this period from Castillo de Teayo; feathers, rosettes and a chignon complete the headdress. These ornaments appear on other goddesses from the area of similar date, but their breasts are bare, as was usual in representations of Huastec goddesses. Here, the breast are hidden under the triangular garment known as the *quechquemitl*.   *m.c.l.*

86. PRIEST ASSOCIATED WITH DEATH AND VENUS

Huastec culture. El Naranjo, Veracruz. Post-Classic (A.D. 900-1521). Stone. Height 140 cm, width 52 cm, depth 22 cm. Gulf Hall. MNA. Cat. no. 3-590. Inv. no. 10-3153.

In Veracruz, "The Priest of El Naranjo" is the name given to this sculpture, which represents a handsome and exceptionally ornamented male. The conical cap, a typically Huastec feature, is crowned by a row of feathers, and adorned at the front by a skull, forming the figure's headdress. The priest also wears spiral shell earflares, like many other Huastec sculptures, and a sort of short tunic, on which sits an enormous pectoral with designs related to the god Quetzalcóatl. Beneath the tunic, at the centre of the body, is a heart-shaped protruberance. The idea of symbolically placing the heart here does not seem so extraordinary when we consider the indigenous traditions that still exist among some Huastec culture groups on the Gulf Coast.

A short richly decorated skirt covers the lower part of the body, and is reminiscent of some of the garments of Toltec sculptures.

The crudely carved legs have the appearance of columns rather than of human limbs. There is a marked contrast between the way in which the upper and lower parts of the body were carved, but in spite of this, the sculpture has a magnificent and imposing look combined with a restful simplicity.   *m.c.l.*

60. VESSEL

61. FIGURE

62. FIGURE

63. SEATED BABY-FACE FIGURE

64. HUMANISED JAGUAR

65. DIGNITARY

66. SERPENT'S HEAD

67. JAGUAR

67. JAGUAR

68. JAGUAR

68. JAGUAR

69. *YUGO* FROM A FUNERARY OFFERING

70. *PALMA* REPRESENTING A CROCODILE

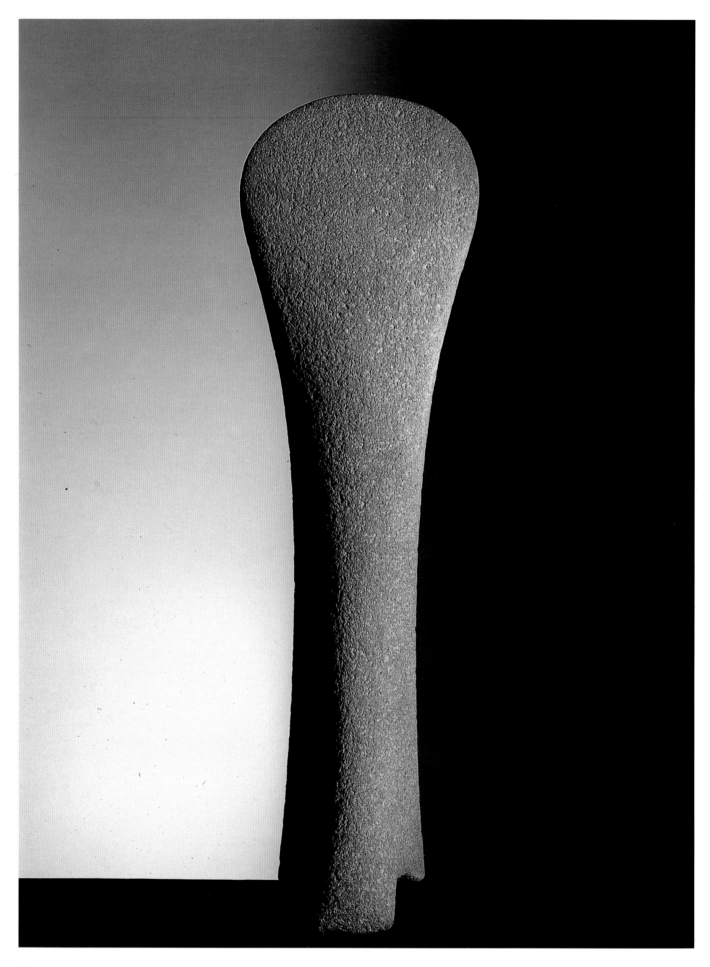

71. *PALMA*

72. VOTIVE *HACHA*

73. PRIESTESS

200

74. PRIESTESS

75. SCULPTURE ASSOCIATED WITH TLAZOLTEOTL, GODDESS OF FERTILITY

75. SCULPTURE ASSOCIATED WITH TLAZOLTEOTL, GODDESS OF FERTILITY

76. PRIESTESS

77. REPRESENTATION OF DUALITY

78. MURAL FRAGMENT FROM LAS HIGUERAS, VERACRUZ

206

79. FIGURINE WITH CHILD

80. SCULPTURE ASSOCIATED WITH FERTILITY

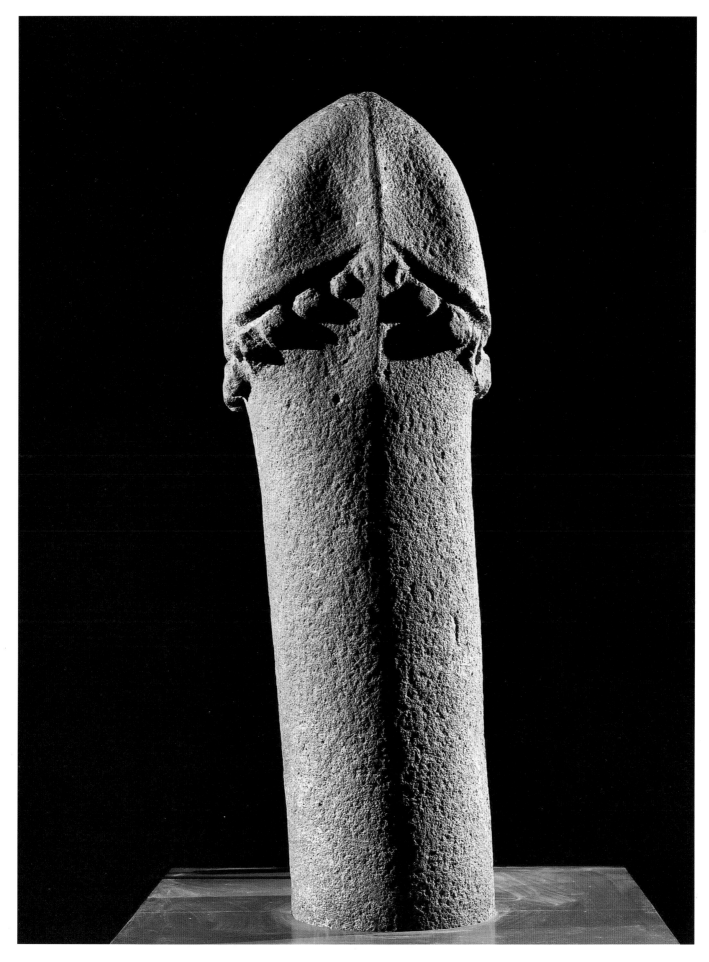

81. PHALLIC SCULPTURE

82. GODDESS OF FERTILITY

83. GODDESS OF FERTILITY

84. PRIEST'S HEAD

84. PRIEST'S HEAD

85. CHICOMECOATL, GODDESS OF FERTILITY

86. PRIEST ASSOCIATED WITH DEATH AND VENUS

13. THE MAYA REGION: LAND OF ARTISTS AND ASTRONOMERS

Amalia Cardós de Méndez

Maya culture flourished in an enormous region of approximately 400,000 square kilometres, whose topographical characteristics cover a range of extremes: there are plains that lie almost at sea-level, as well as high land; limestone deposited on coral, and volcanic areas; country rich in abundant rivers, and landscape that is virtual desert. Vegetation varies from exuberant tropical vegetation to *chaparral* or thicket in dry, arid zones. Vast tracts of coast extend along the Yucatán peninsula, facing the Gulf of Mexico and the Caribbean, while the southern part of the country is washed by the Pacific Ocean. The Maya area includes the whole of south-east Mexico, from the Barra Tupilco in Tabasco to the Ulúa River in the Republic of the Honduras and the Lempa River in the Republic of El Salvador in Central America. Although a common cultural substratum existed throughout this vast territory, other geographical features favoured the development of regional styles; for this reason, the Maya area has been divided into three zones for research purposes: the Northern, Central and Southern.

The Northern zone comprises the Yucatán peninsula – most of the present-day states of Campeche and Quintana Roo, and all of the state of Yucatán; it is stony and semi-arid, with little rain, and its vegetation, particularly in the northern part, is either scrubwood or thicket, except for the low Puuc hills (which rise less than 100 metres above sea-level) on the border of Yucatán and Campeche; the rest of the area is an extensive low limestone plain, barely above sea-level.
The porous nature of the ground has allowed the rapid filtration of rain water, which, when it meets impermeable layers of rock, forms a subterranean drainage system; in some parts, the same filtration has caused the roof of the water deposits to collapse, appearing on the surface of the ground as natural mouths or *cenotes*, allowing access to the water. In general terms, there are neither rivers nor lagoons in this region, so the *cenotes* are the only natural source of water; it is for this reason that settlements were made near these sources.

The Central zone extends from the Barra Tupilco in Tabasco to the Ulúa River in the Honduras, and includes most of Tabasco and Chiapas, southern Campeche and Quintana Roo, Belize and the Guatemalan Petén; rainfall is plentiful, and the climate is warm and humid; apart from the eastern part of Tabasco, southern Campeche and Quintana Roo, as well as the Petén, which is a vast, medium-height savannah, the rest of the zone is higher and mountainous, with tropical forest growing in the valleys. Cedar and mahogany are to be found growing there, interwoven by thick lianas and air plants; rivers, lakes and lagoons, as well as numerous springs, complete the picture. Generally speaking, of the three Maya zones, it is this central area that provides the most advantageous conditions for human habitation.

The Southern zone comprises the highlands and the coastal belt of the Pacific stretching from Chiapas and Guatemala to the western part of El Salvador. Although some areas are hot and humid, most regions are temperate and cold; there are lands of volcanic origin, forming mountain ranges with valleys in the folds of the hills; these hills, some of which rise to more than 1,500 metres above sea-level, are thick with cypresses and pine trees.
The Mayas were to adapt themselves to this country, with its widely contrasting environment, climate and topography, and it was here that from approximately 2000 B.C. the development of a most knowledgeable and refined culture began.

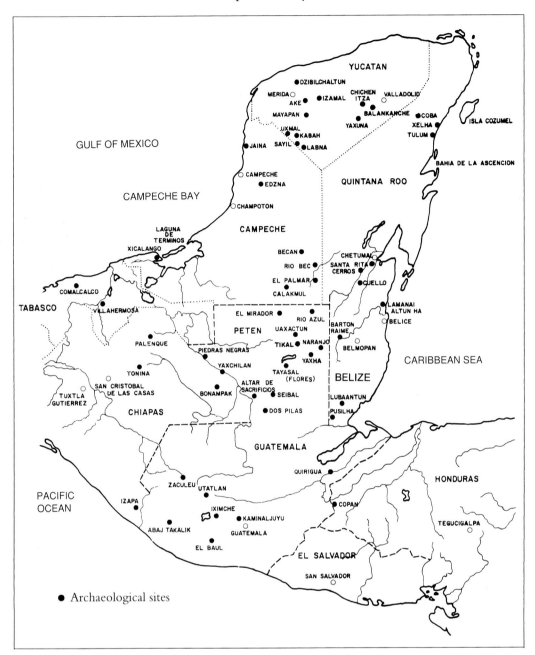

MAYA MAN

The physical characteristics of the Mayas are as follows: they are rather short (the average height of the men is 1.62 metres, and of the women, 1.5 metres) and muscular, with arms that are rather long in comparison to the rest of the body; in general, the head is wide or round, although some of the highland groups have elongated heads, for instance the Tzeltales and the Tzotziles; their hair is straight and dark; the face is wide, with prominent cheekbones; they have aquiline noses; the pronounced eyelid fold gives the eyes an almond-shaped appearance. The Mayas constitute a fairly homogenous group, in so far as these features have become accentuated, or at least preserved.

Several centuries have passed since the Spanish conquest, but nevertheless, this persistent physical type can easily be identified in today's Maya descendants. The only differences among present-day Mayas and extant portraits from the past – in clay, stone, mural paintings, for instance – are due to a series of artificial deformations that were practised in ancient times, either for beautification, or to distinguish them from other groups, and as

an indication of rank or social status. Among the principal deformations are the following:
– The forehead-occipital type, or deforming the cranium, generally achieved by placing two pressurising surfaces (or wooden tablets) on the heads of new-born babies, one against the forehead and the other against the back of the skull, tying them on firmly with rope.
– Dental mutilation, practised by filing the teeth into a different shape, or by boring shallow holes to allow incrustation with some material – pyrite, jadeite or turquoise.
– Intentional strabismus, by hanging a small, light object, possibly a ball of some sort of resin, from the hair of the new-born baby, which dangled between the eyes and forced the child to direct his pupils towards one another. This type of deformation is believed to have been practised on infants dedicated to the cult of the god of the sun.
– Tattooing and scarifications. The latter were achieved by lightly cutting the skin, according to a previously chosen design, and infecting the wound so that a thick, lumpy scar was obtained, leaving a permanent decoration.
There can be little doubt that the most commonly practised and widespread custom was that of the deformation of the skull: by depressing the forehead, the Mayas caused the jaw and nasal part to protrude, giving rise to the classic Maya profile, as seen in Prehispanic representations of humans.
The languages still spoken by modern descendants belong to the Maya linguistic family. Among the principal ones are: Maya, in the Yucatán peninsula; Quiché, Cakchiquel, Quekchí, Mam and Pokomán in Guatemala; Lacandón, Chol, Chontal, Tzetzal, Tzotzil and Chañabal in Chiapas; and Chortí in Guatemala and the Honduras.

ECONOMY

Technology
When the Spaniards arrived, the Mayas – like other Mesoamerican groups – were practically living in the Stone Age with respect to technology; metals, which were only discovered at a late stage (in the tenth century) were used principally for ornament. Carved and polished stone was employed not only for the manufacture of tools and implements for all kinds of work, but also for weapons, vessels, ornament, and for obtaining coloured pigments.
Many of the primary materials were obtained from local flora and fauna to furnish Maya needs. Among those of animal origin are skins, feathers, small seed or cochineal, wax, shell, marine caracols, bones, teeth and some fish spines, used for clothing, tools, musical instruments and ritualistic objects.
Fundamental among basic materials of organic origin are wood (including sapodilla, mahogany and cedar), textile fibres (cotton and henequen), wild palm trees, resins (*copal*, rubber and liquidambar) and certain dyes (indigo and *palo de tinte*), which were used in the construction of huts, weapons, canoes and tool handles, as well as banners, paper, material for clothing, ropes with multiple uses, incenses for ceremonies, adhesives, balms for perfume and substances for dyeing and decorating clothing.
Mineral-based materials included jade, pyrite, obsidian, alabaster, red ochre, alum, haematite and cinnabar.

Agriculture
The Mayas were farmers, and the agriculture practised was (and continues to be today) that of the *milpa*, or maize field, and the *roza*, or slash-and-burn system, which consists of cutting down and burning vegetation to clear the terrain and leave it ready for sowing. This system has the disadvantage of rapidly depleting the land, so that the farmer soon has to seek new ground for his *milpa*.
Recent discoveries indicate that the Mayas may have used certain methods of achieving more intensive cultivation, through the construction of irrigation channels, or sowing along the banks of rivers, lakes, lagoons and swamps. Independently, a theory has been put forward to suggest that the diet of the Maya people was based not on maize but on the fruit of the *ramón* (a type of brushwood), which grows wild in the Petén and in the

Yucatán peninsula; if this was the case, control over a permanent population would have been easier, since the staple food was assured so time was available for the construction of temples and other structures in the ceremonial centres. As well as the basic cultivation of maize, beans and squash, historical sources mention a wide variety of fruits, animals and plants used to complement the main diet, as well as for medicines and for the development of domestic implements; in other words, the Mayas continued to practise gathering, hunting and fishing. Spears, bows and arrows, fishing nets and, in later years, shell and copper fish-hooks were all used for these activities.

Trade

The inhabitants of the separate Maya regions began to exchange basic materials and products from very early times, in order to supplement the deficiencies of their own area. When the Spaniards arrived, according to historical sources, commercial activity had reached a high level of development as a result of the exchange of crude materials and products dating back several centuries. Successful trading led to the rise of professional merchants and market-places for the exchange of merchandise, as well as both land and maritime communication routes.

Numerous pathways, from simple paths to wide paved causeways or *sacbe*, connected the large ceremonial centres, and it is possible that the routes taken by the Spaniards – conquistadors and missionaries – were the same ancient overland routes as those used by Maya merchants. Among the most important routes were the one followed by Cortés on his journey from Tabasco to Las Hibueras (today the Honduras), and the route connecting northern Yucatán with the Petén (Guatemala), taken by Father Orbita y Fuensalida.

The Maya merchants had various gods, the most important of which was El Chuah, patron of the cacao plantations; the merchants generally settled near the temples, and held a sort of merchant court to guard the correct procedures in commercial transactions.

By the time the Spaniards arrived, merchants enjoyed considerable respect, and chronicles record that at some sites, it was customary to "make the richest merchant into a lord".

SOCIAL AND POLITICAL ORGANISATION

Ancient Maya society was divided into social classes; power was exercised by a privileged caste of priests and noblemen, whose material and political needs were seen to by the local community.

The existing ruins of the buildings, temples and "palaces" constituted the ceremonial centre of what must have been the very heart of the city; residential houses were distributed around it, in concentric circles – those closest to the centre being residences of noblemen and priests, those furthest away housing the lower classes, who lived in groups scattered over a wide area; all of these were focused on centres where structures dedicated to ritual and the ceremonies of the gods were built.

Maya territory was probably divided into a sort of federation of politically independent states, which were nevertheless united by strong cultural ties. The government was in the hands of a small select and cultured group of noble priests who, during the Classic period, attained a high degree of scientific knowledge, dominating the population. They justified their economically unproductive position by serving as intermediaries between the people and their gods.

During the time of the Spanish conquest, the ruling class was headed by the *Halach-uinic* (true man) who exercised the highest civil and military power from the "city", which acted as the capital of an independent "state" or territory. A number of minor functionaries performed complementary tasks in public administration, forming a complete bureaucratic hierarchy.

At the head of the priesthood was the *Ahuacan*, which means "serpent lord" – the great priest who, during the Classic epoch, had also performed the civil functions of the *Halach-uinic* – and who was followed by a series of minor priests with specific functions, known in general as *Ah Kin*.

The rest of the nation were *ah chembal-uinicoob*, the common people on whom the economic and material provision of the whole of the population was dependent.

The specialised craftsmen, merchants, farmers and warriors, and all those dedicated to minor offices, such as hunters and fishermen, formed part of this majority group, while the lower echelon consisted of slaves; these last could find themselves labelled as such because of, among other things, delinquency, for being the child of a slave or through being a prisoner of war. Historical documentation suggests that the merchants and warriors who also formed part of this group, while remaining relatively underprivileged during the Classic period, were to emerge as a rich and influential middle class which reached a high social and economic position during the period preceding the arrival of the Spaniards.

ARCHITECTURE

Architectural planning as such did not exist. Ceremonial centres were built according to the natural topography of the terrain, which determined the location of the different architectural complexes. Characteristic of Maya architecture were the false arch, or corbel or Maya vault, used for the roofs of their constructions. Other features included the building of temples around patios or plazas, forming quadrangles. High pyramidal bases, on which temples were sited, were also common, with a stairway up the front of the pyramid facing the temple. The temple façade was generally decorated on the upper frieze with stone and stucco reliefs; an element known as a *cresteria* (crest), or *peine* (roofcomb), was sometimes built on the roof of the temple. The roofcomb was primarily decorative, with the intention of giving greater importance to the temple by increasing its height; it was usually hollow or made of fretwork, thus avoiding excess weight on the roof. Maya architecture also involved the construction of "palaces" or structures consisting of many rooms on an artificial terrace of a certain height; although some consist only of a row of interconnecting rooms, two or three may be distributed on various floors. The use of stelae and altars, although common to other groups, was developed to its maximum by the Mayas. Both elements form part of architectural groupings, and were distributed within the precincts or patios of the quadrangles, at the foot of stairways or in front of temples.

The presence of the Toltecs, Itzas or Putunes from the tenth century in the Northern zone led to the burgeoning of a number of new forms of expression, in architecture in particular. The use of columns and pillars inside precincts enabled much larger spaces to be roofed than was possible using the corbel vault alone. Other innovations were the use of colonnades around pyramidal platforms, precincts with a single storey or built inside temples, and buildings with a central open patio (such as the Mercado at Chichén Itzá). New architectural details also followed, such as *alfardas* and columns in the form of plumed serpents (the head of which rested on the ground, with the tail bent to hold up the lintel) to form the main temple entrance; there were also pillars in the form of warriors, *tzompantlis*, or stone platforms with rows of skulls strung together; stone tablets depicting rows of warriors stalking tigers; eagles and tigers devouring hearts; and sculptures of atlantes, Chac Mools and standard-bearers, among others.

POTTERY

The Mayas were excellent potters, and in the Classic period the simple monochrome ceramics of earlier years became polychromatic and were enlivened by new forms, techniques and decorative motifs; most common were tripod dishes with a flange at the base, small conical or globular supports, and vessels with or without lids. Decorative motifs ranged from simple and geometric (either symbolic or stylised) to naturalistic. Of particular note are vessels on which bands of glyphs are used to frame scenes of people and animals displaying various postures and gestures, full of realism, and faithfully reproducing not only physical appearance but also details of clothing and ornament. Particular mention should be made of the clay figurines made during this period both from moulds and by hand, decorated with appliqué and coloured paint. While these figurines became increasingly complex through the profusion and detail of their dress, others were simple and realistic, as the figures corresponded to all social classes; thus, there are representations of lords and priests, ball-game players, merchants, warriors, musicians, and representatives of the people, some with physical deformities, others normal; at the same time, a large percentage of clay figurines were in fact musical instruments: bells, whistles and ocarinas.

SCULPTURE

The Mayas were proficient in all the techniques of sculpture: engraving, low and high relief and three-dimensional carving of statues, although, as with architecture, each Maya area developed its own style, partly conditioned by the variety of resources available from the different physical surroundings.

Stone, wood and stucco were the materials used. Stelae and altars provide excellent examples of free-standing sculpture or works that have been carved from a single stone, usually carved with reliefs; in Jonuta and Copán, however, sculptures were carved in the round or as statues.

At Palenque, modelling in stucco reached a high level, both free-standing and in relation to architecture; excellent examples are the stone lintels of Yaxchilán and the wooden lintels of Tikal, with magnificent reliefs representing figure scenes.

In Yucatán, where stone is plentiful, sculpture was highly developed for the mosaic work associated with architecture, which emphasised geometric motifs and in which there was an almost total absence of the human figure. Painting also played a part in architectural terms. As well as murals, sculpture too was painted, as many stelae, altars and stone tablets were polychromatic. Paints of mineral and vegetable origin were used, with differing tones of red, yellow, brown, Maya blue, green, black and white.

KNOWLEDGE

A great deal of the Mayas' knowledge was inherited from other Mesoamerican groups – the Olmecs and Zapotecs – and was noticeably developed and improved. Through their understanding of the concept of zero, they were able to establish vigesimal numbering (using 20 as the unit of calculation) based on a positional system. Numbers were written in columns, with their value multiplied by 20 in each new position in ascending order, or, if they were positioned horizontally, from right to left. Although the Mayas used various signs for the writing of numbers, the most common system used dots and bars; the dot represented the unit, and the bar the number 5. By combining dots and bars, they were able to write up to the number 19. The symbol for zero was a form similar to a four-petalled flower, of which only half was usually represented; to indicate 20, it was sufficent to place the dot or unit in the position of the second symbol, although 20 was also written using the symbol of the moon in the first position.

Another form of representing numbers (from 1 to 13) was by means of hieroglyphs known as "head variants", which are representations of the heads of the thirteen gods associated with these numbers. To represent the numbers 14 to 19, a combination which incorporated the features of the head representing the number 10 was used – resembling the combination of words used to write, for example, 28, twenty and eight. Added to the "head variants" are "full-figure" variants, in which the corresponding bodies were joined to the heads. The Mayas' knowledge of arithmetic, their patient observation of the stars and of the periodic recurrence of natural phenomena enabled them to accumulate and pass down through many generations a series of facts and information which ultimately resulted in a considerable astronomical knowledge, including the ability to predict eclipses and to calculate lunar cycles, as well as the duration of the cycle of Venus, among others.

15. Bar-and-dot number system and head variants

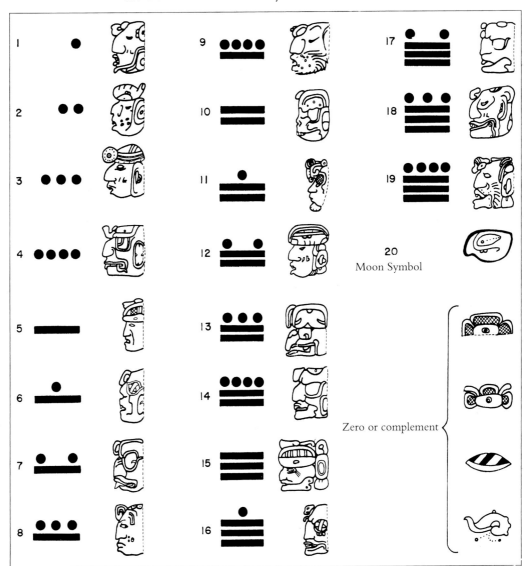

16. Positional numbering system based on the number 20

POSITION	VALUE	MAYA NUMBERS	ARABIC NUMBERS
4.	8,000	(3) x ●●●	= 24,000
3.	400	(8) x ●●● ▬	= 3,200
2.	20	(2) x ●●	= 40
1.	1	(5) x ▬	= 5

17. Names and hieroglyphs of the main units of time

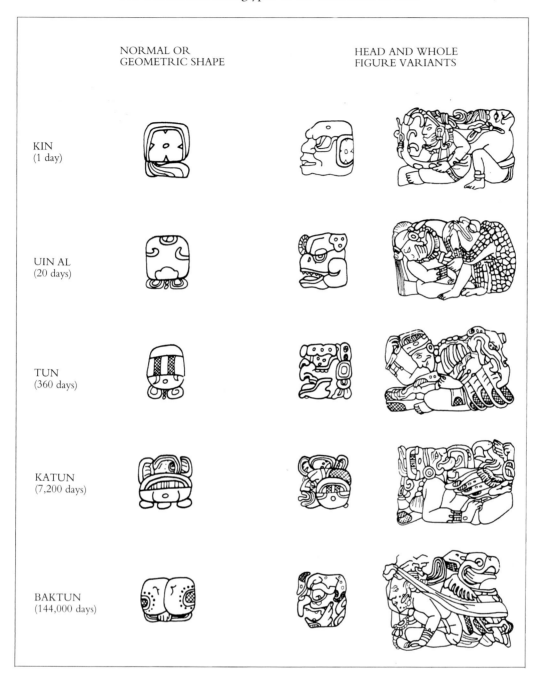

	NORMAL OR GEOMETRIC SHAPE	HEAD AND WHOLE FIGURE VARIANTS
KIN (1 day)		
UIN AL (20 days)		
TUN (360 days)		
KATUN (7,200 days)		
BAKTUN (144,000 days)		

The calendrical system

The Mayas were aware that their civil calendar (of 365 days) did not coincide with the true solar year of 365.2422 days, and that the accumulated error thus had to be periodically corrected; because of this, they made arithmetical calculations and conceived a system of adjustment, which in some cases is more accurate than our own current Gregorian calendar by one ten-thousandth part of the day.

Although the Mayas shared a basic knowledge of the calendrical system with other nations, they managed to develop and perfect it to a greater extent than any other group. They had two different calendars:

The sacred calendar or a cycle of 260 days. This was formed by a combination of the 20 names of the days with the numbers 1 to 13; its functions were of a ritualistic and divinatory nature, and formed the core of the Maya calendrical system. The first day of the cycle was 1 Imix, and in order for the same combination of number and name of day to be repeated, 260 days had to have passed, that is, 20 x 13. For the Mayas, the days represented deities, and the numbers that accompanied them had a similar ranking; thus, matters of personal or general importance were decided according to the omen attributed to each day and its corresponding numeral, as success or failure depended on these.

The civil calendar or year of 365 days. The basis of the civil calendar was the Tun or period of 360 days, divided into 18 periods, or "months", each of 20 days, to which 5 days, the Uayayeb, considered to be ill-omened, were added to complete the 365 days. Each day and each "month", or Uinal, had a particular name, but, like the civil calendar, and other cycles, they had to be coordinated with the sacred calendar or cycle of 260 days. To write a date in the Maya year, the numeral that accompanied each day according to the sacred calendar had to be indicated, together with the one that indicated the position of the month according to the civil calendar. For example:

	(day)	("month")
Dates:	1 Imix	5 Pop
	2 Ik 8	6 Pop
	3 Akbal	7 Pop ... etc.

In the civil calendar, the 20 days bore the same name of each Uinal or "month", and the numeral indicated its position within it. Just as the sacred calendar had ritualistic purposes, the civil calendar was of great importance for agriculture, for the computation of time and for civil and collective activities.

The calendar wheel. The combination of the two calendars formed the cycle of 52 years, or Calendar Wheels, the basis of Maya chronology. As one calendar was larger than the other, for the same date on both calendars to coincide again, 18,980 days, or a period of approximately 52 years, had to have elapsed.

The Mayas also developed a perfect system so that the date of one calendar wheel or 52-year cycle would not be confused with another, through their realisation that the computation of time needed a point of departure. Like our calendrical system, which is based on the birth of Christ and in which we say "so many years before or after Christ", the Mayas chose the date 13.0.0.0.0, 4 Ahau 8 Cumkú (it is not known whether this commemorates a real historical event) as the "era" date in their computation of time, and which in our calendar corresponds to 12 or 14 August of the year 3113 B.C.

As well as the 52-year cycle, the Mayas used other forms of recording dates and computations that covered longer periods, for example:

The Long Count or Initial Series. This is the computation of time that generally appears at the beginning of an inscription, and usually consists of five periods: Baktún, Katún, Tun, Uinal and Kin; the sixth glyph indicates the Kin, or day that is reached by counting the total of days recorded in the whole inscription, starting from the "era" date.

The hieroglyphs are usually placed in pairs, forming two columns and preceded by a very large glyph, which frequently occupies the space of two or four glyphs, and which has been called the introductory or initial glyph;

The Short Count. This is an abbreviated form of the Long Count, used to express the same date; for example, if the Long Count recorded the date 9,16.0.0.0 (9 Baktúns, 16 Katúns, 0 Tuns, 0 Uinales, 0 Kins), day 2 Ahua of the month 13 Tzec, the Short Count abbreviated the figures, much as we do by writing 20/08/89 instead of Saturday 20th of August 1989. The Short Count later became further abbreviated, before the Spanish conquest; if the Mayas knew that the Katún 16 ended on the day 2 Ahua of the month 13 Tzec, it was noted as: Katún 2 Ahua; that is, the Katún which ended on the day 2 Ahua. The period of time that was of greatest interest to the Mayas was the Katún (that is, 20 Tuns or 7,200 days). They believed that the ruler or patron of each Katún exerted the same influence each time it repeated itself, and that likewise historical events, in general terms, also repeated themselves. Because of this, the prophecies related to each Katún had a decisive influence on the events that culminated with the Spanish conquest.

Writing
Examples of Maya writing are found on stelae, altars, lintels and other architectural elements, in mural paintings, on diverse ceramic objects and ornaments, on a variety of

18. Combination of the 260-day sacred calendar and the 365-day civil calendar

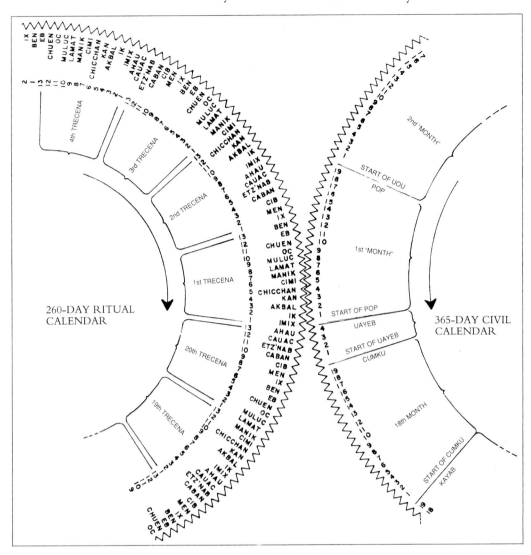

materials and in the only three books or codices that survive, of which only some has been deciphered. The inscriptions refer to computations of time, to astronomical concerns and their associated gods, and, probably, to the predictions and ceremonies that were pertinent to these occasions. In recent years, not only have the names of certain Maya sites or "cities" been identified, but also the dynasties that governed there, as well as individuals and historical events. Maya writing derives from the hieroglyphic type; some signs represent objects that are easily recognisable, but the majority consist of simple geometric shapes or are stylised to such a degree that the objects are unrecognisable. All the signs occupy a rectangular space, which is almost square in some cases and elongated in others; the latter are combined with the former, situated above, below, to the left or right, within a conceptualised rectangle; the distribution of these regular rectangles in an inscription gives it a highly attractive appearance. Many signs represent Maya words, others represent sounds and some have both functions.

RELIGION

Very early in Maya history, Maya religious practices were intimately related to the natural forces that played such a prominent part in their daily life and in the satisfaction of their elementary needs; the ceremonies of the small rural farming communities of that period were probably limited principally to propitiatory rites dedicated to agriculture and fertility, and their most ancient gods were probably the sun, the rain, the moon and, possibly, death. During the Classic period (A.D. 250-900), with the high level of development reached in all aspects, cultural, intellectual and material, a professional priesthood was established which took upon itself the development of the simple naturalistic religion of the earlier period, transforming it into a theological philosophy that became increasingly complex. The majority of known representations of gods date from this time; rarely presented in complete form (except, later, in the codices), they are mostly shown only in part or by allusive symbols. Various of the principal Maya gods have been identified in this form, such as that of the rain (Cháac, the long-nosed god), of the sun (Kinich Ahau), of maize and vegetation (Yum Kaaz), of the moon (Ix Chel), of death (Ah Puch or Yum Cimil) and of the planet Venus (Lahun Chan). For the Mayas, man was made of maize. The myth of creation is narrated in the Popol-Vuh, or the Sacred Book of the Quichés of Guatemala, which relates how the gods wanted to create beings that would worship and adore them. Maize, the principal food of the Mayas (even today) formed their very flesh, and was the object of veneration and worship.

Man's creator was Hunab-Kú, an abstract deity rather than a concrete god, invisible, and elevated to such a degree beyond mortals as to be almost unknown by the people, and of whom no representations seem to exist; he is known to have been the father of Itzam Ná, Lord of the Sky, Day and Night.

19. 260-day sacred calendar

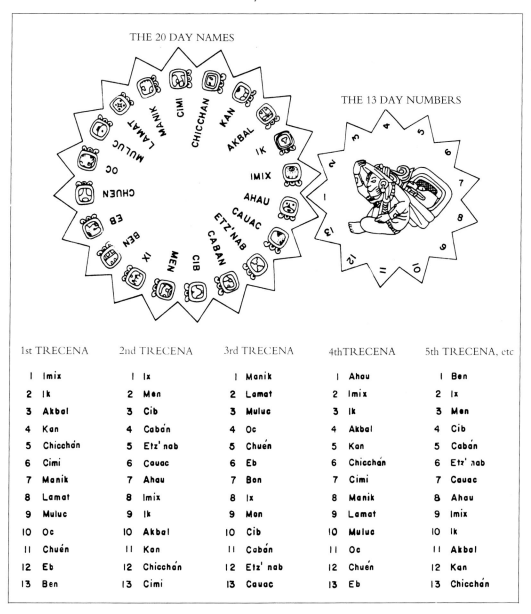

1st TRECENA		2nd TRECENA		3rd TRECENA		4th TRECENA		5th TRECENA, etc	
1	Imix	1	Ix	1	Manik	1	Ahau	1	Ben
2	Ik	2	Men	2	Lamat	2	Imix	2	Ix
3	Akbal	3	Cib	3	Muluc	3	Ik	3	Men
4	Kan	4	Cabán	4	Oc	4	Akbal	4	Cib
5	Chicchán	5	Etz' nab	5	Chuen	5	Kan	5	Cabán
6	Cimi	6	Cauac	6	Eb	6	Chicchán	6	Etz' nab
7	Manik	7	Ahau	7	Ben	7	Cimi	7	Cauac
8	Lamat	8	Imix	8	Ix	8	Manik	8	Ahau
9	Muluc	9	Ik	9	Men	9	Lamat	9	Imix
10	Oc	10	Akbal	10	Cib	10	Muluc	10	Ik
11	Chuén	11	Kan	11	Cabán	11	Oc	11	Akbal
12	Eb	12	Chicchán	12	Etz' nab	12	Chuen	12	Kan
13	Ben	13	Cimi	13	Cauac	13	Eb	13	Chicchán

According to Maya belief, the sky was supported by four gods or "bearers", the *bacabes*, associated with the four compass points and each with a particular colour: red (Chac) for the east; white (Zac) for the north; black (E'ek) for the west; yellow (Kan) for the south. A fifth colour, green (Ya'ax), corresponded to a cardinal point that we do not use: the centre. At each of the four sides of the world was a sacred *ceiba* (a flowering tree), associated with the corresponding colour, and believed to be the tree of abundance that had provided the earliest sustenance for humanity.

The Mayas believed that the sky was divided into thirteen higher levels, on each of which resided particular deities, the *oxlahuntikú* or Thirteen Lords of the Upper World; the underworld, in turn, was divided into nine compartments, each of which was presided over by a god, the *bolontikú* or the Nine Lords of the Night; these were malevolent deities. Little is known of Maya ideas about the shape of the earth, although they seem to have shared the Aztecs' belief in the upper part consisting of an enormous reptile, a type of crocodile, which was the object of a certain cult.

Celestial gods

Itzam Ná was the most important of all Maya gods, and embodied four parts, each assigned to a cardinal point with its respective colour.

The sun was the patron of music and poetry, and was a famous hunter; the moon, in turn, was the divinity of fertility and weaving. Other deities of great importance were the planet Venus and the *chaaques*, rain deities. The *oxlahuntikú* mentioned above also formed part of this group.

Kukulkán, the Maya name for Quetzalcóatl (the plumed serpent, god of wind), seems to have had little influence on the Maya people; although he frequently appears at sites that are representative of Toltec or Itzá influence in the northern Maya zone – principally Chichén Itzá - he did not survive later historical events and changes, and his cult was an ephemeral one, limited to the Post-Classic period, while *chaaques* and other deities are still venerated today.

Gods of the earth

These are principally the gods associated with harvests, such as Yum Kaax, the god of vegetation in general, and of maize in particular, or the jaguar god (equivalent to Tepeyólotl), a deity of both the interior and the exterior of the earth (as both parts coincide or are joined together). The Mayas probably also honoured a group of seven deities associated with the surface of the land, as well as the previously mentioned *bolontikú*, the Nine Lords of the Night, who were the gods of the underworld.

Other gods

Apart from the celestial gods and the gods of the earth and the underworld, the Mayas had other gods connected with specific trades, such as the god of merchants, of warriors, of bee-keepers, of cacao, and of other domestic activities.

They also deified each of their calendrical periods of time, and the numerals, although this type of god had only a minor influence on the majority of the population, and their worship was limited almost exclusively to the priestly caste.

Although the description above suggests a multitude of gods, in reality these consisted of only a few principal deities who were presented as the tutelar patrons of a number of varied concepts or activities, in several different guises.

Rites

Ceremonial practices played an important role in the life of the Mayas, as religion and the worship of the gods formed the axis around which revolved not only daily activities but also major events, gradual changes and the several stages of existence .

The ceremonies included fasts and abstinence (purifications carried out prior to the ceremonies themselves), music and dance performance, orations, the burning of incense (*copal*, an aromatic resin) and sacrifice; the latter varied, and might consist of simple offerings of food, animals and extremely diverse objects, or could involve self-sacrifice, either individual or collective, or human sacrifice using different methods: decapitation, being shot with arrows, asphyxiation through immersion and the extraction of the heart.

The Mayas believed in the immortality of the soul, and in death as something natural, the logical consequence of life. Death was thus not to be awaited with dread, as it signified only the transition to another life, similar to the present one but possibly better. Out of these beliefs, concern arose for the protection of corpses – which might, in the simplest case, involve placing a plate on the head, or, in the most complex, necessitate the construction of tombs - as well as the custom of leaving offerings for the deceased in the belief that these would be useful for them to begin their new life. There can be no doubt that the type of burial was determined by the relative social standing of the deceased, and that this was reflected in the quality of the burial offering.

In the tenth century, invaders from the Central Highlands and the coast of the Gulf of Mexico rudely interrupted the Mayas' peaceful progress, significantly affecting the Maya culture of the peninsular in particular. The presence of these outsiders is clearly expressed in the material remains of the culture dating from the Post-Classic period (A.D. 900-1521), such as monumental architecture, stone sculpture, mural painting, and artistic output such as turquoise, coral, shell and pearl mosaics, the most outstanding examples of which are found in Chichén Itzá, Yucatán.

This evidence underlies the change which became apparent in the Maya culture. It was also the beginning of the Mayas' general demise: civil war, rebellions and enmity were to divide and weaken the unity of the Maya empire.

Militarism was imposed, and artistic and ceremonial activity seems to have ceased; local ceramic production declined, there was greater recourse to importation, and architecture and sculpture dropped in standard. Everything appeared to favour the imminent arrival of the Spaniards and their ultimate conquest of the country

14. THE MAJESTIC ART OF THE MAYAS

Sonia Lombardo de Ruíz

On the island of Jaina, facing the Campeche coasts, multiple burials with offerings were discovered, prompting the belief that the island functioned as a cemetary-sanctuary for the Mayas, and was occupied over a long period.

Among the objects buried in these tombs were found a large number of vessels and figurines, representing a great many different types of individual; in addition to their exceptional beauty, they constitute the richest source of information in existence of an ethnographic nature, providing evidence of physical types, clothing and gestural ornament.

Four figurines are exhibited in this exhibition, two that are hand-modelled, and two made from moulds: many of these were produced in series for votive use.

One of these (plate 87) represents a woman seated with crossed legs, wearing a tunic, necklace and earflares, with short hair combed in an elaborate style and wearing a broad-brimmed hat, apparently made from palm leaves. The simplicity of the various components, graceful and elegant, make this figure one of the "classic" works of the Maya minor arts.

By contrast, in the figurine representing a warrior (plate 88), the expressive language of distortion has been used. The massive body, standing on formidable bird claws, and consisting of flat planes and rolls of clay, generates a great sense of dynamic movement through contrasts of chiaroscuro. The stern, scarified face in the midst of the crudeness of the figurine is highly expressive and has great dignity.

This is not the case with the figurine representing a high-ranking woman or priestess (plate 89), whose overall shape conforms to that of a truncated triangle. The massively rectangular body with rounded corners is wrapped in a simple cape, out of which the feet and hands subtly protude, with one hand clasping a feather fan. The enormous head resting on the body has earflares and an intentionally deformed skull, crowned by a tall headdress. The polychromy that remains implies embroidery on the materials, as well as indicating the practice of facial painting.

A priest is represented similarly (plate 91), although his attire is more complicated. He is also depicted upright, with hands held in a ritualistic gesture, and with a background of ornamentation at either side, as well as on his head, which includes small wings, serpents heads and a descending bird, all of which suggest that he was a great sorcerer with the attributes of a god.

Offerings of *copal*, which was burned to honour the gods, constituted an important part of Maya ritual in the Classic period. It was customary to use clay cylinders with allusive images as supports for the receptacles in which the *copal* was burned. The cylinder in plate 90 has different masks superimposed on it, consisting of conventional forms organised in a varied composition, symbolising earth, rain and night, and which are associated with the principal mask, that of the sun; this iconography clearly reflected the interests of an agricultural people.

The sun mask (plate 93) which comes from Palenque was probably part of a similar cylinder, as its edges look as if it was attached to a larger object. However, as with all the sculpture from Palenque, this face responds to a specific artistic sentiment. In conventional Maya terms, the particular characteristics of the eyes and eyebrows were identified with the sun; however, the rest of the face is modelled with a naturalism that is exceptionally sensual when compared to the mask of the sun in plate 90.

As well as ceramic cylinders, the Mayas also began to produce magnificently crafted clay urns. The example in plate 92 shows a first-rate polychromatic clay figure of a standing priest, wearing complicated attire, with a jaguar face that was intended to transmit religious sentiment to the god of the underworld with a ceremonial gesture.

In effect, during the Classic period the Maya cult of the dead and the conception of "beyond" led them to construct tombs containing luxurious offerings. Outstanding among these are incised or polychromatic ceramics (plate 95 and 96, and plate 94), all with elegant silhouettes and executed with a masterful technique and decorated with glyphs or symbols of deities; almost all of these refer to the gods of the earth and fertility. Masks consisting of greenstone mosaics were often used as offerings (plate 98). This precious stone was associated with the fertility of the land and with life itself, and guaranteed the deceased – according to Maya magical-religious theories – his survival in the afterlife.

During the Classic period of Maya culture, commemorative stelae bore witness to the glory of the Maya rulers during their lifetime: their military feats and most important achievements, such as accessions or initiation into priesthood. These stelae, carved in low relief, were then placed in strategic sites, for instance, at the foot of temple stairways or in the centre of plazas. The individuals were represented in resplendent attire that reflected their status, and in which each element was an emblem and signified their social importance. Hieroglyphic signs completed the commemoration, recording the names of the personages and dates, events and places, as can be seen in the magnificent stela from Yaxchilán (plate 97), or in that of Oxkintok (plate 100), in the northern Yucatán style.

Mural painting was characteristic of Maya culture. Practically all architectural components were painted, and one variant consisted of representations of scenes with human figures. The Bonampak and Mulchik murals are the most magnificent examples of the Classic period, completely covering the internal walls of chambers.

As well as these large murals, smaller scenes survive on the stones that closed off the vaults, which share the characteristics not only of the large mural paintings (but on a small scale) but also occasionally of contemporary codices. In the Classic period, their subject-matter was religious and ritualistic, portraying individuals with the attributes of deities, surrounded by bands of hieroglyphs, as can be seen on the stone from Dzibilnocac (plate 99). The representation is conventional, and the figure is depicted seated in profile, with legs crossed in a lotus position and wearing a fantastic animal mask. A fine calligraphic line characterises the Classic style, defining areas of flat colour; in representations of anthropomorphic figures, the proportions of the body are completely naturalistic.

The peak of development during the Classic period occurred in the Petén area, where the artistic style known as Classic Maya developed; this was to spread throughout a wide area through trade and the diffusion of a complex religion. In the Post-Classic period, development was focused in the northern Yucatán peninsula, and its most important centre was the city of Chichén Itzá.

This site developed its own culture within the overall Maya culture during the Classic period, as is demonstrated by its beautiful Puuc-style constructions. However, towards A.D. 900, the highland peoples began to make an impact, with militaristic organisation and the importation of new deities and ritualistic forms of human sacrifice.

The figure represented in plate 101, from Chichén Itzá, is a priest attired in traditional Maya fashion, adorned with a full bead pectoral, round earflares and a headdresss in the form of a large mask. By contrast, the small atlantean figure (plate 102) and the stone tablet (plate 103) from the same site reveal the influence of the invaders and their art. The clothing is the same as the Toltecs', and the figure on the tablet holds weapons that indicate his military standing. The right hand also holds an object that has been identified as part of the ritual of sacrifice associated with the ball game. Eventually, Maya hieroglyphs were to disappear from stone tablets, to be replaced by animals which, in the Nahua tradition, signified the names of the individual represented on the tablet.

87. FIGURINE

Maya culture. Jaina, Campeche. Classic (A.D. 250-900). Clay. Height 12 cm. Museo Regional de Campeche. Inv. no. 10-290541.

One of the characteristics of the figurines found in Jaina is their infinite variety and the inexhaustable creativity of the Maya potters; no two figurines are the same, and although some are similar, there is always some detail, no matter how small, marking the difference. In this seated female figurine, the remarkable simplicity of her attire, plain and without ornament, except for large earflares with plugs as well as the marks of beads in the necklace on her breast, is compensated for by the headdress in the form of a broad-brimmed hat with a tall crown, which rests on two wide bands that spring from the sides of the head. *a.c.m.*

88. WARRIOR

Maya culture. Maya region. Late Classic (A.D. 550-900). Clay. Height 14.8 cm, width 10.5 cm. In store. MNA. Cat. no. 5-1228. Inv. no. 10-223523.

This clay figurine is another excellent example of the potter's ability to reproduce even the tiniest details of their models, leaving us a clear indication of the identity of the figurines. Judging from its voluminous dress, there can be no doubt that it represents a warrior. The thickness and resistant quality of the clothing is evident not only in the skirt, which is wide and thick, but also in the upper garment that covers the chest and waist, and even in the broad bands that descend from behind the head at the sides onto the shoulders and down the arms.

In his left hand, the warrior also carries a circular shield engraved with ornament, and the right hand, which has disappeared, probably carried a spear. At first it seems strange that the figure is not displaying an equally voluminous headdress, but observation of the head reveals that it is more than usually bare and smooth, like the heads of other figurines which have large detachable headdresses, thus implying that this warrior's headdress must have been the same; unfortunately it has not yet been discovered. Thick boots, apparently made from a ridged or possibly scaly material, complete the figure's attire. The posture, and the expression on the face, which is somewhat damaged or eroded, lend the figure a stern appearance that is even slightly ferocious, which would have been sufficent to terrorise enemies. According to historical sources, warriors' attire had to be thick and padded with cotton or feathers, to afford the best possible protection. *a.c.m.*

89. HIGH-RANKING FIGURINE

Maya culture. Jaina, Campeche. Classic (A.D. 250-900). Clay. Height 21.4 cm, width 10 cm. In store. MNA. Cat. no. 5-1409. Inv. no. 10-222372.

A high percentage of the figurines found in Jaina are also musical instruments, which suggests that as well as functioning as funerary offerings, they must have played an important role in ceremonial activities. This bell figurine represents a women of high social status, judging by her elaborate attire and her bearing, which reveals a certain haughty and severe dignity. Recent studies and new discoveries have redefined the true role of women in ancient Maya society, affirming that power could be passed down through female descendancy; we now know how important certain women really were, not only as the mothers and consorts of the highest civil leaders, but also in their own right. In effect, several women have been identified on stone monuments, tablets and stelae, who at certain times held the position of greatest power within their community or city-state.

The woman represented here shows us what the attire of women of lineage must have been: a long skirt and a wide, low-cut *huipil* (a type of tunic), which is short and rounded at the front, falling over the arms at the sides and descending down to the feet; the figure also wears bracelets, necklaces and earflares with jadeite beads, and a tall headdress, with part of the hair cut into a tiered shape, framing the face, and with long hair tied up with plain bands and adorned with beads. Facial painting and the intentional mutilation of the upper teeth complete the attire. Although the figurine has been slightly eroded, red and blue colouring remains on both the body and the clothing. The figure itself was made from a mould. *a.c.m.*

90. CYLINDER WITH THE FACE OF THE SUN GOD

Maya culture. Provenance unknown. Classic (A.D. 250-900). Clay. Height 94 cm, width 48 cm. In store. MNA. Cat. no. 5-2784. Inv. no. 10-223533.

These objects, found in Palenque or its surroundings, have popularly been called "tubes" because of their basic cylindrical form, which is hollow and open at both ends. At the sides of the tube, two rectangular sections extend which have the same profuse appliqué decoration as the ornamentation on the main front-facing half of the cylinder. It is thought that a plate or vessel was placed on the upper part, in which the aromatic resin *copal* was burnt.

The decoration of this particular "tube" is similar to that of others where the basic motif is constantly repeated: the placing of large masks, one above the other, with the principal one consisting of the solar god Kinich Ahau. At the base of the tube is the upper part of a large mask of slightly fantastic appearance, above which is the principal mask, the largest in size and portraying the face of an old person, with large, smooth eyes, as if blind, and with the superorbital plaques crowned at the ends by a scroll-like shape; the half-open mouth displays intentionally deformed teeth, in this case triangular, although the norm was in the form of a T; the remaining features, such as the high cheekbones, and the expressive lines that run from the sides of the nose to the mouth and jawbone, as well as the scrolls emerging from the corners of the mouth, are accentuated by deep furrows which give the face of this ancient solar god great strength; he also wears in his ears circular ornaments containing plugss, and a bead diadem on his forehead. Above this main face is the upper half of another mask which has a long nose and a slightly grotesque appearance, as well as a wide band or border of beads with a rosette at the centre. The two motifs are repeated again, and are crowned by a small grotesque head, with designs on either side in the form of vertical crossed bands.

At the sides of these main decorative elements, modelled directly on the lateral sections or winglets, is a series of designs executed in appliqué, including crossed bands, jade beads, scrolls, botanical motifs and others that are undoubtedly symbolic in character. Although slight traces of blue paint can be seen, it is possible that, like other tubes, it was originally polychromatic. This type of object undoubtedly had a ceremonial or ornamental function. *a.c.m.*

91. PRIEST

Maya culture. Jaina, Campeche. Classic (A.D. 250-900). Clay. Height 14.8 cm, width 6.9 cm. In store. MNA. Cat. no. 5-634. Inv. no. 10-222282.

One of the principal characteristics of the Jaina figurines was that their creators took great care with the details, which leave little doubt as to the identity and social level of the individuals represented. This bell figurine is an excellent example, as the elements it represents (apart from its hieratic appearance), such as the cruciform-like tablet on which the figure leans, the serpent heads shown in profile and the feathers at each side, as well as the crest on the top section in the form of a bird with outspread wings, inevitably suggest that this is an altar.

The figure represented, a priest or high-ranking dignitary presiding over a ceremony, is in elegant dress. Most noticeable is the wide belt with large caracols hanging from its lower edge − an ornament characteristic of those in high rank. The belt holds up a long skirt made from a rich material, judging by the engraved rhomboid designs and dots that decorate it, which seem to indicate embroidery on the material itself.

The figure wears wide bracelets made from tubular beads on his wrists, and a bead necklace on his chest; similarly, his ears have small earflares, while the hair is indicated with lightly incised lines and is cut in a tiered fashion, framing the face. The figure wears a headdress in the form of a crown of beads and a cap which ends in segments at forehead level. The piece was made from a mould, and traces of blue, red and white paint can still be seen. *a.c.m.*

92. URN IN THE FORM OF A PRIEST

Maya culture. Tapijulapa, Tabasco. Classic (A.D. 250-900). Clay. Height 43 cm, width 23 cm. Museo de Antropología "Carlos Pellicer", Villahermosa, Tabasco.

This type of ceramic object, definitely made with a ceremonial function in mind, was manufactured in Tabasco during the Classic period, particularly in one region. Characteristic features of these urns are the profuse appliqué decoration and the anthropomorphic effigies, sometimes with a slightly fantastic appearance, that decorate the main body of the urn. *a.c.m.*

93. MASK OF THE SUN GOD

Maya culture. Palenque, Chiapas. Classic (A.D. 250-900). Clay, stucco with red paint. Height 21 cm, width 15.6 cm. In store. MNA. Cat. no. 5-1091. Inv. no. 10-222284.

This vigorous face, with its strong features and large eyes, represents the sun god, Kinich Ahau. It recalls the characteristic Maya physical type in many aspects: a wide face, prominent cheekbones, thick, well-defined lips and a broad, straight nose. However, it is the eyes that give us the clue as to the identity of the sun god: the artist has indicated the pupils only lightly but just enough to show that they are crossed; the superorbital plaque is broad and semi-circular, except for the inner part at the top which forms a scroll. The representation of the solar god with large eyes, plain or blind, as well as being cross-eyed, with both pupils indicated by a spiral or a cruciform design, is very common. Deep depressions and ridges define and accentuate each of the features mentioned, as well as the space between the eyebrows and the lines of expression that descend from the sides of the nose to mouth level.

The sun god was one of the most highly venerated of the gods because, like other peoples of similar date, the Mayas considered him benevolent; to them he was a positive deity, a source of life and fertility, despite the fact that at a given time he could be transformed into the opposite, as once the evening declined and night fell, the sun went down and entered the underworld, the world of the dead, and was transformed into a malevolent god. However, with the dawn the sun once again became benevolent. In the myths and legends of certain Maya folklore, the sun is said to have been a great hunter before being transformed into a star, and one story tells of his suffering at the irresponsible and inconsequential behaviour of his consort Ixchel, the moon goddess.

Traces of red and blue paint can be seen on this mask, which was modelled by hand; originally it probably formed part of the decoration of a building, embedded in a wall, stone tablet or decorative element, judging by its shape and the marks at the edges. *a.c.m.*

94. LIDDED VESSEL

Maya culture. Calakmul, Campeche. Classic (A.D. 250-900). Clay. Height 35 cm, diameter 40 cm. Museo Regional de Campeche, Lieutenant's House. Inv. no. 10-290540:/2.

This elegant and beautiful polychromatic lidded vessel is one of the most notable ceramic forms of the Early Classic (A.D. 250-600), and was destined to serve as a funerary offering. It has straight, slightly diverging sides, with an annular base that has a pronounced flange around it, decorated with alternating dots and circles.

The lid and body are elaborately covered with symbolic motifs and serpents alluding to the underworld, in black and red on a cream background. This piece is very similar to others that have been found in the tombs at Tikal, in the Guatemalan Petén, which is not surprising given the relative proximity of Tikal to Calakmul, and that Calakmul shows affinities with other important cities in the same region, such as El Mirador.

This vessel was found together with other regal pieces, such as jadeite and greenstone mosaic masks, in the tomb of an important person buried in Structure III at Calakmul. *a.c.m.*

95. VESSEL

Maya culture. Provenance unknown. Classic (A.D. 250-900). Clay. Height 8.5 cm, width 17.7 cm. In store. MNA. Cat. no. 5-1168. Inv. no. 10-77415.

The serpent is one of the animals most deeply connected with the religious beliefs and mythology of the ancient Mexican peoples; associated with the earth and the rain, it also

233

symbolises the lightning; when it has bird-like elements such as feathers, it is able to fly, rising above the earth and becoming divine. The serpent is used profusely in all forms of art, both because of its symbolism and because its undulating line lends itself easily to any surface. The vessel seen here, burnished black, has a simple semi-spherical form with a flat bottom; its beautiful decoration is based on a design of two serpents, whose twisting bodies display a finely carved reticulated design representing scales, interrupted by occasional empty circles; in some areas, the bodies are curled up, and both heads display the characteristic eyes and open jaws with forked tongue.   *a.c.m.*

96. VESSEL

Maya culture. Provenance unknown. Classic (A.D. 250-900). Clay. Height 9.5 cm, width 23 cm. In store. MNA. Cat. no. 5-1149. Inv. no. 10-76882.

The simple ceramics of earlier periods were enriched with new forms, techniques and decorative motifs during the Classic period; in many cases, a complete or attractive result was achieved without colour. Such is the case of this simple grey clay dish with a composite silhouette and flat bottom. The engraved and incised decoration of simple geometric motifs is extremely effective; the lower half has deep vertical lines converging at the base, while on the upper part is a wide band in which three motifs are repeated again and again: right-angled L-shapes are inverted against each other, with two curved lines and a circle, all within a square.   *a.c.m.*

97. LINTEL

Maya culture. Yaxchilán, Chiapas. Classic (A.D. 250-900). Stone. Height 188 cm, width 75 cm, depth 31 cm. MNA. Cat. no. 5-1774. Inv. no. 10-80371.

During the Late Classic period, one of the outstanding features of Maya sculpture in stelae, altars, lintels, stairways and wall reliefs was the recording of important events, an expression of historical consciousness which forms an accurate chronology.
Here, the hieroglyphs and pictorial representations depict the last ruler of Yaxchilán, Shield Jaguar II, and another individual called Large Skull. The former holds an anthromorphically-shaped sceptre as a sign of leadership (a ruling insignia), and the latter an axe, indicating his military standing. The events depicted date from the second half of the eighth century.
Lintel 58 comes from Building 54 at Yaxchilán, where lintels 54 and 57 were also found, and forms a text interconnected with other inscribed pieces.
Jaguar Shield II maintained close relations with other cities, such as Bonampak in Chiapas and La Pasadita in the Petén , which probably culminated in a political alliance.   *r.g.m*

98. CEREMONIAL MASK

Maya culture. Calakmul, Campeche. Classic (A.D. 250-900). Jade. Height 15 cm, width 13 cm. Museo Regional de Campeche, Lieutenant's House. Inv. no. 10-290542, 10-290543, 10-290544.

This stunning mask of jade mosaic reproduces a human face in perfect form, possibly that of the person buried in Tomb I of

Structure VII at Calakmul, Campeche. The splendid offering found in this tomb also included ceramic objects and over 2200 jadeite pieces. It was discovered in 1984, and is the richest jade offering found to date.
The facial features are extremely realistic; stucco was used for the eyes, with obsidian marking the pupils. Large earflares are formed by a combination of various elements, the largest being a four-petalled form. Although the mask is incomplete, it is undoubtedly the most realistic and the most human found to date, as well as being the most beautiful.   *a.c.m.*

99. ARCHITECTURAL ELEMENT WITH FIGURE

Maya culture. Dzibilnocac, Campeche. Classic (A.D. 250-900). Stone. Height 56.5 cm, width 35 cm. Museo Regional de Mérida. Inv. no. 10-251123.

Particularly characteristic of Maya architecture were the roofs of buildings. Known as the false arch, corbel vault or Maya vault, its name derives from the fact that no keystone was used. At the point when the distance between the two walls (which were built tapering towards each other) could be spanned by a tablet or a regularly shaped stone, such a stone was put in place; these stones have been called "lids" or "seals", as they did not function like the keystones of true vaults or arches. The stone shown here is a good example of a lid or seal, since it also displays the special type of mural painted on this sort of architectural element: a complete scene in miniature. In this case, a deity is shown framed above and below by two bands of glyphs; the seated figure has been identified as the god K; in front of him is a type of pedestal on which stands a basket containing offerings.   *a.c.m.*

100. TABLET WITH REPRESENTATION OF A DIGNITARY

Maya culture. Oxkintok, Yucatán. Classic (A.D 250-900). Stone. Height 84.5 cm, width 43 cm, depth 5.5 cm. In store. MNA. Cat. no. 5-1108. Inv. no. 10-136922.

This tablet was intentionally cut down to reduce its size and weight, so its thickness and original function are unknown; only one of its broad faces has been preserved. The decoration is based on two elements, one human and the other symbolic, the latter consisting of a hieroglyphic inscription of six squares, three above and three below, to the right of the human figure.
The figure is standing and shown from the front, while the head is in profile looking over the left shoulder and the legs are slightly apart with the feet pointing outwards; his right arm hangs loosely at the side of the body, and the left arm is bent and folded across the body, covering part of the belt.
On his head, he wears a large headdress consisting of an impressive zoomorphic mask adorned with beads and a feather crest, the ends of which fall across his right shoulder. The ornament on the ear is large and disc-shaped, with a big plug and a piriform bead hanging behind the lobe. The right cheek is disfigured by a thick scab – possibly the product of scarification, a usual Maya decorative practice. Two strips descend on each side of the neck holding a sort of necklace on the chest which incorporates what looks like a ceremonial rod – the symbol of power or command, but smaller than usual and made from an unusual material which appears to be a hank of

threads or cords; it includes all the usual components, however: a broad horizontal section with "crests" at each end formed by one vertical and three horizontal elements (a straight central element between two curved and opposing ones).

The upper part of the body, aside from the necklace and ornamentation described above, seems to be naked; the lower half is relatively simply attired, apart from the wide belt, adorned at the front with a large human mask; this mask has long, straight hair, divided into two bands that fall at either side framing the face, beneath which hang two large caracols – the usual decorative element among people of importance. The skirt of the main figure is long, and decorated with light, incised vertical lines.

Wide bracelets are worn on the wrists, formed by six plain bands with beads along the upper edge; hanging from the left arm is a long object that curves at the end, which possibly represents the bag for *copal* – the aromatic resin used in religious ceremonies. This suggests that the individual represents a priest, or at least an official, who played a role in the moments leading up to the acting out of some ritual or ceremony. On the figure's feet are sandals of the kind that completely cover the heel and have a wide band that ties at the front around the ankle.

The technique used for this tablet was to carve several different layers of relief, the deepest of which forms the background against which the figure stands out. *a.c.m.*

101. DIGNITARY

Maya culture. Chichén Itzá, Yucatán. Post-Classic (A.D. 900-1521). Stone. Height 89 cm, width 48 cm, depth 50 cm. Museo Regional de Mérida. Cat. no. MM 1986-18:3(1 y 2). Inv. no. 10-25117 1/2.

Representations of human figures with detachable headdresses are relatively common in clay, but not in stone, nor in pieces of the size of the one shown here. This represents a male figure, seated with legs crossed and the right hand resting on the stomach; he wears bracelets, large circular earflares with a plug, and a round ornament on his chest which forms part of a sort of short cape or necklace; the loincloth is simple, with the front band hanging over the crossed legs. The most important part of the figure's attire is the headdress, which presents the large mask of Chaac, the god of rain. Both the figure and the detachable headdress have pegs at the back, which corroborate historical records referring to their forming part of the façade of one of the buildings at Chichén Itzá. Traces of red, blue and ochre paint can still be seen on the figure. *a.c.m.*

102. ATLANTE

Maya culture. Chichén Itzá, Yucatán. Post-Classic (A.D. 900-1521). Stone. Height 90 cm, width 48 cm, depth 32 cm. Maya Hall. MNA. Cat. no. 5-1751. Inv. no. 10-81267.

The sculptures known as atlantes are characteristic of the Early Post-Classic period (A.D. 900-1521) in the northern Maya zone; they are particularly associated with Chichén Itzá, the period's most representative site.

These atlantes stand upright on a plain rectangular base; their arms are held up, with the hands, which are not shown, level with the head, forming a flat surface suitable for supporting something. For this reason they are attributed the function of table or altar supports.

The atlante seen here is very similar to others from the same site, but there are certain differences, not only in the details of the attire but also in the symbols represented. It seems very likely that, as well as features that were shared, there were essential differences which are not obvious at first sight, such as the atlante's association with a particular deity or ceremonial practice.

Here, the figure wears a headdress in the form of a close-fitting cap, with a feather crest running from front to back around the rim; his nose-plug is merlon-shaped, or in the form of an inverted fret, and covers part of the mouth. His earflares are large, each in the form of a double circle with a hole in the middle.

On his wrists are bracelets consisting of six rows of beads, and on his chest is a necklace or pectoral in an inverted crenelated form, made of long tubular beads, from which hang three smaller, identically-sized tubular beads. He wears a loincloth, whose belt consists of a plain, narrow band, with another below it which has squares along its edges.

The piece of material at the front, triangular in shape, is engraved with geometric designs – rhomboids, circles, dots and rectangles. Around the figure's knees are tied bands with a round bead strung on each one and a simple knot at the side. On his feet are sandals of the kind that cover the heel and tie onto the ankle with a plain wide strap or band; this band, which covers the top of the foot, is decorated with a rectangular ornament which ends with vertical incisions that may indicate fringing.

At the back, the figure wears a long cape of wavy feathers, which also appears at his sides. Traces of red paint remain; the atlante has been eroded and is slightly incomplete. *a.c.m.*

103. TABLET SHOWING A WARRIOR

Maya culture. Chichén Itzá, Yucatán. Post-Classic (A.D. 90o-1521). Stone. Height 142 cm, width 44 cm, depth 30 cm. Museo Regional de Mérida. Cat. no. MM 1986-18: 33.

Characteristic of the Yucatán in the Early Post-Classic period (A.D. 900-1250) was the image of the warrior, a major theme taken up by the various artistic manifestations of this date, and of Chichén Itzá in particular. In mural painting, sculpture and even in the decorative motifs used in jewellery, the warrior figure makes a frequent appearance. The stone tablet seen here is a good example; judging by the attire and especially the objects held by this figure in low relief – spear and *átlatl* (spear-thrower) - as well as the shield on his right arm, there can be no doubt as to his profession.

The attire, headdress and ornaments, as well as the treatment of the figure itself and his physical type, are markedly different from the Classic Maya representations of the preceding period, and provide undeniable proof of the changes experienced in Maya culture (in this case by the inhabitants of the peninsula) through the presence of foreign groups who invaded Maya history in the tenth century. *a.c.m.*

87. FIGURINE

88. WARRIOR

89. HIGH-RANKING FIGURINE

90. CYLINDER WITH THE FACE OF THE SUN GOD

90. CYLINDER WITH THE FACE OF THE SUN GOD

91. PRIEST

92. URN IN THE FORM OF A PRIEST

93. MASK OF THE SUN GOD

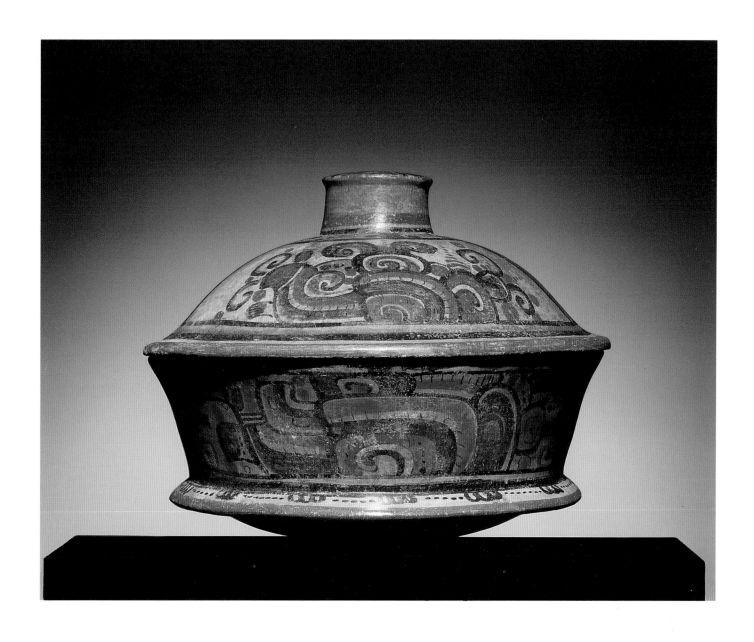

94. LIDDED VESSEL

95. VESSEL

96. VESSEL

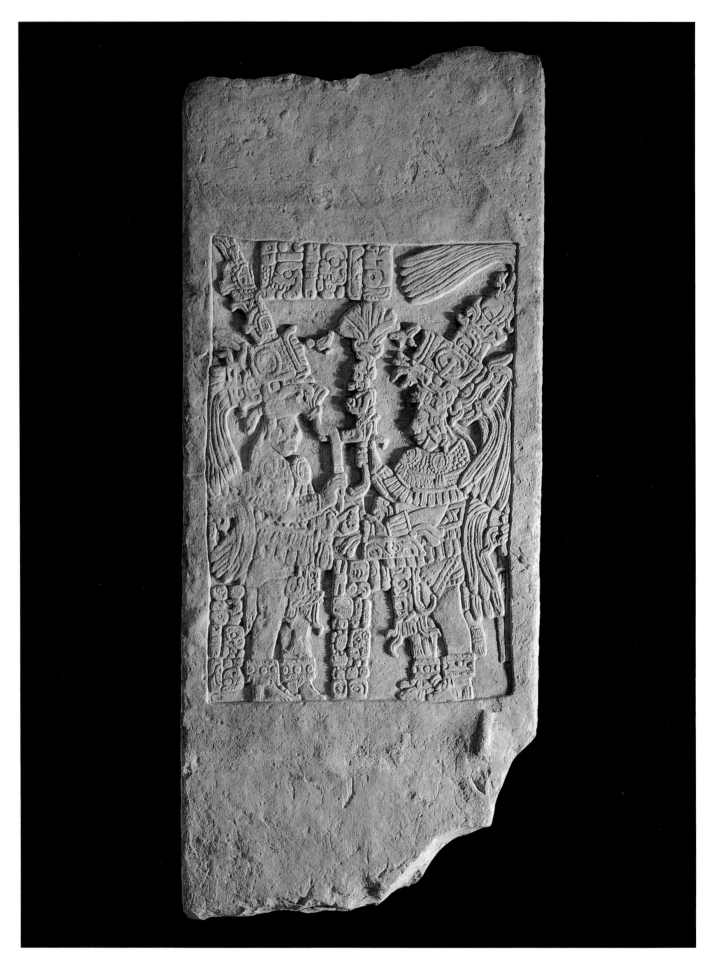

97. LINTEL

97. LINTEL

98. CEREMONIAL MASK

99. ARCHITECTURAL ELEMENT WITH FIGURE

100. TABLET WITH REPRESENTATION OF A DIGNITARY

252

101. DIGNITARY

102. ATLANTE

103. TABLET SHOWING A WARRIOR

15. WESTERN MEXICO: WORKS OF ART IN CLAY

Carolyn Baus de Czitrom
María Dolores Flores Villatoros

The ancient inhabitants of Western Mexico occupied much of the Pacific coast, in an area that includes the states of Sinaloa, Nayarit, Jalisco, Colima and Michoacán, as well as parts of Guanajuato and Guerrero. In archaeological terms, this is one of the least known regions in Mesoamerica; its inhabitants are known to have been sedentary farmers from very early times, producing the ceramic vessels and figurines that were to typify Mesoamerica. However, from 1500 B.C. to A.D. 600, one tradition that was particular to Western Mexico developed there: the use of shaft and chamber tombs. Both the tombs and their associated offerings suggest links with South America.

From A.D. 600, Western Mexico was gradually absorbed into the world of Mesoamerica, in turn contributing important elements to the latter during the periods that followed. During the Post-Classic era, in particular, the West formed an integral part of Mesoamerica, and here the Tarascans played the most notable part in this cultural scene.

During the Pre-Classic period, the western groups lived in villages, cultivating maize, beans and squash. No buildings survive, but the architecture of their houses and temples is revealed by clay models. Their gods are not known, although the shaft tombs indicate that there was a cult honouring ancestors. The site of El Opeño in Michoacán and the Capacha complex in Colima and Jalisco constitute the earliest evidence (1500 B.C. and 1800 B.C. respectively) from the Pre-Classic period.

At El Opeño there are tombs similar to the shaft tombs later used in Colima, Jalisco and Nayarit. The offerings at El Opeño include vessels and figurines, some of which were modelled in a very fine clay and show engraved decoration that appears to indicate tattooing on the body. In spite of being a village-type culture, it was complex and well developed.

A particular type of ceramic distinguishes Capacha. Its shapes, which are most original, include wide-rimmed bowls with narrow waists, vessels in the form of effigies, figurines and a type of stirrup handle in the form of a double-bodied vessel in which the upper vessel is connected to the lower one by two or three tubes. Typical decoration consists of punched holes and wide, incised lines, or areas of colour defined by incised outline. Capacha's importance as regards the study of the origins of civilisation in Mesoamerica lies in its fundamental similarities with South America.

Two important cultural manifestations of the Late Pre-Classic period, the shaft tombs and the site of Chupícuaro, had their roots in Capacha and El Opeño. Chupícuaro was influential throughout an extensive area which included the Central Highlands of Mexico, Zacatecas, Guerrero and Puebla. The archaeological site there was extremely important during the Late Pre-Classic period (800 B.C. to A.D. 200). Today, it lies below the waters of the Solís dam, near Acámbaro, Guanajuato.

The ancient inhabitants of Chupícuaro transformed this site into a large pottery centre, where offerings associated with approximately 400 burials have been excavated. The burials and their offerings paint a vivid picture of the life of the inhabitants, testifying to a numerous population which preferred to settle near rivers or lakes, on land suitable for the cultivation of maize and where, at the same time, they were able to complement their economy by hunting, fishing and gathering.

They built houses using straw and mud on stone platforms; they are known to have ground maize using *metates* (flat grinding stones); the discovery of *molcajetes* (round stone-grinding dishes) suggests that chillies and tomatoes were already part of their diet.

Chupícuaro ceramics display great initiative and a good sense of form and design. The variety of shape and the quality of the pottery from this site make it some of the best of

20. Western Mexico

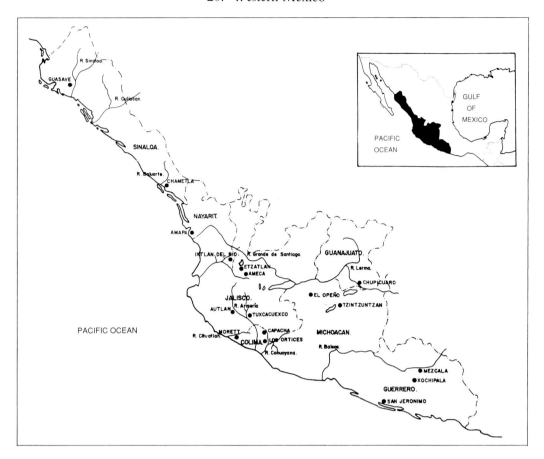

Mesoamerica. Some of the vessels that have been discovered are either two-colour or polychromatic vessels, with anthropomorphic designs using straight and broken lines, and geometric motifs that include frets, rhomboids and squares. Pottery was made in the shape of bowls, jars and tripod dishes, with hollow legs or supports.

Hollow figurines were also produced, decorated in the same fashion as the vessels, and so were solid figurines, modelled by hand and using appliqué. Most represent women, generally naked, with scarifications or ornamental scars on their shoulders, and displaying facial and body painting; many of them take part in maternal scenes. There are also male representations and figurines lying on beds or in cots.

Pottery was used both for domestic purposes and for offerings, as well as for trade or

21. Shaft tombs in Western Mexico

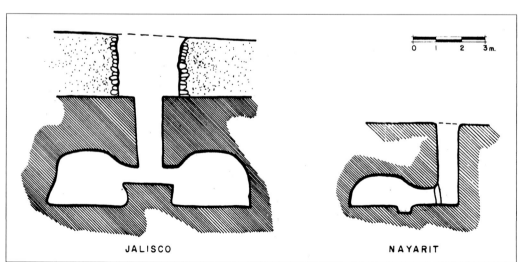

barter with neighbouring peoples. Ceramics was the principal craft, but not the only one, as weaving and basketwork were also practised. Bone was employed to make ornament and tools, such as needles, awls and gravers; knives and arrow heads were made from obsidian.

The tradition of building shaft tombs in Colima, Jalisco and Nayarit lasted from approximately 500 B.C. to A.D. 600. These tombs consist of one or more underground chambers with access at ground-level through a vertical shaft. The deceased were buried in the tombs with offerings that probably had magical or religious connotations. The most remarkable of these burial offerings are large, hollow figures, effigy-vessels and small, solid clay figurines. Hand-modelled, they are faithful and graceful representations of men, animals and plants, and provide a unique source for the study of the early inhabitants and their culture. In artistic terms they are described as Jalisco, Colima and Nayarit styles.

The hollow figures from Colima are highly polished and red or brown in colour. Most have a spout, and were thus used as jars. Subject-matter includes not only a number of human figures, but also vegetation and a wide variety of animals. In contrast to that of Colima, the Nayarit style uses many colours to indicate clothing, ornament, facial and body painting. Most of the subject-matter consists of human figures, almost always with ear and nose decorations made from multiple rings. The third style, from Jalisco, combines modelling and painting, generally in two colours. The figures are almost always human and are characterised by having tall, narrow heads and sharp noses, while eyes and fingernails are extremely realistic. The warrior is one of the more frequent themes in Jalisco.

In general, the solid figurines have the same characteristics, but are more important because of their cultural content. Many are dedicated to a variety of activities, and also show various types of ornament, clothing and implements. The representations of several figures on a single base are of particular interest, showing people carried on litters, maquettes of houses with family groups, and dancers in a circle or a procession. Sick or deformed characters are often represented, particularly hunchbacks and people with rickets, figures with harelips and, of particular interest, figures covered in sores.

The identity of the deities worshipped at this period is not known, but certain objects probably had magical-religious significance. Censers held by human figures and decorated with serpents may have been associated with a god of fire. The richly-dressed figures in dance-postures seem to represent sorcerers, and the flutes, caracol trumpets and bells were almost certainly used for music in rituals and dances. Masks would have had a magical function too.

Around A.D. 600, shaft tombs ceased to be made, and features began to appear that were increasingly identified with Mesoamerica. The Teotihuacán culture was at its peak at this date, although it had little influence on the West. Teotihuacán-style objects appear there sporadically, but probably arrived via trade. However, in El Ixtepec and other sites in the Atemajac valley in Jalisco, and in Tingambato and the region of Huetamo in Michoacán, the architectural pattern of the *talud-tablero,* which comes from Teotihuacán, appears.

At some sites in the state of Guerrero near the Mezcala River basin, an area of stonework specialisation has been located, bearing the same name, where objects such as masks, figurines, double figures, ornaments and trinkets in a variety of forms were manufactured with great skill.

The Mezcala style, sober and schematic, is one in which only the most important features are indicated, expressed through sculpted grooves and ridges. The stone used in this region was principally serpentine and jadeite. Everything is the product of local cultural development. Although there is clear evidence of Olmec and Teotihuacán influence, these traits enable the origin and evolution of the Mezcala style to be situated between approximately A.D. 200 and 800; this stonework tradition seems to have been at its best from the Classic to the Post-Classic periods.

The Mezcala style has brought fame to the archaeology of Guerrero for the variety and quantity of the objects produced, which were made with great art and realism, and which continue in production today. These artefacts were exported from Guerrero to the Central Highlands, though the exact date and context are not known. However, ceramics

PRINCIPAL PRIEST
(Petamuti)

AUXILIARY PRIESTS

THOSE WHO HUNG THE
SACRIFICED VICTIMS UP
BY THE FEET (Hopitiecha)

THOSE WHO CARRIED
THE GODS ON THEIR
SHOULDERS (Thiuimencha)

THE SACRIFICERS
(Axamencha)

appear in Teotihuacán from the Classic period, and in the Post-Classic era they reached the Templo Mayor in Tenochtitlán, in what today is Mexico City. In the Early Post-Classic years, Sinaloa was distinguished for the Aztatlán complex, characterised by *tecali* (alabaster) vessels, clay masks, pipes and polychromatic ceramics. During the Post-Classic period, the most remarkable group was that of the Tarascans of Michoacán, who formed a strong nation that never succumbed to Aztec domination. Tarascan culture developed during the Post-Classic period in the territory of the present-day state of Michoacán. As a military power, it came to subjugate and control a large area in what is now Jalisco, Guanajuato, part of the state of Mexico and Guerrero.

The Tarascans complemented their basically agricultural economy with hunting and fishing, in the region of the Patzcuaro Lake. Their diet was varied and included fish, turtle, trout, duck, venison, rabbit, wild boar and other species.

The state of Tarasco was apparently formed in the year 1370 by Tariacuri, a mythical cultural hero who achieved this through the unification of the villages near the lake. Tariacuri united three originally separate political groupings, whose capitals were Tzintzuntzan, Ihuatzio and Patzcuaro. However, Tzintzuntzan soon began to exert greater political and economic power, and was to be the Tarascan capital until the arrival of the Spanish.

The Tarascans were notable for their metalwork. They were true masters in the field, and became proficient in several techniques, including cold-hammering, melting, the lost-wax technique, the use of moulds and filigree work. These techniques were used to elaborate both ornamental objects and implements, outstanding among which are the copper axes or hatchets that were employed throughout Mesoamerica as a means of exchange – in other words, as money.

Tarascan ceramic vessels came in several different shapes, most remarkable of which are square forms, forms with legs, jars with a handle spout (both basket-type and stirrup), tripod dishes and miniature vessels, with the polychromatic and negative-painting decoration characteristic of this culture. They also made a range of large clay pipes, zoomorphic, anthropomorphic and horn-shaped, which were used for smoking tobacco, a privilege reserved solely for high society. The Tarascan state was organised in a way similar to that of the Mexica state, as its expansion was aimed at finding lands suited to the production of foods needed by its growing population, as well as the appropriation of mineral deposits such as copper, gold and silver, and other products such as honey, cotton, cacao, pelts and resins such as *copal*. Their favourite plunder was the salt deposits at Ixtapan in the State of Mexico, which were continually under dispute with the Mexicas.

The peoples who succumbed to the Tarascans were forced to pay tribute in kind and labour to their conquerors. There were clearly defined social classes, and social mobility was almost non-existent. A firm expansionistic and militaristic structure underpinned the state's monopoly of power.

Within this stratified and complex society were firstly the *calzonci*, the maximum representative of religious, civil and military power, and then higher and lower-ranking priests known as *petamuti*, warriors, merchants, judges, noblemen, artisans and common people such as farmers, fishermen and wood cutters.

23. Tarascan society

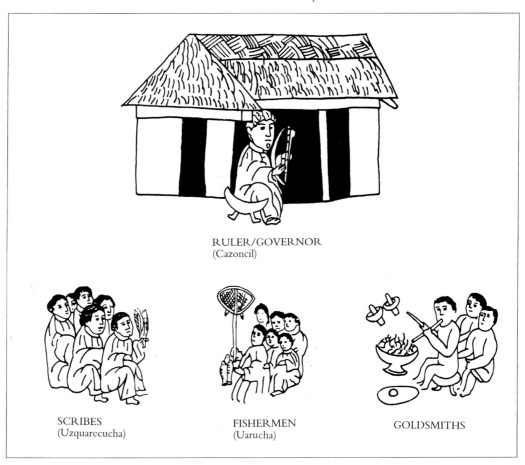

RULER/GOVERNOR
(Cazoncil)

SCRIBES
(Uzquarecucha)

FISHERMEN
(Uarucha)

GOLDSMITHS

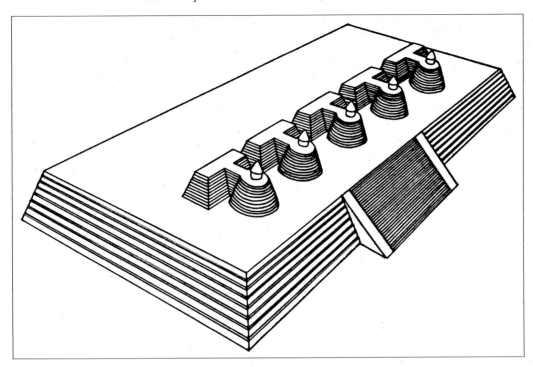

Tarascan sculpture showed little originality. The objects that are still in existence display a marked Toltec influence, an interesting example being the sculptures found at Ihuatzio. Among these, the figure of a coyote (a mammal similar to the wolf) and the Chac Mool stand out. Chac Mools are stone sculptures that represent reclining human figures with their heads raised and their legs bent, holding some sort of vessel on their stomachs. They have been interpreted as warriors or messengers who carried offerings to the gods. This type of sculpture is common in many parts of Mesoamerica, and is found at the sites of Chichén Itzá in the Yucatán, Tula, Hidalgo, and the Templo Mayor in México-Tenochtitlán. The Tarascans did not have images of their gods in temples, nor do the gods appear in paintings or sculptures. However, it is more than likely that they had a vast array of different deities derived from the ancient gods of water, fire and fertility.

The names of some deities are known through sources written in the sixteenth century: Curiacaveri, for instance, was the god of fire and creator of all gods, and Curiavaperi was his female counterpart, the mother of the gods, the deity of life and death and patron of women in labour; Xaratanga, the daughter of Curiavaperi, was not only the young goddess of plant germination and of sustenance, but also the patron of love, whose worship was associated with the observation of the lunar cycles. Urende Quauecaya was the patron of the fishermen, god of the sea and associated with the planet Venus. The Tarascan people shared a knowledge of astronomy and mathematics with other Mesoamerican groups. Although they did not make any original contribution to these sciences, like other cultures they knew how to use them: they employed a common calendar, in which the year had 365 days and was divided into eighteen months, with five ill-omened days at the end of each period, making up the necessary number of days to form the solar year. The festivities associated with the months and years are similar to those that traditionally feature in Mexica religion.

Tarascan architecture is evident in the constructions of Tzintzuntzan and Ihuatzio; both urban sites constituted fairly important ceremonial centres. In the pyramidal bases, called *yácatas*, circular forms were combined with rectangular ones, and had a mud hut on the upper surface, also circular in plan; these were reached by means of stairways situated near ceremonial plazas or patios.

The pyramidal bases were generally filled with loose stones, used without any mortar or other type of fixing element to join one to another. The surfaces of the buildings were faced with thinner stones of volcanic origin, which had a decorative function; there is no evidence of levelling with stucco. These temple groups formed the centre of the Tarascan state's religious worship and political power. The priestly class and the noblemen lived in the ceremonial centres, while the comon people lived in the surrounding areas, in wooden houses that are not very different from present-day ones.

The Tarascan state reached its peak in the fourteenth century, and had no time to experience a period of decline, as the Spanish conquest provoked a total change in the course of its history.

16. EVERYDAY LIFE CELEBRATED IN CLAY

Sonia Lombarda de Ruíz

During the Early Pre-Classic period, the culture of Capacha, in Colima, was to spread through part of the region currently known as Western Mexico, where it was to remain through the periods that followed, by the Late Pre-Classic being contemporary with the cultures of El Opeño in Michoacán and Chupícuaro in the state of Guanajuato; all of these reflected the development of village cultures. One of the features that is both distinctive and diagnostic of the Capacha group is its ceramics: various different types of vessels were produced (plate 105), as well as figurines and hollow figures in which female representations predominate. The example shown in this exhibition (plate 104) is one of the most characteristic. Made from a well-fired high-quality clay, with a polished red finish, it represents a woman in upright posture, with a geometrically-shaped body of unnatural rectangular shape and proportion. The head, which dominates the piece because of its size, has polychromatic facial painting that shows the stepped geometrical designs typical of this site.

In effect, by the beginning of the Classic period the people of the present-day states of Colima, Jalisco and Nayarit had a particular regional culture which maintained the traditions of the earlier village groups of Capacha, El Opeño and Chupícuaro, and which is unrelated to other Mesoamerican cultures, instead displaying links with South America.

As a result, certain aspects of their art are not found anywhere else in Mesoamerica, most important of which are the funerary ceramics from the shaft tombs. Among these are vegetable-based forms, the most common being squash or pumpkins (one of their principal foods), such as the fine example in plate 106.

The animal life that daily surrounded these people was represented with naturalistic forms that acquire graceful rounded shapes when adapted to the function of vessels (plate 108).

Typical sculptures from the area of Colima are the fat dogs (plate 107); because they have been found in burials, they have been seen as antecedents of the tradition taken up by the Mexicas, in which after death individuals were led by the dog on their journey through the underworld. These Colima dogs are modelled in highly polished clay, with rotund heads and bodies and short stubby legs, curled tail and pricked-up ears. The combination of these shapes is extremely pleasing, and contrasts with the open mouth and sharp teeth, which give the dogs an aggressive look.

Representations of men, women and even families (plate 112) are the most frequently recurring motifs in Colima sculpture, and they have been attributed to a cult of the dead. The use of form is very free, and outside any established canons, with gently rounded volumes that are always extremely dynamic. Facial expressions are spontaneous and fresh, with schematic features, so that the mouths, for instance, are lightly indicated by a slit with no further modelling (plate 109). The heads are vertically elongated in the form of a truncated cone.

As was common in Prehispanic societies with magical-religious practices, people with deformities, such as hunchbacks or those born with stumps instead of limbs, were attributed with extraordinary powers enabling them to establish a relationship with the gods, and they often participated in practices of divination and prediction. Their appearance in the sculpture of Western Mexico suggests that they had an important role in these societies. The two examples shown in this exhibition, one in clay (plate 113) and the other in stone (plate 114), express very different styles because of the differences in their media. In the first case, the combination of the malleability of the clay and its function as a vessel result in the sculpture of a small, bulky man, in which the general composition of the body is inscribed within a circle achieved by the position of the arms (with the elbows held out and slightly bent), in conjunction with the crossed legs and the shoulders. The head sits like a pillar on the shoulders; in this case, the facial features are modelled more than usual, and, together with the balanced symmetry of the overall shape, transforms the hunchback into someone of great dignity.

In the case of the stone sculpture, the harder medium meant that the figure was carved using a more abstract language, in which the main elements of the deformed body are structured in the form of a highly dynamic C, with the knees drawn upwards and counterbalanced by the head. The head, defined only in the broadest terms and tilted to face upwards, suggests an attitude of spiritual transcendence.

The funerary ceramics of Nayarit belong to the same culture as the shaft tombs of the Classic period, and the hollow figures of men and women express a particular style that is indicative of a conventional stereotype. It consists of the exaggeration of the shape of the body, adapted to a rectangular format, with extremely robust legs when the figure is represented on foot (plates 117 and 118) or kneeling, and with very thin arms, by contrast.

The female figure in plate 115 is a masterpiece of this type of art in Prehispanic Nayarit. The figure is firmly seated on formidable thighs; stomach and breasts are lightly indicated on the rectangular body, which supports a head with a very fine face, decorated with the typical Nayarit nose-plug in the form of multiple hoops. The general composition is inscribed within a triangle, a symmetrical form that accentuates the verticality of the figure, counterbalanced by the weightiness of the sculpture, which gives an impression of stability. An elegant serenity is expressed by the harmonious proportions of thighs, body and head.

Also in Western Mexico arose a type of stone sculpture described as Mezcala style, produced in a region further to the south in the Balsas River basin. Although there are temple maquettes, masks and decorative objects, it is characterised by representations that are generally of small human figures whose form is usually abstract and geometric, and whose features are extremely schematic (plate 119). Greenstone, to which, as has been mentioned, magical-religious qualities were attributed, was of particular interest to these peoples. Its hardness may have determined the geometric work and rigidly-cut lines (plate 120), but nevertheless, it did not impede the achievement of beautiful sculptural expression. From A.D. 600, the cultures of Western Mexico were gradually absorbed into the Mesoamerican world, contributing important elements to it during the years that followed. In the Post-Classic period, the commercial and military expansion of Tula made itself felt, and it was at this time that certain Mesoamerican traits were introduced into the Western culture, including various religious ideas. The Chac Mool sculpture from Ihuatzio, Michoacán, the messenger who, in Toltec religion, carried the offering of the hearts of the sacrificed victim to the gods (plate 121), presents a clear example of this process. This Tarascan Chac Mool is a schematic and crude regional variant of a metropolitan model, but nevertheless makes an impact through its rather primitive force.

104. FIGURE FROM FUNERARY OFFERING

Western Mexico culture. Chupícuaro, Guanajuato. Late Pre-Classic (800 B.C.-A.D. 250). Clay. Height 35.1 cm, width 14.3 cm. Western Hall. MNA. Cat. no. 2.7-2189. Inv. no. 10-1314.

During the Late Pre-Classic period, Chupícuaro was an extremely important site, which at present lies beneath the waters of the Solís dam, near Acámbaro; the culture to which this piece belongs is named after the site.

This clay figurine is hand-modelled and painted in red and cream, its cheeks decorated with stepped lines, and with two bands of colour, one on the head and another on the legs; the figure is hollow and has its hands on its stomach; it is also naked and without any form of ornament.

The half-open mouth displays its teeth, and there are holes in the earlobes, which may have been used for earrings.

These figurines show us a number of Chupícuaro customs, such as their lack of clothing, their use of body and facial paint, and of turbans or forehead bands, as well as their habits regarding ornaments such as necklaces, earflares and bracelets.

During the Pre-Classic period, most of the figurines represent women, implying a maternity cult and, therefore, a fertility cult of the earth; the sexual characteristics of this figurine are not defined, and the figure may represent a female infant.   *c.b.c.*

105. VESSEL

Western Mexico culture. Chupícuaro, Guanajuato, Late Pre-Classic (800 B.C.-A.D. 250). Clay. Height 39.8 cm, width 22 cm, diameter 12.5 cm. In store. MNA. Cat. no. 2-1796. Inv. no. 10-44650.

Pottery was Chupícuaro's principal craft; it was used both for domestic service and funerary offerings and for trade and barter with neighbouring peoples, and reveals great initiative and a good sense of form and design. The quantity of ceramics from this site makes it one of the best of Mesoamerica, displaying a particular style that achieved considerable acceptance.

The influence of Chupícuaro ceramics was felt in the Central Highlands and in many places in Western Mexico, as well as in Zacatecas, and may have extended to the south-east of the United State. Archaeological excavations at Chupícuaro led to the recovery of offerings associated with approximately 400 burials. This polished black vessel was found in one of these; it is completely undecorated, modelled by hand with straight sides, a flat base, and an oval rim with diverging sides.

Skeletons have been found associated with large fires in the burials, suggesting that fires were made at the time of inhumation. Other burials were sealed by round stones forming a sort of coffin or casket; some individuals had offerings with them, while others had none, which suggests a difference in social class.   *c.b.c.*

106. TRIPOD VESSEL IN THE FORM OF A PUMPKIN

Shaft tombs of Western Mexico. Colima. Classic (A.D. 200-600). Clay. Height 27 cm, diameter 43.5 cm. Western Hall. MNA. Cat. no. 2.4-723. Inv. no. 10-222360.

This is a pot shaped like a pumpkin, with supports in the form of birds. The Colima style is very elegant, and the vessels are generally monochromatic, often red in colour, and highly polished. The very best pieces are found in the valley of Colima, and in the Armería and Coahuayana River basins. Elements of flora and fauna are frequently combined in the vessels, as in this case, where raised vertical sections simulate the segments of a pumpkin, while the three supports represent birds. The birds have elongated tails (their tips pointing outwards where they meet the floor), small wings and a curved beak, and their breasts support the base of the pot.   *c.b.c.*

107. FIGURE FROM FUNERARY OFFERING

Western Mexico culture. Colima. Classic (A.D. 200-600). Clay. Height 28 cm, length 43 cm, width 25.6 cm. Western Hall. MNA. Cat. no. 2.4-382. Inv. no. 10-44395.

The dog-shaped sculptures that come from the shaft tombs of Colima are world-famous today, and the best-known form of Pre-Columbian artistic expression from this state. They are modelled with exceptional realism and grace in clay, as in this case, where a very fat dog is represented in a seated posture. This one has an almost spherical body, with its belly resting on the ground.

The shoulderblades and paws are clearly modelled and incised, as are the muzzle features, with the wide, half-open mouth displaying a complete set of teeth. The round eyes are clearly incised, and the tail curls upwards. The highly polished red finish has been preserved.

The dog was one of the few animals to be domesticated by the indigenous groups, sharing the daily life of all the Mesoamerican peoples. From the beginning, dogs helped man in hunting, and already also served as food during that period. The dog appears in various aspects of Prehispanic religion, personifying the god Xólotl, and is intimately associated with Mictlantecuhtli, god of the dead and of the underworld. It appears in myths of the origin and order of the universe and the underworld, as well as of man's creation.

Some groups, particularly in the West, believe themselves to be descendants of a dog.   *c.b.c.*

108. FIGURE FROM FUNERARY OFFERING

Shaft tombs of Western Mexico. Colima. Classic (A.D. 200-600). Clay. Height 15.5 cm, width 22.4 cm, depth 25 cm. Western Hall. MNA. Cat. no. 2.4-724. Inv. no. 10-228043.

Of all the animal figures, particularly dogs, parrots and ducks, that have been found, the greatest number come from Colima. This pair of ducks in the form of a vessel are pleasing because of the simplicity of their modelling and the sense of volume achieved by beautiful, rounded contours. Fine lines define the few physical traits – beaks, eyes and wings. The spout is at the rear of the piece. The vessel reveals Prehispanic man's intimate relationship with nature, and his love of it.

The clay effigies of the shaft tombs have been preserved in good condition to this day because of the way in which they were sealed in the tombs. After burying the dead, a stone slab or large vessel was used in the form of a door to seal the opening between the shaft and the mortuary chamber; the shaft was then filled with earth to conceal its entrance. In this way, the chamber remained free of earth, while no trace remained at groundlevel of the tomb's existence.   *c.b.c.*

109. FIGURE FROM FUNERARY OFFERING

Western Mexico culture. Colima. Classic (A.D. 200-600) Clay. Height 21.2 cm, width 21.3 cm, depth 22.8 cm. Western Hall. MNA. Cat. no. 2.4-302. Inv. no. 10-77612.

Shaft-tomb offerings include both hollow figures and solid figurines, all modelled by hand, without the use of moulds.
The style of the Colima pieces is refined and realistic. The works are nearly always a red or brown colour, or very occasionally black, and they are highly polished. Most of the hollow sculptures have a spout, and were thus used as vessels for liquids.
This piece represents a seated man, his head resting on one knee, and his left leg bent and resting on the ground. The clothing – a loincloth and a form of shirt – are incised with a fine line. The features are realistically modelled: oval eyes, a large aquiline nose and a mouth formed by a horizontal slash. The spout is on the right shoulder. *c.b.c.*

110. ANTHROPOMORPHIC FIGURE

Shaft tombs of Western Mexico. Colima. Classic (A.D. 200-600). Clay. Height 27.4 cm, width 15.2 cm, depth 4.8 cm. In store. MNA. Cat. no. 2.3-553. Inv. no. 10-224368.

This solid, stylised figure is of the type known as Teco, which is characterised by a high degree of stylisation. The piriform head ends in a tall, thin point, while the shoulders are exaggeratedly wide, the arms long and also tapering to a point, and the legs are slightly bent with knees and feet pointing outwards. The posture is distinctive and the figure has the appearance of a puppet hanging on invisible strings.
The basic shapes within the figure have been simplified, and bear few details.
The head, with its broad jawbone and tapered peak, may represent an artificial deformation. The ears rest on the shoulders, and have holes pierced in them. The eyes are not indicated – they may originally have been painted - and nor is the mouth; the long, narrow nose is aquiline. The figure, which wears neither clothes nor ornaments, is modelled in red clay.
The term Teco refers to the ancient inhabitants of Western Mexico, and the name was given to this type of figure by traders in figurines (*huaqueros*). *c.b.c.*

111. ANTHROPOMORPHIC FIGURE

Culture of Western Mexico. Colima. Classic (A.D. 200-600). Clay. Height 24.3 cm, width 12.5 cm, depth 3.9 cm. In store. MNA. Cat. no. 2.3-595. Inv. no. 10-157328.

This figure is another variant of the Teco type, and has been carefully made, with realistic proportions apart from the extremely broad shoulders. Incised line and appliqué are both used in some small degree for the details, and the figure is shown standing, with arms at the sides and legs slightly bent.
The head is large, with oval-shaped incised eyes, while the mouth consists only of a large gash. The prominent cuneiform nose has a sharp bone. The hair is cut at ear-level, with a chignon on the top of the head.
The shoulders are broad, and the long, pointed arms hang at the sides of the figure. The realistic legs are stylised and the toes of the feet point outwards; the figure, which is made out of brown clay, wears a brief loincloth, and is adorned with a simple necklace. *c.b.c.*

112. FUNERARY OFFERING WITH FAMILY GROUP

Shaft tombs of Western Mexico. Colima. Classic (A.D. 200-600). Clay. Height 17.2 cm, width 18 cm, depth 19 cm. Mesoamerica Hall. MNA. Cat. no. 2-5488. Inv. no. 10-77667.

Many of the pieces from Colima represent aspects of everyday life. However, this scene representing family affection is exceptional: the father is seated at the front, with his hands on the ground, the woman holding him around the waist, and the naked baby lying across the mother's shoulders. Both the baby and the father wear arm bands. The man has long, loose hair, and wears a small loincloth with tassels. The woman wears a skirt and a sort of cap on her head. A tubular spout emerges from the man's back, clearly indicating the group's function as a vessel.
The piece is made out of a reddish clay, and is highly polished, with manganese stains. *c.b.c.*

113. VESSEL FROM FUNERARY OFFERING

Shaft tombs of Western Mexico. Colima. Classic (A.D. 200-600). Clay. Height 32.4 cm, width 25.2 cm, depth 18 cm. In store. MNA. Cat. no. 2.4-244. Inv. no. 57680.

Figures showing signs of disease, such as this hunchbacked dwarf, are a particularly interesting theme in shaft-tomb art. The Mexicas later considered dwarves to be the children of the sun, and attributed supernatural powers to them. Certain opinion holds that they were used as servants in palaces.
This figure is in a seated posture, with his short legs crossed, the left foot on top of the right, and the hands touching the knees. The torso is robust, with clearly indicated muscles, and the head is almost spherical, with small, rhomboid-shaped eyes indicated with appliqué. The nose consists of a triangular wedge, the mouth is open and prominent, and the ears have holes in them. The spout of the vessel is at the top of the head, and the piece, which is made out of brown clay, retains some of its red finish. *c.b.c.*

114. FIGURE

Culture of Western Mexico. El Bajadero de Borregos, Colima. Post-Classic (A.D. 900-1521). Stone. Height 55 cm, width 22 cm. Western Hall. MNA. Cat. no. 2.4-357. Inv. no. 10-81274.

The attitude of this lightly contoured sculpture is clearly apparent despite the lack of detail. The figure represents a seated man with bent legs and hands clasping the thighs. The broad head rises above the body without a neck, and the face – whose features can be clearly distinguished – looks upwards.
This piece was found in a burial associated with ceramics from the Armería Complex, during archaeological excavations along the Central Axis of the state of Colima.
Dating from Colima's Post-Classic period, the sculpture seems schematic in comparison with the elegant style of the clay

figures from the earlier period. However, the presence of this stone figure is exceptionally forceful.

Similar sculptures have been found in regions of the state of Sinaloa, as well as in the southern area of Zacatecas and Durango; it has been suggested that they symbolise a fire deity, which would indicate that they represent the patron who backs the power of the rulers.   *c.b.c.*

115. "CHINESE" FIGURE FROM FUNERARY OFFERING

Culture of Western Mexico. Nayarit. Classic (A.D. 200-600). Clay. Height 70 cm, width 41.2 cm, depth 27 cm. Western Hall. MNA. Cat. no. 2.2-667. Inv. no. 10-78140.

As we have seen, most of the clay sculptures from what is now part of the states of Colima, Jalisco and Nayarit come from shaft tombs with chambers. These tombs, unique within Mesoamerica, comprise one or more subterranean chambers with access from the surface of the ground through a vertical shaft. The dead were buried in these chambers accompanied by rich offerings, most notably ceramic vessels and figures representing men and animals.

The anthropomorphic figures of Nayarit reveal a number of styles, and this one, highly artistic, is in the "Chinese" style, so-called because of the almond-shaped eyes and a certain analogy with oriental art. It represents a naked woman, seated on her heels with her hands on her stomach. She wears a necklace of several strings, as well as a nose-ring and the typical earrings of Nayarit, consisting of multiple hoops. She also has a cord around her waist. The piece is highly polished, and the remains of white paint can be seen on the red clay.   *c.b.c.*

116. FIGURE FROM FUNERARY OFFERING

Shaft tombs of Western Mexico. Nayarit. Classic (A.D. 200-600). Clay. Height 29.4 cm, width 18.2 cm, depth 17.3 cm. In store. MNA. Cat. no. 2.2-1021. Inv. no. 10-77865.

The figures in the style of Ixtlán-del-Río, from the state of Nayarit, are characterised by the number of prominent colours used, which indicate garments, ornamentation and facial and body painting. The figures are made in red or orange clay, with polychrome decoration applied in white, black and yellow. This one is a fine example of this type of polychromy, representing a woman seated cross-legged on the ground, with one foot resting on the other. She has a wide body, with arms folded across her breast and holding a small vessel. She wears a skirt, and her small skullcap is bordered at the lower edge by a twisted cord. The head is oval, with large, prominent, almond-shaped eyes beneath half-moon eyebrows, a sharp, nose, an open mouth and large earflares. The pronounced painted decoration on the body consists of geometric designs.   *c.b.c.*

117. FIGURE FROM FUNERARY OFFERING

Shaft tombs of Western Mexico. Nayarit, Classic (A.D. 200-600). Clay. Height 67.2 cm, width 29.7 cm, depth 18 cm. In store. MNA. Cat. no. 2.2-337. Inv. no. 10-41482.

This standing female figure is typical of the Ixtlán del Río style, with short, very thick and widely separated legs. The feet are

enormous, with well-defined heels and toes. The figure's long skirt displays a single raised vertical band decorated with a geometric relief design; the body is wide, and the breasts are modelled with appliqué nipples. The figure wears bracelets, a nose-ring and earrings consisting of multiple hoops with triangular ornaments. Facial features are crude, with an open mouth displaying the teeth. The figure itself is hollow and made in brown clay, with lines painted in white, orange and black still visible on the skirt. Like other Nayarit pieces, this one almost certainly formed part of the funerary offering for a person buried in a shaft tomb.   *c.b.c.*

118. FIGURE FROM FUNERARY OFFERING

Shaft tombs of Western Mexico. Nayarit. Classic (A.D. 200-600). Clay. Height 73.5 cm, width 43.7 cm, depth 24 cm. In store. MNA. Cat. no. 2.2-341. Inv. no. 10-222299.

The Ixtlán del Río style appears again in this exceptionally large piece. A male of pronounced sex, the figure stands firmly on very short, thick, widely separated legs and over-large, arched feet which balance the figure. The body is wide, large and flat; the thin, bent arms hold a mace in front of it. The figure wears a necklace with a pendant, and the ears display multiple hoops. The bulky protruberances on the shoulders may be indications of scarification; the head is elongated, with prominent cheekbones and well-modelled features. The hair on the forehead and nape, which is short, is finely incised. A polished reddish-orange coating with numerous black managanese markings covers the whole figure, and there is an orifice in the upper part of the head.   *c.b.c.*

119. MASK

Culture of Western Mexico. Balsas River Basin, Guerrero. Post-Classic (A.D. 900-1521). Stone. Diameter 17.3 cm, depth 3.5 cm. Western Hall. MNA. Cat. no. 2.6-640. Inv. no. 10-77643.

An area devoted specifically to stonework has been located at certain sites in the state of Guerrero, close to the Mezcala River basin. The area has been named after the river, and objects such as masks, figurines, temple representations, hatchets with human figures, double figures, ornaments and variously shaped trinkets were manufactured there with great skill.

All of this was the product of a local cultural development; although Olmec and Teotihuacán influences are clearly visible in these pieces, the Mezcala style seems to have come to fruition during the Classic period, although its origins were much earlier.

This solemn and schematised style only admits the most crucial features to be indicated, through minimal carving, as shown by this stone mask.

The archaeology of Guerrero is famous for this particular style, because of the variety and quantity of objects carved in greenstone such as serpentine and jadeite, produced with great artistry and realism and which continue to be made today.

These objects were exported, at an unknown date, from Guerrero to the Central Highlands; the exact context is not known, but they appeared in Teotihuacán from the Classic period onward, and in the Templo Mayor in Mexico City until the Post-Classic period.   *m.d.f.v.*

120. MASK

Culture of Western Mexico. Mezcala, Guerrero. Post-Classic (A.D. 900-1521). Greenstone. Height 24.5 cm, width 21.7 cm. In store. MNA. Cat. no. 2-4857. Inv. no. 10-4751.

Numerous different types of objects in various media were placed as offerings next to the deceased in Western Mexico burials, as they were in the rest of Mesoamerica. Some of the most notable are vessels, figurines and funerary masks like the one shown here.

The features of this sober and elegant piece are formed by incision and grooving, and the mask is carved from greenstone with an extraordinary polish; it is a piece of remarkable beauty.

Greenstone or jadeite was used in Mesoamerica from approximately 1500 B.C. by the Olmecs, and continued to be used up to the period of Spanish contact in A.D. 1521, implying a permanent usage of over three thousand years.

It was employed principally for jewellery and accessories for ornamentation, and in funerary practices. The finest work and the most skilled carving was to be found in these greenstone objects. Greenstone itself was difficult to obtain because instead of mining the deposits, stones were collected from river beds; these stones varied in size and weight, which determined the design of the piece that was to be carved. It is possible that the most accessible sources of greenstone were completely depleted; it is potentially to be found in the states of Guerrero, Puebla, Oaxaca and Chiapas, and in Guatemala there is known to be a greenstone deposit at El Manzanal in the Las Minas Sierra and in the Montagua Valley. *m.d.f.v.*

121. CHAC MOOL

Western Mexico. Ihuatzio, Michoacán. Late Post-Classic (A.D. 900-1521). Stone. Height 84 cm, length 150 cm, width 48 cm. Western Hall. MNA. Cat. no. 2.5-6279. Inv. no. 10-1609.

Chac Mools were generally reclining human figures with head raised and holding a plate or vessel on the stomach; sculptures of this type are frequently found in altars and temple substructures. These pieces originated in the Toltec area in the centre of Mexico, but have been found in other archaeological regions such as Maya and Tarascan sites.

This sculpture, which belongs to the Tarascan culture, comes from Ihuatzio on the shores of the Lake Patzcuaro in Michoacán; it is carved out of basalt, and represents a reclining male figure, holding a dish in his hands, with legs bent, naked and with the sex indicated. His face is shown from the front, and there are very noticeable lines on the forehead and cheeks; around the knees are five bands or bangles.

Tarascan religion revolved around the sun and fire; sculptures from these regions seem to have been related to the cult of the sun, as the receptacle in the figure's hands would have been used to hold ritualistic offerings, consisting mainly of the hearts of sacrificed victims, the divine sustenance of the sun. Chac Mools are thus like warriors or messengers who carried the offerings to the sun god, and because of this they frequently wear bracelets strapping obsidian knives to their arms.

Sculpture was generally intended to complement architecture, and its realistic style was highly descriptive, with a tendency towards marked modelling and elegant design. *m.d.f.v.*

104. FIGURE FROM FUNERARY OFFERING

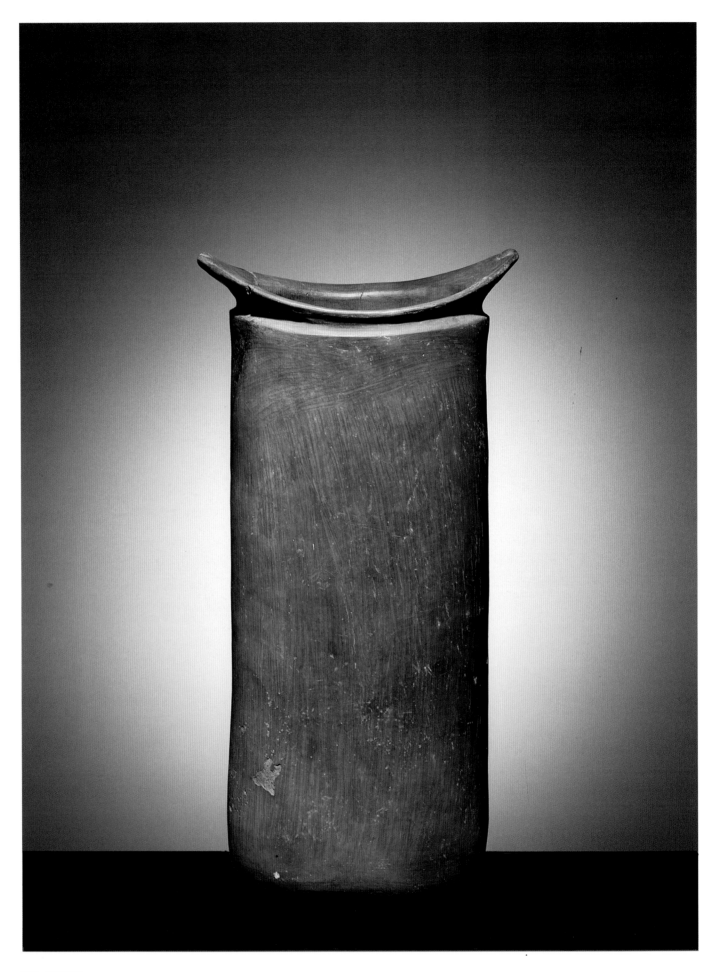

105. VESSEL

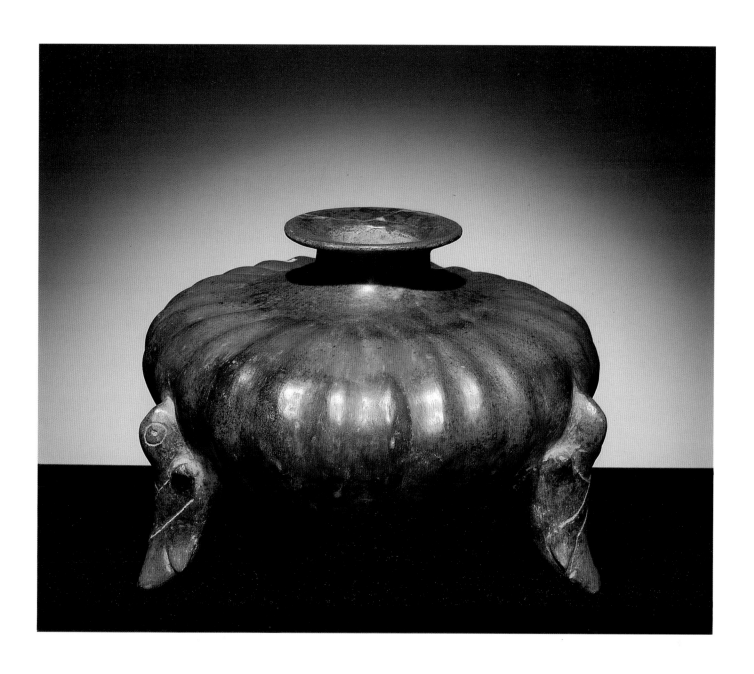

106. TRIPOD VESSEL IN THE FORM OF A PUMPKIN

107. FIGURE FROM FUNERARY OFFERING

107. FIGURE FROM FUNERARY OFFERING

108. FIGURE FROM FUNERARY OFFERING

109. FIGURE FROM FUNERARY OFFERING

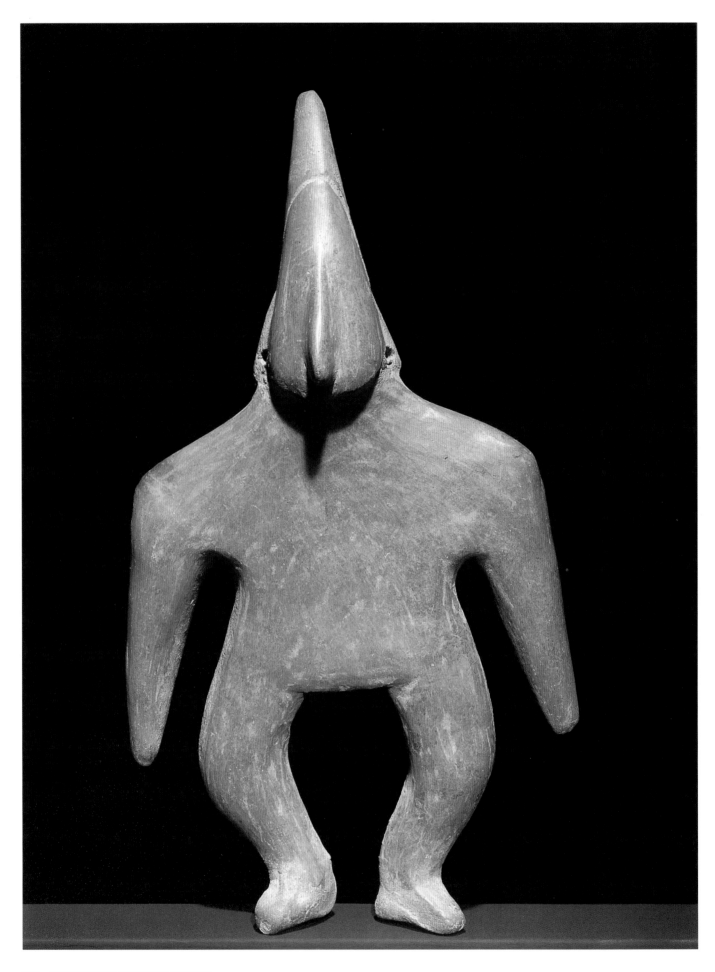

110. ANTHROPOMORPHIC FIGURE

111. ANTHROPOMORPHIC FIGURE

112. FUNERARY OFFERING WITH FAMILY GROUP

112. FUNERARY OFFERING WITH FAMILY GROUP

113. VESSEL FROM FUNERARY OFFERING

113. VESSEL FROM FUNERARY OFFERING

114. FIGURE

114. FIGURE

115. "CHINESE" FIGURE FROM FUNERARY OFFERING

115. "CHINESE" FIGURE FROM FUNERARY OFFERING

116. FIGURE FROM FUNERARY OFFERING

117. FIGURE FROM FUNERARY OFFERING

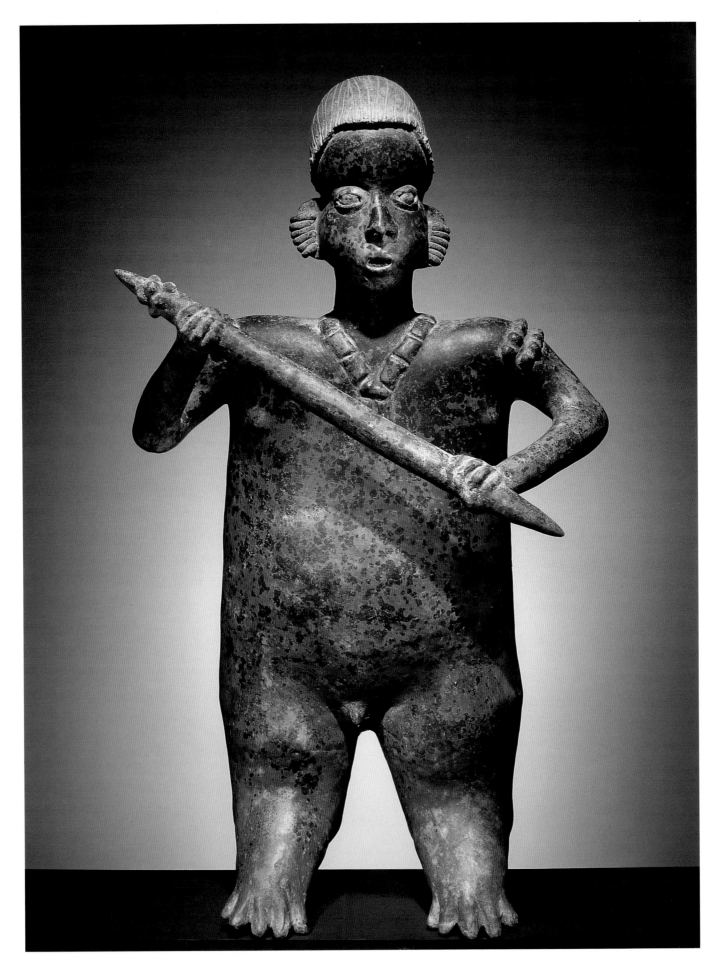

118. FIGURE FROM FUNERARY OFFERING

119. MASK

120. MASK

121. CHAC MOOL

17. NORTHERN MEXICO, BUILDERS OF EARTH CITIES

Jesús Nárez

The northern territory of the Pánuco, Moctezuma, Lerma-Santiago and Fuerte Rivers, up to the border with the United States, constitutes the area known as Northern Mexico. The general landscape of this enormous area is arid, as rivers are few and rainfall limited. There are large valleys and plateaux, with vegetation of cacti, bushes and drought-resistant plants. Two large mountain ranges border this area: to the east, the eastern Sierra Madre, and to the west, the western Sierra Madre, forming an enormous shield broken only by a few mountain foothills that are relatively low. It was here that numerous groups dwelt in the past, known as desert hunter-gatherers because of their way of life, although those who inhabited more hospitable terrain were to achieve greater cultural development.

Their origin is still not very clear, but they were almost certainly descendants of groups that subsisted in the southern part of what are now the United States, where from around 10,000 B.C. to 5000 B.C. there were two clearly differentiated areas: to the east, groups that hunted larger animals, and to the west the so-called Desert Cultures. From 5000 B.C. until 1800 B.C., these groups advanced southwards, penetrating what is now Mexico from the north, and resulting in a fusion of the two currents. During this period, domestication of plants began, as did knowledge of maize-agriculture. From 1800 B.C. to the beginning of the Christian era, the groups that had settled in what is now known as Mesoamerica established themselves through crop cultivation. A cultural centre began to emerge in the north, near the confluence of the present-day states of Utah, Colorado, Arizona and New Mexico, which demonstrated a certain Mesoamerican influence, and which has been called the America Oasis. From this date until around A.D. 1000, however, a noticeable cultural difference was recognisable between the Mesoamerican groups and the Northern groups: in the east were the hunting groups; in the south-west of the United States, the peninsula of Baja California and the northern centre of Mexico were the Desert Cultures. The America Oasis had expanded far afield, stretching across a good part of the United States and, in Mexico, reaching the part that includes the states of Chihuahua, Sonora and Durango. To the south was Mesoamerica, with all its cultural regions: Oaxaca, Maya, the Gulf Coast, Western and Central Valleys.

Towards the north, an area of peripheral Mesoamerica was colonised, with noticeable cultural differences, where more advanced cultures mingled with those of the hunter-gatherers; these groups used various forms of weapon heads (basically carved out of silex and flint), bows and arrows, excavatory rods with their tips previously strengthened or hardened by fire, the *átlatl* or spear thrower, and knives and nets, among other implements; they liked to adorn themselves, and wore necklaces of small bones, caracols, shells and beads, made out of a number of different materials, which they obtained from distant places through barter or trade. They used fibres from local plants such as *lechugilla* (wild lettuce), yucca and agave for all sorts of purposes: bags, sandals, cords; plant and mineral colourants, adhesives made from vegetal resins, and so on. They also made contact with their Mesoamerican neighbours to get hold of several products that they did not produce themselves, such as cotton, *amate* paper, spindles and other items; because of this, foreign cultural elements are often found at their sites. One of their customs was to leave their dead in caves and crevices in gorges, wrapping them in coloured blankets and tying them up tightly. They were sometimes surrounded by offerings and objects that were almost certainly considered to be useful to the deceased in the next life, such as small ceremonial bows and arrows, weapons and venison spears.

Evidence of these people's presence is also found in petroglyphs and pictographs, engraved or painted figures and symbols on the rocks, walls and roofs of caves and ravines. They

25. Mesoamerica and the North of Mexico

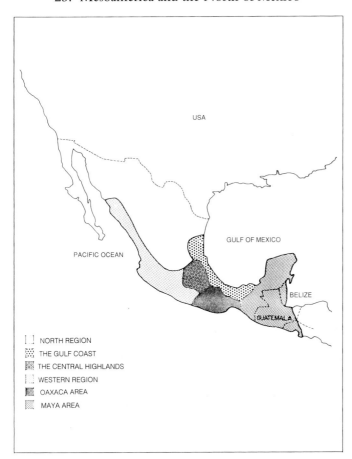

USA

GULF OF MEXICO

PACIFIC OCEAN

BELIZE

GUATEMALA

| | NORTH REGION
| | THE GULF COAST
| | THE CENTRAL HIGHLANDS
| | WESTERN REGION
| | OAXACA AREA
| | MAYA AREA

26. America Oasis

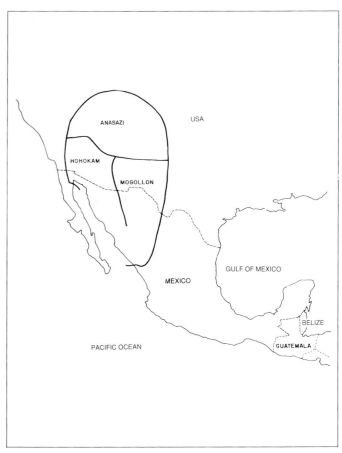

ANASAZI

USA

HOHOKAM

MOGOLLON

GULF OF MEXICO

MEXICO

BELIZE

PACIFIC OCEAN

GUATEMALA

27. Marginal or peripheral Mesoamerica

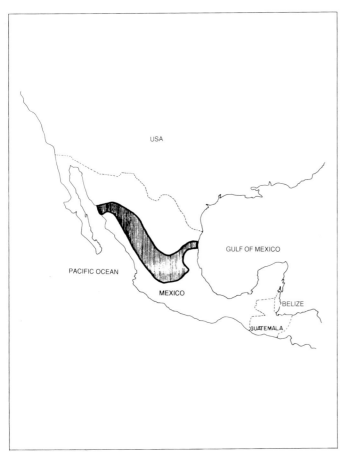

USA

GULF OF MEXICO

PACIFIC OCEAN

MEXICO

BELIZE

GUATEMALA

28. Archaeological sites of the North of Mexico

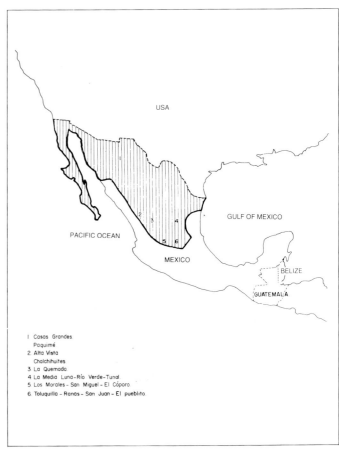

USA

GULF OF MEXICO

PACIFIC OCEAN

MEXICO

BELIZE

GUATEMALA

1. Casas Grandes
   Paquimé
2. Alta Vista
   Chalchihuites
3. La Quemada
4. La Media Luna - Río Verde - Tunal
5. Los Morales - San Miguel - El Cóporo
6. Toluquilla - Ranas - San Juan - El pueblito

were skilled basket makers and weavers of fibre, to such a degree that the baskets were waterproof; these implements were light because of the need to transport them, and could easily be replaced. Heavy items were avoided because of the disadvantages to an errant way of life, which involved following flocks of animals and locating seasonal fruits and edible produce.

Stone-grinding was a technique used to process grain, making the vegetable and seed-based diet more digestible.

Various sites in marginal or peripheral Mesoamerica and in Northern Mexico have been studied: in places such as Los Morales, in the state of Guanajuato, well-finished ceramics and tripod dishes with black decoration on a red background have been found. Another site in the same state is San Miguel de Allende, where clay pipes have been found (proof of influence from the south-eastern United States), as well as beautiful ceramics in red on a chestnut background and vessels finished using the technique known as "raised white". Magnificent shell and stone objects, as well as carefully decorated ceramics, come from El Cóporo, also in Guanajuato.

A very varied collection of stone sculptures has been discovered at Tunal Grande in San Luis Potosí, as well as a number of rather simpler ceramics, while Río Verde, in the same state, has a wide variety of both stone and ceramic artefacts and numerous unique male votive figurines representing ball-game players, which come from the Media Luna Lake. Stone pipes have been found there which were also influenced by the south-eastern United States.

In Querétaro are the sites of El Pueblito, Toluquilla, Ranas and San Juan del Río, where a strong Mesoamerican influence is apparent both in the buildings and in the materials that have been excavated.

In Zacatecas and Durango, settlements were characterised by their ceramics, which included vessels with basket-type handles and cloisonné decoration. Fascinating archaeological sites such as Alta Vista-Chalchihuites and La Quemada have come to light, with large constructions made from adobe bricks of compressed earth and stone, which allowed natural surface-level differences to be taken into account. The groups that constituted the Chalchihuita culture were great astronomers, as is proven by the observatories that have been found at Alta Vista and La Quemada. These people also organised trade across enormous distances, exchanging both basic materials and manufactured goods. Most of their religious representations were comparatively unimportant and made from perishable materials, and only a few stone sculptures have been preserved.

Casas Grandes, in the State of Chihuahua and also known as Paquimé, is unique, corresponding to the cultural area of the America Oasis. The marked influence of the Anasazi, Hohokán and Mogollón groups is noticeable there; around the time that these groups began to decline (by A.D. 800), they united to become one group, and advanced southwards forming new settlements as they went. Casas Grandes is one of the most remarkable of these. The site's most notable feature is its architecture, consisting of a huge agglomeration of rooms and houses of one or more storeys or levels. These were made of mud, which was placed in large wooden moulds to form the walls. At ground level and on the first floor, these walls were up to two metres thick, diminishing with each new level. To finish off, the walls were covered with a fine layer of mud and painted in white, yellow and ochre. Some dwellings had a fire or oven, and there was an ingenious system of canals for distributing water throughout the city, as well as another system for the disposal of sewage water. The city must have been impressive to look at, reaching a size of over 60 hectares.

There were some variations on the basic model of construction, such as the cliff-houses that, taking advantage of natural outcrops, were built in gorges, and *kivas*, semi-subterranean circular constructions with a wood and hay roof, where certain ceremonies and initiation rites were carried out.

The ceramics of Casas Grandes are diverse and very beautiful; they display great sensitivity and skill. The shapes used are extremely varied, with anthropomorphic, zoomorphic, botanical and plain vessels rendered with a pure technique; they are decorated with geometric lines and highly stylised representations of serpents and birds, with black and red predominating on a cream background.

The Casas Grandes inhabitants cultivated maize, beans, squash and other plants; evidence of large bird-breeding sites has been found here, with birds such as the wild turkey, *guacamayas* and parrots (for the supply of feathers) used in beautiful mosaics and weavings. The parrot appears frequently as an ornamental motif on ceramics, represented in relief or in stylised drawings.

Trade was important and well-organised, and Casas Grandes served as a meeting place or corridor between Mesoamerica and the south-eastern United States and vice-versa. Because of this, elements from distant areas are often found, including those from coastal regions (shells and caracols, principally from the Californian Gulf), which were used in ornaments such as necklaces, earflares, pectorals and bracelets. The inhabitants also knew and worked copper, using the techniques of beating cold metal, moulds, the lost-wax technique and filigree.

The organization and government of Paquimé or Casas Grandes was theocratic rather that military, and within a pronounced social division, master craftsmen, merchants, those who worked in the fields or built houses, shamans and many others, all co-existe; they were definitely not a nation of warriors. At the beginning of the fourteenth century, they were attacked by nomadic groups who routed them and burnt their settlement, which was abandoned once and for all.

Palettes for pigments, carved out of greenstone or serpentine, or made out of clay – some elaborate and some simple – are frequently found in the north, as are numerous ornaments made in a variety of semi-precious stones such as turquoise and natural crystals.

One feature that is particularly noticeable is the absence of any monumental representations of deities. Northern groups, like others, worshipped all natural manifestations: the sun, the moon, the rain, thunder and lightning, and water, but their symbolic representations were made in the form of pictures, using coloured earth, sands, various seeds and flower petals. These representations were not considered very important, and were only made when necessary, to ask for rain, to favour hunting and sowing, or for curative or thanksgiving purposes.

The Northern Mexico groups clearly had a long, rich history and a particular cultural heritage, but they have not been studied with as much attention as they merit; however, the desert, caves, gorges and mountains of this vast area are gradually yielding their secrets and their evidence, which testify to the presence of the number of groups that inhabited the area so long ago.

18. THE ASYMMETRICAL GEOMETRY OF NORTHERN MEXICO

Sonia Lombardo de Ruíz

Although the culture of the Northern Mexico peoples is characterised by both Mesoamerican and America Oasis traits, this exhibition presents only pieces from the last era – presisely because of their difference from the rest of the objects on display - which prolong the tradition of the ancient Desert Cultures.

Many of the objects hand-made by these peoples relied on perishable materials which came from local resources, principally fibres and textiles. As a result, information about their sculpture can only be provided by their ceramics and a few stone sculptures.

The site of Casas Grandes, which was occupied over a long period, was initially linked to the cultures of the southern United States. In its middle and late periods, well-finished ceramics with an extraordinary sense of decoration were produced.

The vessels, which have spherical bases, are of differing diameters, sometimes forming bowls (plate 123), and sometimes elegant pots with narrow mouths (plate 122). Occasionally animal heads are placed on the upper edge, as in the vessel in plate 124; at other times, the vessel becomes a human figure, with its proportions grossly distorted because of the vessel's necessary bulk; the figures have short legs, thin arms and very large faces, as can be seen in plate 125. Great ingenuity is expressed in both anthropomorphic and zoomorphic vessels.

The background is generally cream-coloured, which allows the foreground designs, in black and earth colours, to stand out (plates 122 and 123). The designs consist of wide continuous diagonal bands, running at different angles to each other, with rectangles containing stepped frets and semi-circles or zoomorphic figures appearing in the spaces in between. The shapes are always geometric and placed asymmetrically, producing remarkably dynamic designs full of contrast.

In the stone sculptures of Northern Mexico, human figures are schematic, nearly always seated on the ground with crossed legs and full-frontal features (plate 126), crudely carved and with little detail, though these aspects appear to be intentional. Other types of sculpture connected with Mesoamerica are marginal variants but by comparison with these examples, they are of less interest.

122. POLYCHROMATIC POT

America Oasis culture. Casas Grandes, Chihuahua. Middle Post-Classic (A.D. 900-1521). Clay. Height 38 cm, diameter 41 cm. Northern Hall. MNA. Cat. no. 12-1-982. Inv. no. 10-81178.

This monumental polychrome pot is exceptional for its size. Its decoration in based on geometric lines, rhomboids, rectangles, frets and a highly stylised bird's beak, almost certainly that of a parrot, in black and red on a cream background. The city of Casas Grandes, one of the most important archaeological sites of Northern Mexico, was built out of earth. Stone was rarely used in its constructions, but was later adopted as a result of the influence of Toltec groups, who maintained strong commercial trading links with the Paquimé groups around 1000 A.D. *j.n.*

123. DISH

America Oasis culture. Casas Grandes, Chihuahua. Late Post-Classic (A.D. 1060-1340). Clay. Height 10.5 cm, diameter 15.8 cm. In store. MNA. Cat. no. 12-1-4. Inv. no. 10-54904.

The external decoration of this clay dish is based on lines and rhomboids in colours of black and sepia on a cream background. The quality of the work conveys the great skill and sensitivity of the Casas Grandes or Paquimé craftsmen, who also left magnificent examples of shell and caracol, out of which necklaces, pendants, pectorals and ritualistic objects were made. *j.n.*

124. ZOOMORPHIC VESSEL

America Oasis culture. Casas Grandes, Chihuahua. Middle Post-Classic (A.D. 900-1521). Clay. Height 15.5 cm, width 17 cm. Northern Hall. MNA. Cat. no. 12-1-466. Inv. no. 10-228057.

A feline head, with notably long whiskers, appears on the rim of this polychrome zoomorphic pot. The body of the pot is completely covered with lines and geometric motifs, in black and red on a cream background. The Pueblo groups that inhabited Casas Grandes were fond of making zoomorphic representations in ceramics, so we have been left many pieces, which are a great help in understanding the animal life that was familiar to them. *j.n.*

125. ANTHROPOMORPHIC VESSEL

America Oasis culture. Casas Grandes, Chihuahua. Middle Post-Classic (A.D. 900-1521). Clay. Height 15.5 cm, width 17 cm. Northern Hall. MNA. Cat. no. 12-1-466. Inv. no. 10-228057.

This clay vessel represents a woman with her hands on her stomach, seated on top of a figure lying on his back. There is only one pair of legs, which could belong to either character. The overall piece is very beautiful, decorated with geometric lines and motifs in black and red on a cream background. As we have seen, Casas Grandes (Paquimé) is the largest and most important site in Northern Mexico. Its clay architecture is one of the most impressive in America because of its size, proportions and conscious urbanism; its location in a desert area also makes it interesting. Casas Grandes emerged around A.D. 800, and reached its zenith between 1000 and 1200, only to go into decline around 1300. Heir to the Anasazi, Hohokam and Mogollón groups, it extended the America Oasis influential sphere very far south in Mexican territory. *j.n.*

126. SCULPTURE OF SEATED FIGURE

Chalchihuita culture. Cerro Moctezuma, Zacatecas. Classic (A.D. 100-800). Stone. Height 41.5 cm, width 18.5 cm. Northern Hall. MNA. Cat. no. 12-3-1021. Inv. no. 10-228059.

The stone sculpture shown here represents a deity or some other individual in a seated position, resting his arms on his knees. He has a band or sash across his forehead, a detail that was characteristic of the inhabitants of Northern Mexico.
Marginal or peripheral Mesoamerica is situated between Mesoamerica and Northern Mexico. The groups living there were influenced by the highly developed cultures of the south, as well as showing traits common to the barbarian groups of the north – a clear indication of the area's function as a place of contact. The region suffered constant changes, as the southern groups sometimes penetrated very far north, while at other times the Chichimeca groups advanced towards the south, destroying the Mesoamerican settlements and forcing the inhabitants to abandon their villages. Stone sculptures are very scarce in the north, although not lacking in aesthetic value. This piece from Zacatecas, which reflects the Chalchihuita culture, is typical. *j.n.*

122. POLYCHROMATIC POT

123. DISH

302

124. ZOOMORPHIC VESSEL

125. ANTHROPOMORPHIC VESSEL

125. ANTHROPOMORPHIC VESSEL

126. SCULPTURE OF SEATED FIGURE

126. SCULPTURE OF SEATED FIGURE

Jorge R., *El palacio del Quetzalpapalotl,* Mexico, Instituto Nacional de Antropología e Historia ("Memorias", 10), 1964.

Armillas, Pedro, "Notas sobre sistemas de cultivo en Mesoamerica: Cultivos de riego y humedal en la cuenca del río de Las Balsas", *Anales,* Mexico, Instituto Nacional de Antropología e Historia, 1949.

Bernal, Ignacio, *El mundo olmeca,* Mexico, Editorial Porrua, 1968.

Blanton, Richard E., *Monte Albán. Settlement Patterns at the Ancient Zapotec Capital,* New York, Academic Press, 1978.

Caso, Alfonso, *El tesoro de Monte Albán,* Mexico, Instituto Nacional de Antropología e Historia ("Memorias"), 1969.

Caso, Alfonso and Ignacio Bernal, *Urnas de Oaxaca,* Mexico, Instituto Nacional de Antropología e Historia ("Memorias", 2), 1952.

Castillo Tejero, Noemí and Felipe Solís Olguín, *Ofrendas mexicas en el Museo Nacional de Antropología,* Mexico, Instituto Nacional de Antropología e Historia ("Corpus Antiquitatum Americanensium", 8), 1978.

Castro Leal, Marcia, "La coleccíon de esculturas huaxtecas en piedra del Museo Nacional de Antropología: un ensayo de interpretación", *XLII Congreso Internacional de Americanistas,* Paris, 1979, vol. IX-B, pp. 57-66.

Covarrubias, Miguel, "Tlatilco: El arte y la cultura preclásica del Valle de México", *Cuadernos americanos,* 9/3 Mexico, Editorial Cultura, 1950.

Davies, Nigel, *The Toltecs: Until the Fall of Tula,* Norman, University of Oklahoma Press, 1977.

Di Peso, Charles C., *Casas Grandes. A Fallen Trading Center of the Gran Chichimeca,* Dragoon, The Amerind Foundation, 1974.

Diehl, Richard A., *Tula, the Toltec Capital of Ancient Mexico,* London, Thames and Hudson, 1983.

Garcia Payon, José, "Arqueologia de la Huasteca", *Los pueblos y señoríos teocráticos. El período de las ciudades urbanas (segunda parte).* Mexico, Instituto Nacional de Antropología e Historia, 1976, pp. 62-126.

Grove, David C., *Chalcatzingo: Excavations on the Olmec Frontier,* London, Thames and Hudson, 1984.

Kelly, Isabel, "El oeste de Mexico y la Hohokam", *El Norte de México y el Sur de Estados Unidos,* Mexico, 1943.

Kubler, George, "Studies in Classic Maya Iconography", *Memoirs of the Connecticut Academy of Art and Sciences,* New Haven, September 1969, vol. 18.

Lister, Robert H. and A.M. Howard, "The Chalchihuites Culture of Northwestern Mexico", *American Antiquity,* XXI, 1955, pp. 123-29.

Lombardo de Ruíz, Sonia et al., *La pintura mural maya en Quintana Roo,* Mexico, Instituto Nacional de Antropología e Historia, Gobierno del Estado de Quintana Roo (Colección Fuentes), 1987.

Lumholtz, Carl, *El México desconocido,* New York, 1904.

Medellín, Alfonso, *Cerámicas del Totonacapan: exploraciones en el centro de Veracruz,* Jalapa, Universidad Veracruzana, Instituto de Antropología, 1960.

Miller, Arthur G., *The Mural Painting of Teotihuacan, Mexico,* Washington, D.C., Dumbarton Oaks, 1973.

Millon, René (ed.), "Urbanization at Teotihuacan, Mexico", vol. I, pp. 1 and 2: *The Teotihuacan Map,* Austin, University of Texas Press, 1973.

Morris, Earl H., Jean Charlot and Ann Axtel, *The Temple of the Warriors at Chichén-Itzá, Yucatán*, 2 vols., Washington, D.C., Carnegie Institute, Washington (Publication no. 406), reprint of 1931 edition. 1931.

Museo Nacional De Antropología, *El juego de pelota, una tradición prehispánica viva*, Mexico, Instituto Nacional de Antropología e Historia, 1986.

El preclásico o formativo: Avances y perspectivas, ed. Martha Carmona Macias, Mexico, Instituto Nacional de Antropología e Historia, 1989.

Niederberger, Christine, *Paleopaysages et Archeologie Preurbaine du bassin de Mexico*, Mexico, Centre of Mexican and Central American Studies, 2 vols.

Paddock, John (ed.), *Ancient Oaxaca*, Stanford, Stanford University Press, 1966.

Parsons, Lee, *Pre-Columbian Art*, New York, Harper & Row, 1980.

Pasztory, Esther, *Aztec Art*, New York, Harry N. Abrams Inc. Publ., 1983.

Piña Chan, Román, *Las culturas preclásicas de la cuenca de México*, Mexico, Fondo de Cultura Económica, 1955.

"Algunas consideraciones sobre las pinturas de Mulchic, Yucatán", *Estudios de cultura maya*, vol. 4, Mexico, Universidad Nacional Autónoma, Mexico, 1964.

Los Olmecas antiguos, Mexico, Consejo Editorial del Estado de Tabasco, 1982.

Quirarte, Jacinto, *The Santa Rita Murals: A Review* (version mecanografica), 1981.

Robertson, Donald, "The Tulum Murals: The Ancient International Style of the Late Post Classic", *Verhandlungen des XXXVIII Internationalen Amerikanisten-kongresses, München August 1968*, Munich, 1970, August, vol. II, pp. 77-78.

Sejourne, L., *Arquitectura y pintura en Teotihuacán*, Mexico, Siglo XXI Editores, 1966.

Solís Olguín, Felipe, "The Formal Pattern of Anthropomorphic Sculpture and the Ideology of the Aztec State", *The Art and Iconography of Late Post-Classic Central Mexico*, Washington, Dumbarton Oaks, 1982.

Townsend, Richard F., *State and Cosmos in the Art of Tenochtitlan*, Washington, Dumbarton Oaks, 1979.

Whitecotton, Joseph W., *The Zapotecs: The Princes, Priests and Peasants*, Norman, University of Oklahoma Press, 1984.